And if ... ... he di ...

whacked.

In the M ... ...

above you ... ... in your ...

in loan sh ...

bers rackets, prostitution, drugs, stolen jewelry, sports memorabilia, Internet pornography, or any other criminal enterprise. Peter "Petey Chops" Vicini ran a highly successful gambling and numbers operation in the Bronx that netted him millions of dollars. As a made member of the Gambino crime family, he was responsible for sharing some of that wealth with his capo, the individual to whom he reported, along with the "administration" of the family—the boss, the underboss, and the consigliere.

Nobody can touch a Gambino, or a Lucchese, or a member of any of the other families that make up La Cosa Nostra in New York. No one can move into his territory, steal his shakedown victims, or interfere with his moneymaking activities. But operating under the protection of a crime family comes at a price. The Mafia soldier must kick up. He must share what he makes with those above him. A Mafia soldier must also report to his superiors regularly. Some capos insist on meetings every day. And the soldier had better come with money to kick up the line. Failure to do so is a capital crime in the Mafia, and for months now Petey Chops had been avoiding his responsibilities. He wasn't kicking up. He was in hiding from the rest of the Mafia.

Making Jack Falcone

AN UNDERCOVER FBI AGENT TAKES DOWN A MAFIA FAMILY

JOAQUIN "JACK" GARCIA
with MICHAEL LEVIN

P★ POCKET STAR BOOKS

NEW YORK   LONDON   TORONTO   SYDNEY

Pocket Star Books
A Division of Simon & Schuster, Inc.
1230 Avenue of the Americas
New York, NY 10020

Copyright © 2008 by Jack Garcia

All rights reserved, including the right to reproduce this book or portions thereof in any form whatsoever. For information address Touchstone Subsidiary Rights Department, 1230 Avenue of the Americas, New York, NY 10020

First Pocket Star Books paperback edition October 2009

POCKET STAR BOOKS and colophon are registered trademarks of Simon & Schuster, Inc.

For information regarding special discounts for bulk purchases, please contact Simon & Schuster Special Sales at 1-866-506-1949 or business@simonandschuster.com.

The Simon & Schuster Speakers Bureau can bring authors to your live event. For more information or to book an event contact the Simon & Schuster Speakers Bureau at 1-866-248-3049 or visit our website at www.simonspeakers.com.

Harbor and cranes © Corbis.

Manufactured in the United States of America

10 9 8 7 6 5 4 3 2 1

ISBN 978-1-4391-4991-1
ISBN 978-1-4391-6668-0 (ebook)

*For my loving wife and precious daughter,
my wonderful parents, family, and friends—
I thank you for your encouragement, support, inspiration,
and understanding through the years.*

*For all the men and women in law enforcement
who risk their lives daily while working undercover—
may God watch over you and keep you safe.*

Nessun dorma! Nessun dorma!

. . .

Ma il mio mistero è chiuso in me,
Il nome mio nessun saprà!
No, no, sulla tua bocca lo dirò,
Quando la luce splenderà!

Ed il mio bacio scioglierà.
Il silenzio che ti fa mio!

No one shall sleep! No one shall sleep!

. . .

But my secret lies hidden within me,
No one shall discover my name!
Oh no, I will reveal it only on your lips
When daylight shines forth!

And my kiss shall break
The silence that makes you mine!

"Nessun Dorma," *Turandot*, Puccini

PART ONE
insertion

PROLOGUE

The Battle of Bloomingdale's

Petey Chops wasn't kicking up.

And if he didn't start soon, he was going to get whacked.

In the Mafia, "kicking up" means sharing with those above you in your crime family the money you make in loan sharking, construction scams, gambling, numbers rackets, prostitution, drugs, stolen jewelry, sports memorabilia, Internet pornography, or any other criminal enterprise. Peter "Petey Chops" Vicini ran a highly successful gambling and numbers operation in the Bronx that netted him millions of dollars. As a made member of the Gambino crime family, he was responsible for sharing some of that wealth with his capo, the individual to whom he reported, along with the "administration" of the family—the boss, the underboss, and the consigliere.

Nobody can touch a Gambino, or a Lucchese, or a member of any of the other families that make up La Cosa Nostra in New York. No one can move into his territory, steal his shakedown victims, or interfere with his moneymaking activities. But operating under the protection of a crime family comes at a price. The Mafia soldier must kick up. He must share what he makes with those above him. A Mafia soldier must also report to his superiors regularly. Some capos insist on meetings every day. And the soldier had better come with money to kick up the line. Failure to do so is a capital crime in the Mafia, and for months now Petey Chops had been avoiding his responsibilities. He wasn't kicking up. He was in hiding from the rest of the Mafia.

The Gambino boss was Arnold "Zeke" Squitieri, an old-style Mafioso who avoided the limelight the way his illustrious predecessor, John Gotti, had sought it. Squitieri was a convicted felon due to his involvement in the narcotics trade; so much for the Mafia's "code" that forbade dealing drugs. Squitieri had assigned Petey Chops to Greg DePalma, another old-school Mafia guy who had been a Gambino capo, or captain, since the 1990s and a made man in the family since 1977. Greg was in his early seventies when he emerged from prison after serving time for shaking down Scores, the Manhattan strip club made famous by radio shock jock Howard Stern.

The Mafia and the FBI both considered Greg a relic, a washed-up has-been or, in the colorful language of the Mafia, a brokester, a broken-down valise. Yet Greg was anything but a broken-down man. Within months of his release, he was riding high once again among the Gambinos. So high that the boss of the family, Squitieri, assigned Greg, among many other tasks, the responsibility of meeting with and collecting from the prize Gambino soldier and cash cow, Petey Chops.

Petey Chops had become a thorn in Greg's side. He simply wouldn't report. Petey Chops always made excuses. He'd say things like "Greg, I can't meet you. I'm being watched. I'm under investigation. I don't want to take a pinch."

Meaning he didn't want to be arrested.

"Hey," Greg would respond, "we're all being watched! Now get over here with the money!"

Still no Petey.

Months went by. DePalma grew tired of Petey's whining. And then he had an idea.

He heard that Petey Chops and his girlfriend went to eat at the restaurant buffet in the Bloomingdale's department store in White Plains every Monday night at six. On February 21, which happened to be the Presidents' Day holiday, the Old Man, as Greg was called, decided that he, his Gambino soldier Robert Vaccaro, and I would find Petey at Bloomingdale's and straighten him out.

Who am I? An FBI undercover agent who had managed to infiltrate Greg DePalma's crew. Greg thought I was Jack Falcone, a big-time jewel thief from South Florida, and he had made me part of his crime crew. He had no idea that I was only the second FBI agent in history to deeply infiltrate the Mafia on a long-term basis. Joe Pistone, playing the role of Donnie Brasco, was the first.

I knew that the matter had been festering with Greg, because money was important to him. It was also the principle of the thing—to benefit from your privileged position in an organized crime family and not share the wealth . . . it's a fatal mistake.

That Presidents' Day, Greg, Vaccaro, and I sat in La Villetta restaurant in Larchmont, New York, when Greg turned to me and rasped, "Listen, we're gonna go for a ride."

As usual, Greg didn't tell me our trip agenda. I always became a little anxious at moments like that because I wasn't in control. I could be taken anywhere— out on a hit, or even to my own demise. I never knew.

"Where are we going?" I asked, trying not to show my concern.

"Don't worry about it," the Old Man told me. "Let's go to White Plains."

What could I do? I drove a Hummer at the time, as befit my role as a successful South Florida jewel thief. FBI agent Bim Liscomb, a member of the FBI surveillance team, was covering me. Like me, he didn't look like an agent. He was African American, heavyset, and he wore a beard, which was anathema in J. Edgar Hoover's time. Actually, in Hoover's day, that entire package would have been three strikes and you're out. I opted to have him cover me because he didn't look anything like an agent, and because he didn't drive one of those brand-new cars with the tinted windows that always gave surveillance teams away. What do I look like? I'm six foot four, 390 pounds. I don't look like an FBI agent either.

We left La Villetta, and the three of us piled into my Hummer. I couldn't get on the phone and say, "Bim, I'm going to White Plains. Follow me." Instead, I hoped that he would notice us heading away in my H2 and discreetly follow us. I drove slowly, as usual, so I wouldn't lose my tail. My torpor behind the wheel always drove Greg crazy.

"You drive like an old lady!" he complained. "Hurry up, Jackie boy! It takes you a fucking hour to drive what it takes me half an hour!"

"I always go slow," I told him. "I get flashbacks from an accident I had when I was a kid."

If Greg had been in a hurry, he would have told me, "We gotta get there fast. You're not fucking driving." I'd follow him and pretend to get lost, just to zing him. But that wasn't happening this time. We were all in one car, my car, and I still had no idea what we were doing.

On the way, Greg finally explained the nature of our mission.

"We're going to Bloomingdale's," he said. "We're going to find that cocksucker Petey Chops."

Okay, so today's not my day to get killed. That's a positive. But why would we look for a recalcitrant Mafia soldier in a department store? Greg volunteered no more information, and as a member of his crew, I was in no position to inquire.

We arrived at Bloomingdale's and didn't know

where the hell the restaurant was. There were housewares and rugs all around us. By nature, we weren't
the kind of people conversant with the layout of department stores. Mob guys don't buy retail. The three
of us definitely didn't look like shoppers. We looked
like Mob guys—dressed to the nines, manicured and
barbered to perfection.

It took us a while, but finally we found the restaurant, and we waited for Petey Chops.

At 6:00 P.M. there was no sign of Petey.

Ten after six. Still no sign of him.

Six-fifteen. Nothing.

That's when one of the waiters recognized Greg.
The waiter had the slick look of a guy comfortable
leaning on the rail of a racetrack or hanging around a
Vegas sports book. If you had any reason to be in contact with organized crime in Westchester County, you
knew Greg DePalma, and this guy certainly did.

"You guys want a table?" the waiter asked Greg
cautiously. Everybody was cautious around Greg, who,
even in his seventies, would reach out and slap someone he considered disrespectful.

"We just ate," Greg explained, disgusted that Petey
Chops wasn't there.

At that moment, I felt good because regardless of
what was about to happen, I knew it wasn't a hit on me.

Meanwhile, Greg muttered under his breath, "That
cocksucker, where is he?" He called the waiter over.
Whenever we were in public, he comported himself
with stereotypical Mob guy behavior.

"You know my friend Pete that eats here on Mondays?" Greg growled.

The waiter nodded. "He usually comes in with his girl," he replied carefully, not knowing what answer might be the wrong answer.

"When this guy comes here again," Greg told him, "tell him that he is to see me tomorrow at the nursing home in New Rochelle."

The nursing home, the United Hebrew Geriatric Center, was where Greg's son Craig lay in an unconscious state. Craig had been comatose for several years, after a prison suicide attempt. Craig, a made member of the Gambino crime family, had been convicted along with Greg in the Scores case, but he had cooperated with law enforcement in exchange for a reduced sentence. To an old-school Mob guy like Greg, his son's actions were reprehensible. He passed a note to Craig to that effect, and Craig, full of shame, had tried to take his own life. Instead, he had put himself into an irreversible coma. Greg regularly did Mafia business in front of his son's body, on the correct assumption that the FBI would not have the bad manners to bug his comatose son's room.

The waiter nodded.

Greg glared at him. "Tell me what I just said!" he said menacingly.

"Meet you at the nursing home in New Rochelle," the wide-eyed waiter repeated.

Greg nodded, and we figured that was that. Petey wasn't showing, so we left the restaurant and began to make our way out of the store.

Just as we passed the housewares section, there he was! Petey Chops in the flesh . . . with not just one girl but two at his side. He saw us and got nervous. As well he should have.

"There's that jerk-off!" Greg exclaimed, heading toward him.

Robert and I fell back. Greg walked up to Petey, who kissed him on the cheek, and then turned to Petey's two companions.

"Ladies, do you mind?" Greg asked, to the point as always. "I gotta talk to him."

"Girls, get a table at the restaurant," Petey told them nervously. "I gotta talk to these guys and I'll be right there."

The ladies obviously realized that they did not need to be a part of whatever was going to happen next, so they took off.

Greg and Petey leaned against the wall and started to talk. Their conversation was quiet at first. Meanwhile, Robert and I were looking over the items for sale.

"Look at this!" Robert said, astonished, picking up a vase. "They want $400 for this piece of shit!"

So I teased him. "Hey, you drop it, you bought it!"

I was trying to keep in a jocular mood, because I didn't know what was going to happen, but I sensed that it would be something bad. By now DePalma was raising his voice.

"What's the matter with you?" he demanded in a voice loud enough for Robert and me to hear. Shit, half of Bloomingdale's could have heard him, he was so loud.

Petey said nothing.

"You ain't showing up!" Greg exclaimed, his anger rising. "I'm asking you over and over to come in, and you ain't reporting to see me!"

"I can't show up, I'm telling you!" Petey said, looking uncomfortably at Greg, Robert, and me.

"I want the money that's owed me!" Greg insisted.

I later learned that Petey had invested his gambling and numbers income in a marble mine in Guatemala, of all places, and the mine had gone belly-up. Maybe in Petey's mind it was okay to offset his Guatemalan mining losses against his Mob-related income.

"I'm being watched," Petey replied belligerently, his voice rising, "and I don't want to be seen meeting anyone!"

He was loud and he was animated. In my twenty-four years as an undercover agent, I had never seen a subordinate speak so inappropriately and disrespectfully to a boss. At that moment, had I been a real wise-guy or Mafioso and not a member of law enforcement, I would have given him a crack! I was thinking, What a fucking asshole Petey Chops is! Listen, if you wanna be in the Mob, you gotta pay your dues! You're getting protection, you gotta pay up!

I was into the moment. I know I was an FBI agent, but this guy wasn't playing by the rules. It was a confrontation, and I was siding with my capo, with Greg. The guy was acting like a jerk-off. I couldn't believe he was loud, rude, and disrespectful to a capo of the family he's sworn to uphold.

"Keep it down," Greg ordered him. He must have been equally surprised by Petey's belligerence. After all, Greg was the capo, and Petey was a soldier, and people were around. We were in a very public place.

"This is bullshit," Greg snarled. "You gotta start coming in. You gotta start reporting."

"I don't want to be seen!" Petey said, increasingly nervous. "What do you want?"

"What do I want!" the Old Man exclaimed, as if he had just been asked the stupidest question in history. "I want you to start reporting like you're supposed to!"

Now the discussion became even more animated. This wasn't going down in some back alley somewhere. We stood in the housewares section of Bloomingdale's in White Plains at 6:15 P.M. on Presidents' Day. People were everywhere, shopping, milling around, whatever. I was clueless—I knew this guy was acting disrespectfully, but I still had no idea where all this was headed.

"I want you to meet someone," DePalma said, motioning toward Vaccaro, the new acting capo in our crew. An "acting" or "street" capo represents the interests of the boss in public places, sparing the boss the risk of detection by law enforcement. Many crime family leaders are on parole for one violation or another and could be returned to prison if seen in the company of other known criminals.

"I don't want to meet anyone," Petey protested, but the Old Man didn't care. I watched warily, knowing that the situation could turn violent at any moment.

"No, you *gotta* meet him," DePalma insisted. "This

is Robert. He's *a friend of ours.*" That expression—"a friend of ours"—is the special way of introducing one made man in the Mafia to another.

"He's good friends with the boss," Greg added, to emphasize Robert's importance in the Gambino family.

"I don't give a fuck who he is or what he does or who he knows," Petey responded. "I'm not reporting. This is bullshit."

Robert seethed.

I watched warily, positioning myself to hear everything they said.

"Hey, tough guy!" an annoyed Robert said, entering the fray. "Keep it down!"

"Fuck you guys!" Petey shouted as shoppers and clerks turned to look.

I was surprised. Nobody talked like that to a skipper like Greg.

That set Robert off. He grabbed a solid glass Kosta Boda candleholder, nearly a foot in length,* from the nearest display and whacked Petey over the head with it. When it connected, I heard a *pop* like a broken cantaloupe. Bystanders gasped. Petey Chops dropped to the floor, unconscious, blood gushing from his head.

Suddenly my emotions changed—I went from "This

---

* To be precise, 11⅛ inches. According to Bloomingdale's website, www.bloomingdales.com, "Cool candleholders from Kosta Boda offer a contemporary lighting option. Clear crystal shaped into clean, simple columns has a bubble effect which is showcased to perfection when lit." The candleholder lit Petey Chops up pretty good, I'll say that.

guy's an asshole and needs a crack" to "Holy shit, I'm an FBI agent and I just saw a guy get assaulted. I've got to protect him from getting killed."

If Robert had just grabbed him by the lapels and yelled at him, okay, that would be one thing. But this was an assault with apparent intent to kill. He had a yelling coming to him, not a freaking beating. That one blow alone could have killed him.

Robert was about to hit him again while he was down, so I grabbed the candleholder out of his hand and threw it down.

"Get up, you motherfucker!" Robert shouted at Petey. "Get up, tough guy! What's the matter, you're not so tough now, are you? Go ahead! Say something! Say something, you piece of shit!"

"Yeah, you cocksucker!" Greg shouted, getting into it.

This was insane. I had to get these guys away from Petey Chops—they were going to kill him, right there in the housewares section of Bloomingdale's.

"Come on!" I yelled to Vaccaro and DePalma. "We gotta get out of here! We're gonna take a pinch!"

But they didn't move a muscle. Getting arrested doesn't frighten wiseguys. Instead, Robert turned on a barely conscious Petey Chops.

"You're not so tough now, are you?" he taunted. "Say something, tough guy! Come on already!"

"What did you do that for?" Petey Chops asked, coming to. He was completely dazed and blood continued to gush out of his head.

"You're gonna get shelved!" DePalma snarled at him.

This meant that he would be stripped of all Gambino family protection for his criminal operations. Another Gambino could take over his business. The punishment was not permanent, but its revocation depended on his demonstration of remorse for his actions. Short of getting killed, this is one of the worst things that can happen to a mobster.

Suddenly I realized that Robert and Greg had to be surprised and disappointed that I was not participating in Petey's beating. But DePalma also looked concerned. Petey was a made guy, and no matter how disrespectful he might have been, Robert didn't have the right to crack him. I stood in the middle of all this thinking, If I don't participate, I'll blow my cover, but if I do get involved, Petey could get killed.

Petey sat up, covered in blood. He asked Vaccaro and DePalma again, "Why did you do that for? Come on, I was only kidding!"

"You weren't kidding," DePalma replied, disgusted. "You were being a jerk-off."

Petey wasn't used to being spoken to that way, even by his capo. Incensed, he rose and came toward us, but Vaccaro grabbed a knife from a tabletop display of Ralph Lauren Polo place settings.*

---

* The knife was from the Equestrian brand Flatware Collection by Ralph Lauren. Again, from the Bloomingdale's website, it "takes its inspiration from the classic beauty of a leather bridle, featuring rich texture and intricate detailing. Stainless steel. Dishwasher safe."

"I'm gonna stab you, you motherfucker!" Vaccaro yelled.

By now people had gathered around, witnessing this astonishing public display of brutality. Greg was oblivious to his audience.

"You better show up tomorrow or you're gonna get shelved, do you understand?" Greg told Petey.

My FBI training to save lives kicked in, and I somehow managed to get the knife away from Vaccaro and threw it back on the table. I finally got Robert and Greg on the down escalator, away from Petey; otherwise Vaccaro would have stabbed Petey in the eye or in the heart. But Petey kept coming. He bled all over my fucking coat and yelled as he approached us on the escalator, "What did you do that for! I don't understand what you did that for!"

"Listen, asshole," I told him, "get the fuck outta here, 'cause you're gonna get hurt."

Petey jumped on the escalator behind me, getting more blood all over me. Somehow he spun me around—and how a little guy like that did that to me, I'll never know. He got close to Vaccaro and DePalma.

"You're gonna get hurt!" I shouted at Petey. "Stay the fuck away!"

Too late.

First, Robert said, "Jack, keep this motherfucker away from me!"

He then yelled at Petey, "You cocksucker! I oughta kill you!"

He cold-cocked Petey with one punch, just dropped

him . . . and now Petey sat on the down escalator, unconscious, blood still streaming out of his head from the blow with the candleholder. The only thing missing were those little cartoon canaries spinning and chirping around his head. I didn't know what to do. Interfere and risk blowing my cover? Or do nothing and let a man be beaten to death in a public place, before my very eyes?

On top of that, I was afraid Petey was going to get trampled to death at the bottom of the escalator. We weren't alone there—Bloomingdale's probably had some big sale going on, and the store was busy!

So I picked up Petey Chops with one hand, woke him up, and yelled, "What are you, a stupid jerk-off?"

At the bottom of the escalator, security people scrambled toward us. DePalma, thinking quickly, didn't miss a beat. He pointed to Petey and yelled at the guards, "Hey, this poor guy just fell down the steps! He's gonna sue you!"

I've got to give Greg credit. That was a good line.

The security guards were looking around like, What the heck is going on around here?

I was still busy yelling at Petey.

"Listen," I told him, "you fucking jerk-off, get the hell out of here now."

With that, Vaccaro, DePalma, and I took off from the store, but not before DePalma looked back at Petey and yelled, "That's it, you're shelved!"

How none of us got arrested as we left Bloomingdale's, I don't know.

Back at the car, I saw Bim, my loyal guy, waiting for me in the shadows. I gave him a look like, You're not gonna believe what just happened.

I'd been running with the Gambinos for almost two and a half years at that point, and even *I* didn't believe it.

As I drove us back to the restaurant, I was deeply worried. Maybe Robert and Greg didn't like the fact that I hadn't participated in Petey's beating. It wasn't just I didn't give Petey a lick or two myself. I even tried to break up the fight, and I'd expressed my concern that we might have gotten arrested. What real wiseguy would do things like that? Were they on to me? Had I just unwittingly given away my true role—as an undercover agent?

On top of that, I had witnessed one made man hit another. From Greg's and Robert's perspective, I could go around telling other guys in the crew what I saw, and that would cause endless trouble. Knowing the Mob as well as I did, one natural resolution of this situation would be for them to whack me, in order to silence me. Or if the matter were taken to the boss of the family, they could blame me instead of Robert for hitting Petey Chops. I'd be the sacrificial lamb, and I'd get whacked at that point.

Either way, I would be killed.

What if they made a move on me right now? Robert sat in the backseat and Greg sat beside me in the passenger seat. I'm driving the car. If Robert makes a move, I decided, I'll give him a football elbow and knock him out and then punch Greg in the throat. I'd been in enough street fights growing up in the Bronx and working in my youth as a bouncer to know that if you punch a guy in the throat, he's going down.

Or if they pulled a gun on me, I would smash my truck into the first building I saw.

Or crash it into Bim's car.

That way I'd be in control—because I knew a crash was coming and they didn't. I could escape.

Or I could drive them to a police station.

Or right to the White Plains office of the FBI, which was just two hundred yards from Bloomingdale's.

Greg finally broke the deeply uncomfortable silence.

"Now listen here," he rasped, "if we get stopped by the cops, this jerk-off fell down the steps. And Robert, you gotta go see the boss tomorrow. You've got to go on record with this."

"Going on record" in this context means documenting the incident—telling the boss what happened. He's got to know. He can't be blindsided by the news. He must be kept abreast.

"Yeah, I know," Robert said sullenly.

The twenty-five minutes back to the restaurant were agonizing. I drove slowly, bracing myself for an assault. I knew that I had royally fucked up, but I had no other choice. Had I blown the whole case? Would I be whacked as a result of my actions? And when would I find out? And even if I survived, would Greg still continue with his attempts to have me inducted into La Cosa Nostra?

How exactly does a Cuban-born FBI agent end up pretending to be Italian and part of a Gambino family crime crew? How was I able to protect my identity for almost two and a half years while working undercover in four other major cases, involving terrorism in New York, corrupt cops in Florida, corrupt public officials in Atlantic City, and an international smuggling ring that brought in counterfeit cigarettes, weapons, and "Supernotes"—fake hundred-dollar bills we were told were printed in North Korea? And why would the FBI terminate the Gambino case just two weeks before the ceremony that would have transformed me into a made member of the Mafia in my own right, with the ability to vouch for undercover agents infiltrating every Mob family in the nation?

I'm still wondering about the answer to that last question myself.

CHAPTER ONE

Come Fly with Me

"This is Special Agent Joaquin M. Garcia of the FBI, and I'm consenting to record my conversation with Greg DePalma and others as-yet unknown . . ."

Then I turn the music up loud and sing along. I usually pick arias from operas like Puccini's "Nessun Dorma," or some Frank Sinatra and Dean Martin classics, or maybe a little Tony Bennett. I sing to get myself in the mood and also to entertain the poor bastards back at FBI headquarters who have to transcribe every word of these conversations.

I've been an undercover agent in the FBI for more than a quarter of a century, and I've put hundreds and hundreds of bad guys in jail: dopers, terrorists, bad cops, dirty politicians, you name it. The difference between most agents and me is that I work multiple major cases simultaneously as an undercover, sometimes juggling five or six different identities and roles. I did this for approximately twenty-four years out of my twenty-six years of service, working an FBI record of forty-five long-term major undercover investigations and countless short-term undercover operations.

Each day I speak these introductory words into the recording device strapped to my body with which I will pick up the conversations among Greg DePalma and others in his world.

Greg suffers from every serious ailment under the sun, from heart disease to lung cancer to who knows what else. But in just a few months out of prison, this man, whom both the Mob hierarchy and the FBI considered nothing more than a washed-up old brokester, a complete has-been, has reasserted his authority within his crime family. He has taken back control of the loan sharking, extortion, and gambling enterprises that once were his and is currently fighting like a bastard to resolve the issue of a hit he ordered on another wiseguy.

Every week I see the "tribute" envelopes full of cash passed to him by the members of his crew and the construction company owners and other business owners to whom he provides protection. I estimate that Greg DePalma is pulling down at least a quarter of a million dollars a year, all of it tax-free. This is not to mention the sports memorabilia, art, jewelry, watches, and everything else that he steals and sells. Greg, like the rest of the modern Mafia, is all about the money. He's spent his life in and out of prison because he has rarely taken a plea, never ratted anyone out, always went to trial, and never, ever allocuted (the legal term for admitting) to his membership in La Cosa Nostra. He never betrayed the Mob by acknowledging its existence in court. That's why I call him a stand-up mobster of the old school.

He is also among the most cautious, careful, and colorful of Mafiosi ever to grace the streets of New York. You don't get to be seventy-three and a wiseguy by making mistakes or trusting the wrong people.

Indeed, Greg DePalma has only made one serious mistake when it came to whom he trusted, whom he let into his confidence, whom he admitted to his world.

Me.

I'm on my way to meet Greg right now, for another day of eating, meetings, and the planning of beatings. It's just another day in the Mafia, just another day building a case against "Greg DePalma and others as yet unknown."

I couldn't be happier. As Sinatra sings, "Come fly with me."

CHAPTER TWO

Serpico Sent Me

When I was a kid, the last thing I ever imagined was that I'd be an undercover agent of the FBI. I was born in Havana, Cuba, in 1952 into an affluent home with nannies, housekeepers, and a government chauffeur for my father, who was an important official in the Cuban Treasury Department. My mother was an opera singer who would perform "Ave Maria" at almost every high society wedding in Havana. I had an older brother and a younger sister, and we were a tight-knit, loving family, living in a beautiful home in an elegant neighborhood. My father was six feet four inches tall and weighed 240 pounds. I always remember him working hard at the huge home office he maintained in addition to his magisterial government office. It's hard to recall him without a cigar—he would smoke at least ten a day. In Cuba he was known as Señor Garcia, and everyone loved him. He was a great guy, and my mother was an angel.

In 1959 Fidel Castro began his revolution and tossed out the Batista government, in the name of eliminating corruption from the island nation. My father, fearing for his life, contacted his counterparts at the U.S. Embassy in Havana. One night in 1959 he awakened us, kissed us good-bye, and was escorted out by the FBI attaché in Cuba. The next day Castro's militia came looking for him, but he was already gone. Had he stayed one more night, he might well have been taken out and killed.

My father had to work three jobs in Manhattan in order to raise enough money to get the rest of the family out of Cuba. He worked the midnight shift as a bookkeeper in a hotel and took backbreaking, menial jobs during the day. He took anything that he could get, working around the clock for a year to raise the money to get us out. In Havana, feelings about Castro divided families. Whenever my father called, he and my mother talked in code, because they knew that the calls to and from the United States were being tapped. It cost a fortune for us to call the United States, so we waited for my father to call from New York. The phone calls, always monitored, were disconnected if my parents' conversation ventured into territory that was considered too controversial by the Cuban censors.

My father eventually put enough aside so that my mother, my brother, my sister, and I could make the short flight from Havana to Miami, where our father escorted us to New York. I'll never forget that as a nine-year-old, I was strip-searched for contraband at the Havana Airport by Castro's soldiers. The irony is that the FBI, for many years during the 1960s and '70s and even into the early '80s, was wary of taking on Cuban-born individuals as Special Agents, fearing that we might be moles planted by Castro's regime. In fact, the opposite was the case. Just about anyone who left Havana in those years hated Castro with an abiding passion, because of the way he divided families, destroyed livelihoods, and imprisoned and killed so many people. I was appointed as a Special Agent of the FBI in 1980, only the second Cuban to achieve this honor.

I was always an outgoing person, even as a kid. So I quickly learned English, American culture, how to make friends, and all about American life. My given name, spelled Joaquin and pronounced Wakeen, was too hard for most of the Americans I met, so they called me Jock because I loved to play sports. Remember, Joaquin Phoenix was not even born yet!

The 1960s was a time when people wanted to assimilate, instead of keeping out of the mainstream and identifying primarily with their ethnic origin, as is the case today for many. Back then I was embarrassed by my accent. I would say "choos" for shoes or "shins" for chins, or "jello" for yellow, and my friends would make fun of me. To this day, if I get overly excited or immersed in a Spanish-speaking setting, my accent will come out. My wife will laugh at me and call me Ricky Ricardo.

My father eventually established his own successful accounting firm and was like the godfather of the community—everybody loved "Mr. G," as he came to be known in New York. He walked the streets with his big cigar and helped people solve their problems—with taxes, with accounting issues in their own small businesses, with whatever they needed. He even wrote a book called *El Income Tax y Usted* (Income Tax and You) to help the Hispanic community understand the American tax system. He was a great man and everybody loved him. I'm sure I derived my sense of community service from the way he went about his business.

I became a typical teenager and cared most about football. At six four and 240 pounds, I was built for the game and loved being part of a team. I played on a championship team in high school and was voted All-Conference. As a result, I got a lot of scholarship offers to play football. I have to admit that my grades were poor, something that really angered my parents, and the best of the schools from an academic perspective was one in Texas. Now, that was an eye-opening experience for a Cuban boy from the Bronx, let me tell you! The school was in the middle of nowhere, and it offered me my first real experiences with prejudice and bias.

I would tell people, "I'm Cuban."

They would respond, "No, you're Mexican. Your name is Garcia, so you must be a Mexican."

I tried to explain that there were Puerto Ricans, Dominicans, Cubans, and Mexicans, each with our own different culture, but nobody cared or understood. If you had a last name like Garcia, you were Mexican, and that was the end of the discussion. I think what kept me sane was playing football and the many friends on the team. That's how it was in the Panhandle of Texas in 1970.

After a successful freshman year, I decided to move back home and transfer to a junior college in New York that won a national championship, where I also played football. I then received a full football scholarship to a powerhouse school in Virginia, where I played football and from which I graduated. About this time, two events conspired to make me start thinking about the FBI. First, two brothers who played ball with me in Virginia had a father who was an FBI agent. So that got me thinking about it. And then the movie *Serpico* came out, and that changed everything for me. Al Pacino played a New York City undercover cop named Frank Serpico, who infiltrated the world of drug dealers and other criminals going under the name Paco. He had long hair and a real tough, cool-guy attitude, and I couldn't get enough of that movie.

After my experience as a child with the lawlessness of Castro's Cuba, I had developed a visceral hatred of crime and corruption in all forms. In *Serpico* I saw a guy who had the ability to go inside the barricades, to mingle with the criminal element, catch them breaking the law, and put them in jail. I loved *Serpico*! It was one of those moments where I suddenly saw my whole future, what I was meant to do with my life. And if I'm going to be in law enforcement, let me shoot for the stars and be part of the most prestigious law enforcement agency in the world: the FBI. So that became my life's goal.

I applied for the FBI but I heard nothing for a long time. One day I was watching Spanish-language TV and the FBI was advertising for Spanish-speaking agents. That's bizarre! Here I am, a Spanish-speaking applicant in good standing who met all of the Special Agent requirements, and I hadn't heard anything! So I called the FBI recruiter.

"How come I haven't heard anything regarding my application?" I asked.

His answer was very simple.

"You aren't a citizen," he told me.

I couldn't believe it! Okay, I'll go and immediately file my application for naturalization! I'd love to be an American citizen! I'd lived here practically all my life, so I already felt as though I was an American, although I was proud and remain proud of my Cuban roots. So I took the test, passed, and was on my way to be sworn in. I'll never forget when I went down to Newark, New Jersey, to raise my right hand along with hundreds of other immigrants from around the world who were also becoming U.S. citizens during the 1976 celebration of the nation's Bicentennial. The scene was comical, and I swear it happened just the way it does in the movies. We were given small American flags and the official swearing us in told us to raise our right hands and repeat after him. "I" . . . and we all said "I" . . . and then he said, "State your name," and sure enough, everybody responded, "State your name!"

I shook my head, looked around, and thought, Oh my God. Did I just hear that right?

With my citizenship in place, I contacted the FBI, and they scheduled me for the battery of entrance exams. These were really tough tests with a lot of hard-core math. I'm no genius at math and I wasn't the greatest student. When I finished the math part, I thought to myself, Well, there goes *that* career. What else could I do? But I'm a believer in destiny, and it turned out that I did very well on the test. I guessed at a lot of the questions, but I somehow got good scores.

That brought me to the next level of the application process to become an FBI agent—panel interviews with other agents. They reviewed my accomplishments, the opportunities I had created for myself, and my goals. I could tell from their expressions that they were impressed, and I later learned their input elevated my total score. As a result, in February 1980 I was admitted to an FBI training class and headed off to Quantico, Virginia, for sixteen weeks of training at the FBI Academy.

My parents were not thrilled by my career choice. They were hoping that I might become an accountant or an attorney, like my siblings. My mother expressed her concern that I could be injured or killed while working the streets. My father had been in law enforcement early in his career in Havana, but he didn't especially want me to follow the same career path. Yet they somewhat reluctantly gave their blessing to my decision. Their attitude was, This isn't what we would have wanted for him, but at least he's doing what makes him happy.

I had received some law enforcement training while working briefly at the Union County, New Jersey, Prosecutor's Office as an investigator. At Quantico, they told us, "Whatever you know about law enforcement from past experience, forget about it. We're going to teach you the FBI way—in forensics, in firearms training, in everything. And just because you are admitted to the sixteen-week program doesn't mean you're automatically appointed to the FBI. You can be called out of your classroom at any time and cut from the program—for any reason. You're gone, just like that." So we were always on our toes.

The physical aspect of the training—running, push-ups, sit-ups, pull-ups—did not present a problem. I was out of shape when I arrived, but I knew from my football experience that I could quickly round into shape. Firearms—not a problem. The FBI prides itself on the ability of its agents to shoot, but I was decent even before I got to the academy. I'd gone to the range with my buddies on occasion over the years, and I had received some firearms training with the Union County Prosecutor's Office. A passing grade in firearms at

Quantico was 85; my scores were consistently in the low 90s. By FBI standards, I was a good shot if not a great one.

My real weakness was academics, so I found some smart guys in the class to help me out, tutor me. When I was in college playing ball, I was just out there having fun. I never took schoolwork seriously. My parents stressed education, but I never did. So now I really had to hit the books. What's the Bill of Rights? What's search and seizure? By the time the tests came, I was prepared, and I did well. This was the first time in my life I had to study, and that didn't come easily for me.

Unfortunately, an assistant director at Quantico took an instant dislike to me because of my appearance. At the time, the FBI placed a lot of emphasis on looking like Director J. Edgar Hoover's ideal image of the G-man—in great shape, well dressed, the whole thing. The assistant director running our group told me that I was overweight. Well, that wasn't exactly news to me! According to the medical charts, as an individual six feet four inches tall, I should have weighed 210 pounds. Hey, I had never weighed 210 pounds in my life, except maybe when I was fifteen years old!

Two weeks after arriving in Quantico, this supervisor pulled me out of class.

"You've got to resign," he told me flatly, "because of your weight. If you don't resign, you'll be fired with no possibility of being reinstated. If you do resign, you can drop the weight and get into the next training class."

I was outraged! How come nobody told me this ahead of time? I'd already had a going-away party at my former job, and now I faced unemployment! I was faster and stronger than some of the other agent trainees in my class who weighed much less than me. But I had no choice. I resigned and went home, embarrassed and depressed.

My class counselor, Special Agent Jim Pledger, got in touch with me.

"You got screwed," he told me. "Lose the weight, get back here, and prove them wrong."

My depression vanished, and suddenly I turned into Rocky. I lost forty pounds in two months, got weighed in, and then was sworn in again as an FBI trainee in May 1980. I even walked up to the assistant director and said, "See, I told you I could have done this. There was no need for you to do this to me."

He couldn't look me in the eye. Typical bureaucracy. But no matter. I passed Quantico with flying colors, with the constant tutoring of my best friend, T. J. Murray, who, sadly, has since passed away. I helped him with firearms and he helped me with academics. I was admitted to the FBI. I was on my way.

CHAPTER THREE

The "FNG"

There's a complicated system allowing agents to express preferences about offices and assignments that all FBI agents must follow. It would take too long to go through the whole thing here, but the FBI does have a very comprehensive approach to soliciting agents' desires and then determining how best to deploy them. The only problem is that they totally ignore the system. If you ask the average FBI agent, he'll tell you that the way the Bureau assigns people is that they've got a monkey in a room who throws a dart with your name on it at a U.S. map on the wall. People who want to go East get sent West. People who want to go West are sent East. The whole thing is ridiculous.

An agent can't switch once a decision has been made, and there's absolutely no logic to any of it. It goes back to the Hoover days. J. Edgar wanted agents away from where they grew up so they wouldn't be corrupted. But that's really crazy! The smart thing is to send agents home where they have connections and street knowledge. Otherwise, every agent wastes time figuring out every city—what neighborhoods are good and bad, what the "rules of the road" for the community are, and so on. It's ridiculous.

I was lucky—my dart landed near home. My first assignment was Newark. Typically, rookies get lousy squad assignments. FBI field offices are broken down into squads, which each handle specific violations, such as bank robberies, applicants, white-collar crime, and so on. The FBI is organized into divisions, and the size of the division determines the number of squads. The Newark division had about twenty-five squads. A squad supervisor handles all of the cases in his region that fall under the rubric of his particular squad. Individual case agents in the squad run each case, and the rest of the squad helps the case agent achieve the goals of the investigation. Let's say I'm in Newark and I get a lead about a bank robbery in Alabama. I'll pass that on to the squad supervisor and case agent down in Mobile, so they can take action.

Of course, divisions sometimes get territorial. I might be working a dope case in Newark and I'll identify the source of a conspiracy to import cocaine. Let's say the source is in the Bronx. So I'll send that information to the appropriate agent in the New York office, but the New York office may try to steal the case, take it from us. That happens all the time. Ideally, we ought to be thinking about one FBI, one overarching set of law enforcement goals, a team effort.

New agents rotate through various squads and usually end up on some boring, low-level squad. Yet someone or something was watching out for me. After just three or four weeks on squad rotation, I was assigned to the finest, most important, most coveted group of all, the Fugitive/Bank Robbery/Terrorist Squad, C-1. I'd be learning from seasoned veterans right out of the gate. I was the envy of my new fellow agents stuck working stolen cars and other low-level cases.

My first few weeks, nobody in the entire squad asked me to do anything. I would just sit there at my desk, from 7:00 A.M. until 6:00 P.M., when everybody went home and all the radio chatter among the agents working in the field dropped down to a trickle. Nobody wanted to use me for anything. Nobody even wanted to talk to me. I was the loneliest guy in the FBI.

My nonofficial title in the squad was "FNG," which stands for fucking new guy. Who was I? the other agents wondered. How did I get assigned to this desirable position? "What are you," they'd ask me, "the SAC [Special Agent in Charge]'s pet?"

I kept my mouth shut and just waited for the opportunity to be a part of something. Time and again, word came in that a fugitive was holed up in an apartment somewhere in Newark or a bank robbery was going down. All the agents in the room saddled up—shotguns, vests, handcuffs, all the tools of law enforcement. I'd ask plaintively, "Can I go with you guys?"

The answer was always the same. "No, kid. You stay here."

It was eating at me, just killing me that I wasn't allowed to participate in the action with my fellow agents. It wasn't that I had nothing to do. The problem was that I had nothing *meaningful* to do. Like all rookies, I was given files to read, but these files were on cases that were referred to as "old dogs"—fugitives who were out there for so long, the idea of ever catching them was just a joke. They'd even wrapped the assignment file of one case with an Alpo dog food label, just to emphasize what a dog that case really was.

Here I was, a lowly GS-10, a rookie getting coffee and sandwiches for twenty guys, with nothing else to do. When I saw the guys talking about heading out for a drink at the end of a workday, I'd say, "You guys going out after work?" "No—sorry, kid!" was always the response. They were going out, but they just didn't want me to tag along. It was okay. That's just how things were back then. I had to pay my dues.

One day, when I had been on the job for a couple of months, one of the agents had a hot lead on a fugitive who had closeted himself away in a house in a bad neighborhood in Jersey City. The agent was Pat Johnson, who had the nickname "Superman" because he looked just like Christopher Reeve. Johnson looked around for somebody to come with him to make the collar. He was considered a "heavy" agent—which means that he would be called on to react to a crisis situation, like a bank robbery in progress. "Heavy" was an FBI term of approbation for the bravest agents who worked the most dangerous cases.

I saw him looking around, so I said, "Need help?"

He shook me off. "Nah, we got it, kid."

He must have seen my face fall, or maybe there just weren't any other agents available at that particular moment.

"All right, come on," he said to me, in the tone of voice you reserve when your younger brother wants to tag along on a date. I was so excited I could barely contain myself.

We went out to Jersey City, and it turned out that all the information was correct. The fugitive was indeed hiding in this particular house. So we went in, just like in the movies. My heart was pounding, I was so excited. We had a guy watching the back door, and then Johnson yelled, "FBI! Open the door!"

We heard noises from inside the house—the guy was getting ready to take off. So Pat, who was extremely strong, hauled off and kicked the door in. Or at least he tried to. He didn't budge it.

"I got it! I got it!" I yelled. There was no restraining me. I hit that door like I was taking down a tackle on the football field. No problem. I flattened the thing. We found the guy upstairs, and we arrested him.

It was the first time I had participated in a collar—the arrest of a suspect. More important, after what I had done to that door, I was *in*. I was finally accepted by the other agents on the squad.

Johnson couldn't resist ragging me. "I loosened the door for you, kid."

He had to say that, because all the other agents were teasing him, saying "Hey, Superman, you let the FNG show you how to knock down doors!"

From that moment on, I had become one of the guys. Soon I was involved in terrorist cases involving the anti-Castro group Omega 7, the Weather Underground, the New World of Islam, and FALN, a group that agitated for the independence of Puerto Rico. To my surprise, I found myself mentioned on a "wanted" poster that the group distributed and hung up throughout the Union City, New Jersey, area. It said at the top *"Condenados a Muerte"*—Condemned to Death. The targets were primarily FBI informants, along with agents of G-2, the Cuban equivalent of the FBI. But I was also named on that wanted poster for having recruited an FBI informant.

The most important thing that happened to me in these first few years of my career with the FBI, involved the search for a top-ten most wanted fugitive, Ronald Turley Williams. This case was so big for me because it provided me with my first taste of undercover work. Ron Williams was known for frequenting massage parlors in the New York area, and he favored one particular masseuse above all. It was our mission to find that masseuse, because she could lead us to Williams. We instituted surveillance on massage parlors in Manhattan, and we even sent a few agents to the parlors, to gain admittance and seek information. But they were all turned away. They looked too much like cops.

The FBI is a very conservative agency. We're the guys—at least we used to be the guys—in the suits with the narrow lapels, the narrow ties, the white shirts, and the wing-tip oxford shoes known as thousand-eye shoes. You didn't need the gun, the handcuffs, the radio, or the badge—when you went on the street dressed as a typical FBI agent, everything about you screamed "FBI." There's an expression in Spanish that captures it completely—it's *tiene la pinta de un policia,* and it translates as "he has the color of a cop." In other words, if someone painted a law enforcement officer, we'd be the guy in the painting.

When I first got into the Bureau, I absolutely radiated law enforcement, from the way I carried myself to the way I spoke—there was no mistaking what I did for a living. I was a Cuban émigré and my family had absolutely nothing when we were lucky enough to come to this country. And now I was a Special Agent of the FBI. Talk about living the American dream! All I wanted to do was knock down doors, lock up fugitives, and arrest bad guys! I know that sounds almost childlike in its innocence, but that's how I truly felt. And that's how I still feel, after almost thirty years on the job. I might not have been going undercover at the time, like my childhood hero Serpico. But I was working complex investigations and learning from the best agents in the Bureau: Ed Petersen, Pat Johnson,

Dan McLaughlin, Ron Romano, Ron Butkiewicz—true FBI legends. But in every other way, I was living my dream.

And then one day they asked me to go undercover and gain admission to the massage parlors.

I thought they were crazy. "They're going to read me!" I exclaimed, stunned. "They're going to see *la pinta* of a cop! They'll make me in two seconds!"

They ignored my protestations and sent me in. I took off my tie, my white shirt, my oxfords, and I put my sneakers on and a polo-style shirt that I had in the trunk of my car for when I went to work out. An agent can't go to a massage parlor wearing those thousand-eye government-issue oxford wing-tip shoes!

The first massage parlor on my list was located in a brownstone in the East 20s. Back then the massage parlors in New York were pretty much all in brownstones. That way there wasn't a nosy doorman snooping around. If a client wanted to go inside, he had to have an appointment, or he had to be known to them. So I'm standing there, nervous as hell, barely breathing, and I knocked on the door. A small screen opened.

I knew I was being looked at.

"Yes, can I help you?"

"Let me in," I said, my heart literally trembling. "I want to come in."

A moment later I heard the door unlocked, and I was in.

The place was nothing special. It wasn't filthy,

beat-up, or seedy, but it certainly wasn't super high-end either. The main room, which must have been a living room when the place was a private home, had two couches, a table, and a bar. There were a couple of guys drinking at the bar. They looked like your neighbors—businessmen, professionals. It wasn't a place where they were sneaking around or had furtive expressions on their faces. The customers were totally relaxed. They came in, had a couple of cocktails, did what they had to do, and then they'd go home to their wives or girlfriends.

Nobody was doped up or lying on the floor or anything like that. It was a very low-key operation. Girls would come out dressed in gowns. You picked the one you wanted, and you'd go off to a back room with her. At the time, a massage would cost fifty to seventy-five dollars. Back then massage parlors were like the United Nations—you had women of every race and ethnicity. Today it's mostly Asian, but then it was a mix.

A very attractive girl came out in a gown and escorted me to a back room.

"Get undressed," she said.

"I—I'm just looking for a friend of mine," I stammered.

"No problem," she said. "Just take off your pants."

I felt like Jackie Gleason playing Ralph Kramden—all that came to me to say was "Hummina, hummina, hummina." I didn't know what to do. I certainly hadn't gotten any training for moments like this.

So I took off my pants. I stood there in my Hanes

boxer shorts and I said, "Look, I really don't want a massage. I'm just trying to find this particular girl whose name is China. She's a friend of mine and I've got some stuff that belongs to her. Do you know where she is?"

"I know her," the girl said, "but I wouldn't know how to find her. She used to work here, but she works someplace else now. Where that is, I couldn't tell you. You sure you don't want a massage?"

I've got to tell you, the girl was really beautiful—long brown hair and a great body. But I was there on official FBI business. A massage was not on the menu. So I put my pants on and headed out. As I was leaving, I saw that she was talking to the bouncer about me, but I didn't get into any sort of trouble with anybody. I just took my leave, and that was it.

Once I got back to my fellow agents, they wanted to hear the whole story. I told them about how I took my pants off, and they roared with laughter. They thought it was the funniest thing they ever heard—me standing in my underwear interviewing a masseuse. They asked me what she looked like and whether I got aroused, the typical things guys would say to each other. But the main thing was that I had gotten in—and they hadn't made me for a cop.

That was a revelation for me.

I soon repeated the process at a second massage parlor a few blocks away, and this time I felt a little more confident as I approached the door of the brownstone. I knocked on the door not like a scared

FBI agent but like a typical business guy who went to massage parlors every week of his life. No big deal. They let me in there as well. And this time I struck pay dirt. I found a girl who knew where China worked. As a result, we were able to track her down and, through her, discover the whereabouts of the fugitive for whom we had been searching.

By the time they found Williams, shortly after my initial forays into undercover work, I had been sent to Puerto Rico to work on the FALN case. My brother agents Dan McLaughlin, Eddie Petersen, and Ron Butkiewicz arrested Williams in a violent shoot-out in a New York City hotel. Williams was shot five or six times by several different agents. Thank God none of our guys was hit in the violent exchange of fire. Had I been there, I could have been shot and not been here to tell this story.

It turned out that I had a strong ability for under-cover work. At that time, few agents in the Bureau had any experience going undercover. It wasn't something Hoover had thought much of, and the Bureau tended to rely on informants for their information about criminal activity. But it became obvious to me that information from informants was always suspect—you never knew if they were telling you the truth, whether they were being self-serving or looking out for your interests, or even if you could find them when you needed them. If you went undercover, you had control over the process for creating your own information about what was really going on. I had a sudden taste for undercover work, and I wanted to do more of it. The Bureau put me on a three-and-a-half-year undercover investigation on a national security matter that I am still not at liberty to describe. It gave me a nice apartment, a nice car, and an expense account, and in all the time working that case, I never went into the office once. I did good enough work on the case for the Bureau that I could choose any city in the United States for my next assignment.

So I put in a request for a transfer to Miami, where there would be plenty of opportunity for a Cuban-born FBI agent to go undercover to solve crimes.

So, of course, the Bureau sent me to Philadelphia.

CHAPTER FOUR

Tipping the Scales of Justice

For me, before the Gambinos, there were the Badlands.

The Badlands neighborhood of North Philadelphia is one of the most dangerous and drug-infested communities in the nation. The neighborhood is overrun with drug dealers from Colombia, the Dominican Republic, Mexico, and elsewhere. It's about as dangerous a place to survive as an undercover law enforcement agent that you'll find. And for four years, I was Manolo, a Mercedes-driving, Bacardi-and-Coke-drinking, cigar-smoking drug dealer and money launderer. Or at least that's the role I played.

My entrée into the Badlands came thanks to the hard work of my fellow FBI agent W. Van Marsh, who had developed a case against one of the leading bookies in the neighborhood, a man called "Tony Oro." Van Marsh had arranged for Tony to broker the sale of two kilos of practically pure cocaine to another of Van Marsh's sources. Once the deal was done, Van Marsh revealed his identity as an FBI agent, took Tony to breakfast, and gave him a choice: cooperate with the FBI, or spend the next few decades behind bars.

Tony was not a large man, but he carried himself with the swagger of the streets. He was in his early fifties, a father, and a very wealthy man, thanks to his sports betting and numbers operations. Tony wore a huge necklace and pendant with an Aztec god embedded with diamonds, rubies, and emeralds. It must have been worth half a million dollars. Tony displayed it proudly and fearlessly in the Badlands—after all, who was going to bother *him*? When he ran short of cash, the outsize piece of jewelry served as an emergency bank account—he could hock one of the precious stones and pay off his debts.

The exterior appearances of drug neighborhoods can be deceiving. The homes may look like tenement row homes from the outside, but on the inside, many of the drug dealers and other high-level bad guys live in astonishing splendor. Inside, the houses of some of the main targets in the case—the people who controlled the drug trade in a given neighborhood—looked like electronics store showrooms, with the latest and best TVs, sound systems, and appliances. They had fine furniture, rich carpets, and luxury cars. Tony, for example, drove a Rolls-Royce Corniche. Some even had cockfighting rings in their homes.

Living in the neighborhoods where they dealt drugs

offered both a sense of security and a steady supply of trustworthy assistants. Drug kingpins hired relatives and friends to prepare the drugs, sell them, take care of the money, and perform other tasks related to the illicit sale of drugs. They were very happy living there because everybody in the neighborhood looked out for them—the same way mobsters benefit from the protection of the community in the five boroughs. These narcotics traffickers could live anywhere, but they choose to remain in these neighborhoods because they feel protected. There was obviously a lot of money to be made taking bets and brokering drug deals.

At the time, in the late 1980s, a kilo of nearly pure cocaine could be purchased on the streets of Philadelphia, or any major city, for that matter, for between $17,000 and $25,000. Yet the street value of that cocaine was astronomically higher. First, you could cut it with baby lactose, inositol, or some other chemical, thus doubling its weight. This is a process drug dealers call "stepping on" the drugs. So now your one-kilo, or 1,000-gram, investment yields you two kilos, or 2,000 grams, to sell. If you're especially greedy, you can step on it again, and now you've got three kilos, or 3,000 grams. The average consumer, who is desperate for a quick high, is less concerned with purity than availability, and accepts the risk of buying diluted cocaine, usually in a "dime bag," which contains one gram, for $100. So do the math: 3,000 grams derived from that initial, 95 percent pure kilo of cocaine, stepped on twice, yields enough product to make 3,000 grams, which retail for $100 a gram. That's $300,000 worth of gross income coming from that initial investment of $17,000 to $25,000.

A lot of dopers don't even put down the full amount of the purchase price when they buy, creating financial leverage that investors in real estate or the stock market could only envy. A few thousand dollars' "down payment" on a kilo yields a return one hundred times the size of the investment. Or to put it more simply, after all the expenses are taken into account, a drug dealer can net a quarter of a million dollars pure, untaxed profit for every kilo he buys.

Of course, there are certain challenges in making a living as a drug dealer. First, you're dealing with a supply network that's heavily armed and thinks nothing of killing people over the smallest of suspicions or disagreements. Second, although you might not be able to tell if you wandered into an urban, sidewalk drug supermarket, it's against the law to buy and sell dope. It's impossible to tell whether a "customer" is a law enforcement agent. And that's where I came in.

At my height and weight—by now I was three hundred pounds—I did not fit a drug dealer's picture of what a law enforcement agent looked like. And that's what we were banking on when Tony the bookmaker became Tony the FBI cooperating witness.* Van Marsh introduced him to me, because Van Marsh wanted

---

* In FBI terms, a cooperating witness, unlike an informant, wears a wire, and can be called to testify in open court.

someone to replace him in handling Tony, running the case and doing the undercover work, while he took on a well-deserved promotion at the FBI Academy.

Tony had a new mission in life: Convince individuals with whom he did business that I was a legitimate bad guy, a drug dealer, and a money launderer. And for the next few years, Tony risked his life helping me to create that image in the community, and I risked my life, by working the Badlands, often seven days a week, seeking to put bad guys behind bars.

In order to foster the image that I was Manolo, a bad guy's bad guy, Tony started to take me around the community. Initially, our forays into the underworld of the Badlands consisted of multiple daily visits, sometimes as often as four times a day, to a restaurant/nightclub in the heart of the area known as El Kibuk. The owners of the club were Cuban drug dealers, and the club was a hangout, meeting place, and trading floor for the dealers and other lowlifes of North Philadelphia.

To burnish my image, I drove a new, luxurious, customized SL500 AMG package Mercedes-Benz that the Bureau had seized from drug dealers in Miami. I always flashed a huge, FBI-supplied bankroll. I quickly learned from Tony how to comport myself on the streets and in clubs. Tony would always say, "Power perceived is power achieved." Bad guys never asked for a check when they went into a restaurant or bar. They might get a cup of coffee or a drink, but they would never pay for it directly. That would break the bad guy code. Instead, I learned from Tony to leave a fifty-dollar or a hundred-dollar tip for that cup of coffee. A bad guy would never go into a bar and ask, "What kind of beer do you have?" Or "What do you have on draft?" That kind of question is for losers.

A true bad guy knows exactly what brand of beer he drinks. Give me a *llave*, Spanish for key. This was a signal for the bartender that you wanted a Beck's, because there is a key on the top label of a bottle of Beck's beer. Similarly, as a Cuban, if I wanted a rum and Coke, my drink of choice as Manolo, I wouldn't ask for a Cuba libre, which translates to "free Cuba," as that drink is commonly known. Instead, I'd ask for a *mentira,* Spanish for "a lie," because everybody knew that as long as Castro was in charge, there was no such thing as a Cuba libre. And I would immediately get rid of the straw. No self-respecting tough guy sucks on a straw!

A guy my size is hard not to notice, especially when I'm driving that big Mercedes, dropping in four times a day at El Kibuk, and hanging out with Tony, a known quantity in the Badlands. After just a few weeks, people began to approach Tony and ask about my bona fides. Was I a bad guy? Could I be trusted? What did I do? What was I looking for? In order to convince the suspects that I really was a dangerous person and one of them, we had a mug shot taken of me indicating that I was wanted by the FBI for drug distribution and murder.

Tony put that photo out on the street, claiming that he got it from some dirty cops. It wasn't long before other bad guys started to approach me to do deals. Other FBI agents would show their informants the same photo and ask, "You seen this guy around?" This added to my bona fides, because the bad guys now had additional "evidence" that I was a bad guy too.

Was it frightening? Of course it was. Some of the higher-level drug dealers, who buy and sell dozens or hundreds of kilos of cocaine or heroin at a time, are businessmen indistinguishable in manner or appearance from the men you might see on a commuter train heading to work in the morning. Most would never have imagined using drugs themselves. It was strictly business for them, and while I never felt entirely safe around them, I never felt especially threatened in their presence.

But by the time the drugs reached the street, the dealers were cut from an entirely different cloth. They were invariably addicts themselves, always armed, always suspicious to the point of being paranoid, a state no doubt fueled by their drug use. They represented a constant, lethal danger and would have killed me as soon as looked at me. For example, one dealer killed someone who owed him for some kilos by dumping him into a barrel full of lye, sealing the barrel up, and disposing of it in the Schuylkill River.

I took what precautions I could. For example, when I was on the phone with a dealer I'd never met face to face, I'd tell him, "They call me Flaco [Spanish for "skinny"]. I'm five foot two and I weigh a hundred and fifty pounds. I'll be wearing jeans and a T-shirt."

That way I'd have the advantage. The target wouldn't know who I was, and I certainly wasn't a little guy wearing jeans and a T-shirt. If I didn't like the situation, I could walk away without the target making me for law enforcement.

I did roughly forty-five separate dope buys in the Badlands, which were divided into turfs. Each corner had its workers, lookout guys, and "stash houses." Despite my height and my girth, and despite the fact that Tony was vouching for me, every once in a while some hard-core paranoid dealer would ask me whether I was a cop. They usually ask any newcomer in their midst this question. Many drug dealers live under the misapprehension that if they ask an undercover officer whether he is a policeman, they are not criminally liable for any acts that follow once the officer says no. Of course, that's not true, but it's tough to get these guys to abandon a concept like that. One lowlife even asked me for a driver's license! Naturally I told the guy what he could do with his request for a driver's license. He never saw it, we did the deal, and he went to jail.

At one point, the owner of El Kibuk actually gave me a device called a wire detector, which you can buy at spy shops. It's a little black box the size of a pager. It can detect the radio frequencies emitted by the kind of wires that I wore as an FBI agent. The owner was trying to do me a favor—help me identify whether a guy I was supposed to meet was an informer for law enforcement. Fortunately, he gave me the device while it was turned off. Otherwise, it would have detected the wire *I* was wearing, and I might have found myself floating down the Schuylkill River in a barrel, like that other poor bastard!

My role as Manolo was time-consuming, requiring me to spend vast amounts of time in character with Tony and with the always-dangerous cast of characters on the streets of North Philly. Tony himself was a cocaine addict, and his behavior was as erratic as one might expect from a longtime user. I used to think of him as Dr. Jekyll and You Better Hyde. When he was clean and sober, he was as nice a guy as I might wish to meet. But when he was using, he was crazy, despondent, suspicious, murderous, an absolute nightmare to be around.

On top of that, in order to remain in character, I had to be available to take his calls at any time of the day or night. He might call at three or four in the morning with someone for me to meet or just to ramble on in a drug-induced state of paranoia. It drove my wife crazy that I would be spending more time with Tony than with her, that I would spend entire weekends with him, and that I lived at Tony's beck and call. The high demands my role as Manolo made definitely put a strain on my marriage. My wife didn't like the danger I faced every day, and she didn't like the long hours I had to spend on the job. It's not easy being married to an undercover agent.

At the same time, I was being pressured by my new supervisor in the Philadelphia field office of the Bureau, an ex-Marine we'll call Martland. For whatever reason, he took an immediate dislike to me. He was a by-the-book Marine, and he brought his love of regulations to his role as supervisor in the Philly field office. In his eyes, because of my weight, I was a number-one offender.

The emotional toll of playing Manolo and the strain in my marriage caused me to put on the pounds. Hey, I'm a nervous eater. Some guys get anxious, they reach for the Jack Daniel's. Me? I go for the Apple Puff Entenmann's. So the question quickly became this: What was more important, the weight of the cocaine and heroin we were trying to take off the streets, or the weight of FBI Agent Joaquin Garcia?

From Martland's perspective, the only thing that mattered was that I was too heavy to match the image of the perfect FBI agent, and something had to be done about it. He tried to put me on a scale, but at 350 pounds, I was too heavy for any typical bathroom scale. So, ignoring all his other responsibilities as supervisor, Martland devoted a considerable amount of time to finding a scale large enough to weigh me!

The scale he found was in the basement of the Federal Building, and he ordered a female ex-Marine nurse on the office staff to weigh me every week. It sounds funny now looking back, but at the time, it was absolutely humiliating. Here I was risking my life for the Bureau and for American citizens day after day, night after night, sometimes around the clock, and the only thing my supervisor could think about was finding a scale big enough to measure me.

I had to get weighed every week, and I was expected to drop at least a pound a week. I found a doctor in nearby Camden, New Jersey, who put me on diet pills, which did help me lose some of the weight, but they made me even more jittery as I tried to deal with my responsibilities as an undercover agent. Before long, despite the diet pills, my nervous eating was causing my weight to go even higher. I knew that if word of this got back to Martland, he'd pull me from the investigation and perhaps even try to have me booted out of the FBI. So I discovered a scam of my own: If I went and bought my own scale, I wouldn't have to go to the basement of the Federal Building to be weighed.

I put the case on hold—no bad guys, no drugs, no Tony—and went shopping! I must have gone to every department store in Philadelphia and South Jersey testing every scale they had. Finally I found the one, the Holy Grail, a scale that registered my true weight. But if I leaned just a little bit on the side, I could cheat and it appeared that I lost a pound when in reality my weight had either stayed the same or had actually gone up. For the first month or two, my scam worked perfectly. The ex-Marine nurse would be down on her hands and knees, trying to see the number on the scale, while I would be vigorously leaning off to the side in order to fake her out. Sometimes I felt like the leaning Tower of Pisa!

Unfortunately, as the months went by and my weight continued to rise, one day I leaned a little too far . . . and while she's down on her hands and knees, I fell off and landed on top of her! My scam was revealed, and Martland had the ammunition he needed to have me tossed off the case and out of the Bureau. He immediately had me placed on probation, held up my pay raises, and began the process of personally monitoring my weight loss in order to pursue possible dismissal. It's funny how I sometimes worried more about how much I was going to weigh than my personal safety on the streets. I knew I could talk myself out of dangerous situations in the Badlands, but inside the FBI office in Philadelphia, I was running scared.

My saving grace was that in my role as Manolo, I had already begun to produce results. Tony, to his credit, played his part to perfection. I don't think anyone in the Badlands ever suspected that he was an informant or that I was an undercover agent. I'm grateful to Tony, because the lessons he taught me about how to walk among bad guys made an important difference for me throughout the rest of my career, especially when I was undercover with the Gambinos. But back then I was a relative novice at the world of undercover investigation. And, one by one, we began to pick off the drug dealers of North Philadelphia.

Drug dealers, like businesspeople in any line of work, tend to talk. They talk about business, they talk about new customers, they talk about suppliers, they talk about prices. Under those circumstances, it would have been impossible for me to simply go to one drug dealer after another on the streets of North Philadel-

phia and do a buy-bust—arrange for the purchase of
a kilo of cocaine or heroin and then take them down
one by one. The word that Manolo was an undercover
agent would get around the Badlands like wildfire.

Even if we intended to make buys and hold off on
making the arrests until we had a large enough number of criminals to take off the streets, it still wouldn't
have worked. First, the FBI didn't have enough cash
lying around to spend $18,000 to $25,000 to buy a
kilo of cocaine from every bad guy in town. Second,
if I purchased a kilo from one guy, word would get
around to the other dealers. It would look suspicious
for me to move away from supplier number one and
instead seek to do business with suppliers number
two, three, four, five, and so on. Only an undercover
agent would buy from one guy, abandon him, and try
to buy from a bunch of other people in succession. So
that wasn't going to work.

Instead, we hit on a scheme that allowed us to
take down multiple drug dealers without having to
spend a ton of the Bureau's cash and without running
the risk of my being exposed as an undercover agent.
It worked this way: Tony introduced me around as
a money launderer. After all, drug dealers operate in
an all-cash environment, and their customers pay in
small bills—ones, fives, tens, and twenties, all of the
bills dirty, and all of them invariably dusted with drug
residue. Let's say a dealer moved four kilos of cocaine
in a short period of time. He ends up with a million
dollars of cash in small bills. Getting that cash out of

North Philadelphia and into someplace safe—a bank vault in another state, a safe house, or back to the supplier to buy even more—was a dangerous operation. The dealer could be robbed and killed for the money, and even if he didn't meet a bad end, he still had the problem of transporting duffel bags full of cash, reeking of drug residue.

Manolo to the rescue. I told these dealers that I had a connection at a bank that laundered money. For a 1 or 2 percent fee, I could transform their small bills into hundred-dollar bills. A million dollars in hundreds fits neatly into a briefcase. Good-bye, duffel bags of cash that can only attract the wrong kind of attention, both from other criminals and from law enforcement. I was able to make deals with countless drug dealers to launder their money.

It usually worked this way: I went up to a guy and said, "I know somebody who is looking to buy a few kilos of cocaine. What if I brokered the transaction for you?" And we might or might not make the deal. They always came back and said, "No problem. I'll sell you a key."

"What's in it for me?" I replied. "Where's my taste?"

In other words, "If I help you out, who is going to help me? One hand has to wash the other. What are you going to do for me? Throw me some money-laundering business, and we might have a deal here."

The more money they brought in, the easier it was for us to identify the size of their drug-dealing operation. In so doing, the FBI was able to "launder" millions of dollars of drug money from the streets of Philadelphia, thus creating an airtight case against drug dealer after drug dealer. We called the operation BT Express. The B stood for Bureau, as in Federal Bureau of Investigation. The T stood for Tony, the informant. Express didn't stand for anything. That was just for fun. There was a music group by that name at the same time, but there was no connection between the two. We took out a storefront in North Philly, in the heart of the Badlands. Tony conducted his bookmaking operations in the front room. The back room was where drug dealers went to launder their cash or sell us their kilos of cocaine. They didn't have any idea that the conversations about drugs and drug money were under video and audio surveillance. Drug dealers popped into BT Express's offices with duffel bags full of drug money and kilos of cocaine and heroin, and they walked out ready for prosecution.

Incidentally, when Martland, the ex-Marine who was so hot and bothered about my excess weight, came on board, he hated the operation name BT Express and wanted to change it . . . to Warthog, of all things. I went ballistic. There was no way we were going to call our beautiful operation Warthog. I later learned that Warthog was the name of a Marine reconnaissance vehicle, so I understood his attachment to the term. Ultimately, the operation did get a new name— Metroliner, because some of our drug connections took the Amtrak train either up from Washington or down from New York in order to consummate deals.

For an entire year, my life consisted of heading into the Badlands day after day, making deals with street-level, armed, paranoid, and dangerous drug dealers, stopping by El Kubik four times a day for coffee or drinks, staying out till all hours with Tony and his pals, and then going back to the FBI office each evening to write up reports on everything I had seen and done. And then I'd have to get up early the next morning and start the whole thing over again, while somehow watching my weight and keeping my marriage alive. It wasn't easy but it was rewarding. By the time we brought BT Express Metroliner to a conclusion, we provided enough information to the prosecutors to hand up eighty-five indictments against Colombian, Cuban, and Dominican drug dealers.

The indictments were served on the same day in cities from Philadelphia to Los Angeles. Eighteen of the accused fled the country. Of the sixty-seven who remained, sixty-two were convicted and received lengthy sentences for drug dealing and money laundering, two were acquitted, and one died during the course of the trials. For the year after we shut down BT Express Metroliner, I was testifying in one case or another day after day. It was one of the biggest drug busts in the history of law enforcement.

By the time the case concluded, I knew that I had to get out of Philadelphia. Martland's vendetta against me continued unabated, despite my long hours, hard work, and the success of the case. He continued to hassle me and tell me that I was breaking rules and regulations. Finally, one day, I exploded. "What about you?" I asked. "You're still in the National Guard; didn't you have to resign your commission as part of the FBI's hiring practice? Why don't you mind your own business!"

Despite Martland, we managed to put a substantial number of bad guys away and to disrupt the flow of drugs from not one but two of the leading Colombian Cali drug cartels operating in the United States. For our efforts, the case agents and undercover agents whom Van Marsh and I introduced into the operation were honored by the FBI with incentive awards and with accolades from the United States Attorney's Office for the Eastern District of Pennsylvania.

The FBI incentive award read in part: "SA Garcia, it was through your bravery and remarkable skill as an undercover agent that you were able to gain the complete confidence of the subjects." The United States Attorney's office also wrote a beautiful letter to then-FBI Director Louis Freeh on my behalf that read in part: "Special Agent Garcia's ability as an undercover agent also deserves special praise. He thinks quickly and adroitly in dangerous situations, understands criminals, speaks their language and wins their confidence easily. While the FBI has many fine agents who have the ability to function in undercover roles, SA Garcia has to rank in the top flight of this elite group. He is an extremely valuable agent who has the ability to make large numbers of high impact cases."

How brave was I really? I was freaking afraid to

get weighed, for fear that I would lose my career in the Bureau!

My marriage had somehow survived this rocky period, as had my career. The undercover work was as exhilarating as it was exhausting, and I knew that I had truly found my niche not just in law enforcement but in life. Despite the difficulties I encountered in terms of lack of support from my Bureau supervisor, I knew that my life's mission was to work undercover and keep taking bad guys off the streets. I was under no illusion that my efforts, or anyone's efforts, could deliver a fatal blow to drug importation and distribution in this country. But I also knew that a lot of bad guys were behind bars because of the efforts of me and my fellow agents.

I put in for a transfer, and this time, I got my wish. I was going home to New York.

CHAPTER FiVE

Welcome to New York

I arrived in New York with two aspects of my history in the FBI preceding me. The first was my experience as a Spanish-speaking undercover agent, and the agents in the New York office who worked dope cases were clamoring for me to get on their squad. Unfortunately, the other thing that followed me from Philadelphia was my repeated run-ins with Supervisor Martland, and Martland, it turned out, had friends in high places in New York who tried to embarrass me. I had just completed what may have been the largest and most important drug case in the history of the Bureau. But thanks to the markers Martland was able to call in New York, there were to be no drug cases for me. Instead, I was assigned to what FBI agents pejoratively refer to as the Plaster Police squad. The Plaster Police squad doesn't arrest anybody. They don't go after dopers, terrorists, bank robbers, or even joy riders. What they do is supervise the construction and remodeling of FBI facilities. Hence the name Plaster Police, and that's where they wanted to stick me.

I howled. I put my foot down. I explained to anyone who would listen that this was insane—I had a calling as an undercover agent. It would have been a terrible waste of Bureau resources to have me watching a bunch of contractors do Sheetrock all day long. I had to call in the help of some of my friends who were able to convince New York management that I was not whatever Martland and others in Philadelphia must have labeled me. Fortunately, the Bureau came to its senses, and before long I was assigned to C-13, the New York field office's premier FBI–New York Police Department Narcotics Task Force. This squad had been responsible for celebrated cases like the Pizza Connection case, one of the biggest organized crime cases in Bureau history. This was like reliving my FNG days in Newark. The guys on the squad were hardworking and respected agents. The cops were all highly decorated detectives from the NYPD's elite Organized Crime Bureau. The whole squad worked together as a team with one common goal—as we liked to say, "to put bad guys in jail." C-13 was the best the Bureau and NYPD had to offer, and I was grateful that I became part of it.

I was working undercover on several major cocaine and money-laundering operations in our squad. In each case I played a different character. It was a special challenge for me to play the role of an Italian mobster when I was among Spanish-speaking people. I understood what they were saying, so I always wanted to jump in and engage in conversation with them. Instead, I had to wait patiently for the informant to "translate" for me. I almost made that mistake on many different occasions. Along the same lines, when dealing with Jamaicans, I would pose as a Colombian drug lord who spoke poor English. I didn't find it credible, but fortunately, they did.

As those cases were developing, we also did about thirty "quick-hit" buy-busts while I was assigned on C-13. I worked with Detective Paul Caroleo as the case officer and Agent Craig Arnold in charge of my security. We seized a lot of kilograms of heroin and cocaine and, more important, we put some really bad guys in jail. We all loved quick hits—they were an adrenaline high and team-building exercise. The whole squad would go out together—I'd do the undercover work, other guys would do the arrests, and so on. It was a blast for all of us.

Shortly after I was assigned to C-13, a confidential informant told our squad that there were a couple of gangbangers at 123rd Street and Lenox—Ground Zero for the narcotics trade—who were looking to sell major amounts of cocaine on behalf of the Colombians. That intersection is about the most dangerous place an undercover agent could go. So I sent word back through the informant: "I'm a willing buyer, but I won't meet the guys uptown." Instead, I would only meet them on turf that was considerably friendlier or safer for a guy like me—central Queens.

Word came back—no problem. We arranged a meeting that night at the Georgia Diner, near the Queens Center Mall, where Queens Boulevard crosses the Long Island Expressway.

That night I met the gangbangers, and they were hard-core criminals who ran street operations and were more terrifying than the dealers I'd met in the Badlands. They promised me fish-scale cocaine. "Fish scale" indicates a level of purity and quality that's hard to beat. The name derives from the appearance of the cocaine—when you open the package, it's very shiny and white, like the scales on a fish out of water. The gangbangers from 123rd and Lenox wanted to do the deal that night, right there and then, but I said no way. I told them that I only bought large amounts of cocaine during the day, when there were more people around, so it would be easier to melt into the crowd. They didn't have a problem with that, and we agreed to meet again the next morning.

By the time of our second meeting, the area surrounding the Georgia Diner had turned into what we in law enforcement call a set—a backdrop for an encounter between criminals and law enforcement. There were agents and detectives with recording and listening devices in a van parked outside the diner. Undercover agents and detectives were parked and ready to seal off exit routes in all directions in case things turned to shit. There was even an agent lying on the sidewalk against a garbage can, clutching a bottle in a brown paper bag, pretending to be a drunk homeless guy, ready to watch the whole thing go down. Agents placed in this position are called ghosts—they're right there in plain sight, but they blend into the street scene so naturally that the bad guys never notice them. And I was there, of course, waiting for the gangbangers to arrive. We had everything we needed . . . except for the drug dealers.

That's because dopers don't operate with the same sort of respect for time that you'll find in the military or in law enforcement. Dopers show up when they show up. The good news is that the gangbangers arrived only forty-five minutes late, not bad for doper time. And that's when things started to go wrong.

The agreement was that I would buy nine kilos of fish-scale cocaine, but the gangbangers didn't have any drugs on them. Suddenly we were doing the Scarface thing: "You got the stuff?" Meaning, you got the drugs?

And they responded, "You got the money?"

Nobody had anything, and it was turning into a standoff. My sixth sense told me that the situation was not going to turn out well.

The subjects told me that the dope would be there any minute, and five minutes later, a Colombian arrived. So we walked over to meet him—the two gangbangers from 123rd and Lenox whom I had met the night before and myself. The Colombian wanted to know whether the intermediary who brought us together could be trusted. I said that I had never met him but my partner had. Trust, never in great supply in drug deals, was rapidly breaking down. More and more people came onto the scene—another three partners of the Colombian drug dealer. Suddenly there was a whole circle of guys in the side parking lot of the Georgia Diner.

Keep in mind that the lunchtime rush had begun, and tons of civilians were straying through our set. So now we had six bad guys, me, and the two CWs, the confidential witnesses who began this whole thing. Nine guys stood around in a circle, and nobody knew what was going on or what would happen next. This guy was vouching for that guy, that guy was vouching for this guy . . . and the Colombians didn't like it at all.

"Listen, guys," I said, my exasperation mounting. "Are we doing this or not?"

I didn't want to look like this was my first time. I wanted to regain control over the situation.

"Not here," the Colombians replied nervously. "There's too many eyes out here. We've got a safe house around the corner. We have all the dope there, and you can sample and take any nine kilos you want. Leave one guy behind as collateral with one of my guys and let's go."

The gangbangers loved that idea and insisted that I go with the Colombians to the safe house and they would provide protection. For whatever reason, the Colombian surmised—accurately, as it turns out—that law enforcement was on the scene. He didn't realize that I was undercover, but *his* sixth sense that he had honed through his experience dealing drugs must have told him that not everything was as it should have been. In the safe house, we would be able to complete the transaction without any prying eyes. In keeping with common practice with drug dealers, one person would be left behind as human collateral. If the deal went bad for any reason, that guy would get whacked.

Here's where my experience as an undercover agent, particularly in the Badlands, paid off. There was no way on earth that I would ever leave the safety and security of the set, where we law enforcement officials had the upper hand, to go off to some safe house where God only knows what could happen. A younger, more gung-ho agent might have leapt at the opportunity to go to the bad guys' lair. This is great, he would think. We're gonna get not only the nine kilos but the whole mother load at the stash house! Think what this one operation is going to do for my career! Instead, I thought about what acceding to their request to move to the safe house might do to my life expectancy. And it wasn't good.

I had to think quickly.

"There's no way I'm going," I told the Colombians. "I consulted my *madrina* last night, and she said to do the deal here, at the diner."

Now, a madrina is a priestess or seer in the cult of Santeria, which is a folk religion common in many Spanish-speaking communities. If your madrina told you to do something, you did it. You ignored her guidance at your peril. I often dressed as a *santero,* wearing the colorful Santeria necklaces and gold jewelry of an adherent of the religion.

The Colombians were displeased. They had as little intention of doing the deal there at the diner as I had of leaving with them and going off to the safe house. To break the tension, I told them I wanted to have a conversation with my partner, the confidential witness. As I'm talking with him, I walked toward the parking lot, and I passed by the FBI van with the C-13 Task Force members inside monitoring my transmitter. Since the entire deal was going down in Spanish, they had a translator in the van as well. I walked so I could tell the guys inside that this deal was not looking good. On my way to there, I noticed two cars full of bad guys watching me. In one of the cars, there was a bad guy pretending he was reading the *New York Post* . . . but he was holding it upside down!

This is getting dangerous, I thought. Who knows how many other bad guys are monitoring this transaction for the dealers? I decided I'd better not go to the van, so I returned to the pack, where the Colombians were waiting for my decision. Would I come with them or not? The gangbangers were salivating, insisting on the safe house. What do they care if I get killed?

"I can call my madrina," I said, buying time. "Maybe it'll be okay for me to come with you."

The Colombians, who evidently respected Santeria, nodded their assent and allowed me to go into the diner, where there was a pay phone in the front vestibule. I called the FBI, which patched me through to the van in the parking lot. This was in the era before cell phones.

"It's looking real ugly," I said.

"It's a dangerous situation," SA Arnold said. He was our on-scene commander and probably one of the best agents I have ever had the pleasure of serving with.

"We know about the two vehicles," he added. "Stay where you are. We're going to take them down right now."

I hung up the phone and stayed where I was, in the vestibule. Suddenly agents and New York City cops came flying from every direction. I didn't know it, but back at the office, they'd gone into the-shit's-hitting-the-fan mode. They had everybody drop everything, pick up their weapons, and haul ass to the Georgia Diner. By now the bad guys—a dozen in all—were leaping out of cars and running in every direction. Keep in mind, again, that we were in one of the busiest parts of downtown Queens, and it was the middle of the day. Our Task Force members sealed off every street radiating from Queens Boulevard, and they collared every single one of the bad guys, as they leapt through windows, jumped fences, did whatever they could to escape from our guys. One agent was running down Queens Boulevard with an MP5—a machine gun–like weapon used by SWAT teams—chasing after them.

Ultimately, ten were arrested. Inside their vehicles and on their persons were a Tec-9 machine gun, a .357 Magnum, a 9 millimeter, a huge Jim Bowie knife, lots of duct tape, and rope. (They were going to tie me up, but I guess they were delayed in coming to the meeting because they had to stop at Home Depot to get more tape and rope after seeing my size the night before!) We took statements from the two guys from 123rd and Lenox, the gangbangers who had put the whole deal together. Once we had gone to the safe house, it was their intention to rob me of my money and to rob the Colombians of their dope.

There really is no such thing as honor among thieves. The situation would have been so volatile at the safe house that, without my Badlands experience, I would have almost certainly gotten myself killed. Instead, we made a great case in just two days. Out of the ten arrested, nine were convicted. These were significant drug suppliers from the Colombian cartel. The tenth person arrested was a woman who law enforcement ultimately decided was a nonparticipant in the event. Ten arrests, nine bad guys taken off the streets, and no heavy lifting. We always referred to this case as the Nine Kilo Nightmare.

Welcome to New York.

CHAPTER SIX

Making $2 Million on Our Lunch Hour

At the risk of stating the obvious, the world is awash in dope and dope money. At any moment, billions and billions of dollars of drugs—and the money to pay for those drugs—is in transit around the world. The drugs come down by mule from the farmland in Colombia, where they are transported by truck to the ports, from which they move by water or by air to Miami or other gateway cities in the United States and then on to major distribution centers like Los Angeles, Chicago, and New York, then to the hinterlands.

Everybody's making money—those who grow and refine the drugs, those who transport them to warehouses in their countries of origin, those who ship them, those who arrange international transportation, those who distribute the drugs, those who store the money that the drug cartels earn, and those who launder the money, shipping it back to the countries from which it came. It's the job of law enforcement to somehow stick a finger in this billion-dollar dike, put the bad guys away, seize the money, and keep the drugs away from our neighborhoods and our children.

In my time in the Bureau, I've seized millions and millions of dollars in cash from drug dealers. It gets to be like pieces of paper after a while—it means nothing. And yet no matter how much money we seize, no matter how many bad guys we put away, the frustrating, maddening thing is that we will never eradicate the drug problem. It's hard to root out the supply part of the equation as long as there are so many people in this country and around the world who want to take drugs.

That may be the nation's attitude, but law enforcement agents on the ground feel differently. We risk our lives to get drugs and drug dealers off the streets. One time we were working a drug case in Queens when one of the best NYPD detectives on our squad, Paul Caroleo, received an anonymous tip in the form of a letter written in broken English. The letter told us that a particular apartment and a particular luxury highrise in the "Little Colombia" neighborhood of Jackson Heights, Queens, was being used as a drug safe house. Okay, let's take a look, we figured. What did we have to lose?

During a lunch break, a few of us Task Force members—Detective Caroleo, Special Agent Paul Cassidy, and me—went into the building and knocked on the door of the apartment, where we were greeted by a stunningly attractive young Colombian woman wearing a bathrobe.

"We're law enforcement," Detective Caroleo explained. "May we come in?"

"Sure," she said, ushering us into the apartment.

We looked around, and the girl definitely didn't match her surroundings. The apartment was decorated in that style I like to call "early Ralph Kramden"—just the bare minimum of mismatched furniture. No one was living here like the other, law-abiding tenants in the building. This was a drug hideaway, nothing more.

"We received a tip," Special Agent Cassidy told the young lady. "One of your neighbors says that there is money and drugs here in the apartment. May we look around?"

Detective Caroleo showed her the letter, and she read it.

"Go ahead," she said. "Feel free."

So we did a quick plain-view search and noticed that she was getting nervous and was staring at the dining room closet door. I then asked, in Spanish, the question that we always ask when we enter apartments or houses that we suspect to be drug safe houses.

"What's in the closet?" I asked casually.

She shrugged. "I have no idea."

From a legal perspective, she might have been wondering why we didn't have a warrant. The answer is that if we have consent to enter a place, we don't need a warrant. And the young lady had already given

us consent, freely and willingly. So there were no issues of illegal search and seizure here. And when she
told me that she had no idea what was in the closet,
my antennae were definitely up.

If somebody were to ask you what you had in a
closet, wouldn't you know what was in it? If you got
pulled over by a police officer and he asked you what
you had in the trunk, wouldn't you know? If you had a
huge duffel bag stuffed with something in your trunk,
wouldn't you know what it was? Well, dopers will
answer the same way: "I've got no idea what that is. I
don't know whose it is. I don't know how it got there. I
don't know anything about it."

Mobsters, on the other hand, will tell you, "I don't
know nothing, I didn't see anything, I wasn't there,
and if you say I was there, I must have been sleeping!"
All criminals have their own defense.

Either the person is suffering from amnesia, or
he's a doper hiding something. There really aren't that
many other possibilities. And when a person tells me
that he or she doesn't know what's in the trunk, or
what's in the closet, that constitutes probable cause to
seize that item, should it turn out to be something that
we might suspect to be drug money. Obviously, if it's
drugs or unlicensed weapons, we can seize them, no
problem. It's against the law to have those things. It's
not against the law to keep a million dollars in a duffel
bag in the trunk of your car or in boxes in your closet.
If a guy doesn't trust the banks and that's how he likes
to keep his money, more power to him. But he better

be able to tell a law enforcement agent that he knows what it is and he knows how he got it. Otherwise, it can be seized . . . legally.

I asked the young lady whether it would be okay if we could see what was in the closet. Again she gave us permission. Maybe she truly had no idea. The people whose money it was probably didn't tell her very much. Why would they?

So we went into the closet and we found six of those boxes that contain a dozen reams of copy paper, the kind you'd buy at your local office supply store. We opened up each of the boxes. They were each jammed with twenty-dollar bills. She had over two million dollars' worth of twenties in boxes in her closet, and she had no idea what it was.

Now she got a little nervous!

"Don't you need a warrant for this?" she finally asked.

I shook my head. "You gave us consent."

The young lady was living in this apartment with minimal furniture and two million dollars' worth of twenties in boxes in the closet. If that doesn't sound like a drug safe house to you, then you don't have a future in law enforcement.

So what did we do? We took the girl and the money, and we brought them down to the FBI office. We photographed her and took her information and then we bundled the money and took it to the bank where the FBI takes money under such circumstances. We gave the young woman a receipt for the two million dollars. Legally, the burden had now shifted to her—or her friends—to prove that the money was legitimate and that there was some credible reason why she was keeping all this cash in boxes in a sparsely furnished apartment in a known drug neighborhood.

The woman was released. She hadn't committed a crime, and we had no reason or desire to keep her. Yet we waited for someone—anyone—to call or bring the receipt back to our office and claim the money. No one ever did. Two million dollars in cash, forfeited to the government. Just a cost of doing business in the billion-dollar drug trade.

Two million dollars may not be a lot to a doper, but to the FBI, that's real money. The cash goes to the Treasury or the U.S. Marshals Service, and a piece of the action goes to any law enforcement agency involved in the case. The term is "equitable sharing of seized assets," but it's really just like the Mafia—everybody gets a taste! Well, everybody except the FBI, for reasons I've never fully understood. Still, not a bad haul—two million bucks in cash, and we seized that money during our lunch hour, while we were working another case!

This was a minor matter compared to the cases against the drug networks we were trying to take down, though. By the late 1990s, the Mexicans had begun to control the drug distribution network, the pipeline that led from Colombia and other drug-producing countries into the United States. Previously, the Mexicans had been small-time players in the

transportation of drugs. They had gotten wise to the
amount of money they could make by not taking cash
for transporting and distributing cocaine and heroin
but took a piece of the action instead—a percentage,
often a large percentage, of every shipment of drugs
they transported from Colombia, through Mexico, and
into the United States.

The Mexicans were now demanding—and receiv-
ing—as much as 45 percent of every shipment of drugs
and thus were able to increase their profits exponentially. If I pay a transporter money to move a shipment
of dope, that person makes a predetermined amount
for the kilos he or she is contracted to deliver. Transporters can make anywhere between $500 and $3,500
per kilo, depending on distance and speed in their
delivery. But if I pay that person with a kilo of dope,
that kilo can bring him or her as much as $200,000
or $300,000 on the street. The Mexicans were on to a
good thing now, and they knew it. They were moving
hundreds of millions of dollars of cocaine and heroin
into the United States every year.

Of course, when you're moving that much product,
you've got to find a way to get your money back to
Mexico and into Colombia. As mentioned, everyone
gets a piece, a taste—from the grower, to the manu-
facturer, to the mule driver, to the warehouse owner,
to the shipper, to the distributor, and finally down to
the dealer on the street corner in your neighborhood.
But even with all those mouths to feed, there was
still plenty of money to be shipped out of the United

States. And that's where a money launderer steps in, to take that cash and turn it into legitimate wire transfers from banks inside the United States to banks in other countries.

This situation gripes me considerably, because the banks have to have some idea of what these millions and millions of dollars they are transmitting on behalf of the dopers back to their native countries must represent. And yet they turn a blind eye, because they're getting paid. It's tough to have a war on drugs when practically everyone is bought off, either under the table or, in the case of the banks, in a totally legal manner.

As in the Badlands, dopers can't simply bring a million dollars in dirty, scrunched-up twenty-dollar bills to the bank at the corner and ask for a wire transfer to Latin or South America. Instead, they have to find a money launderer they can trust, someone who can take those millions of dollars in cash and magically transform them into wire transfers that cross the border and end up in the bank accounts of the cartels that manufacture the drugs. And that's where I came in.

From 1999 to 2004, in New York, I worked a series of cases that were known as Telewash I, Telewash II, and Telewash III, for Special Agent Reynaldo "Rey" Tariche and NYPD detective Frank Berberich. These cases were part of the FBI–DEA/NYPD major case initiative called Operation Reciprocity. We learned that an individual named Amado Carrillo Fuentes ran one of the leading drug cartels in Mexico. Carrillo Fuentes had dispatched one of his trusted lieutenants to the New York City area to head the distribution of his cocaine empire in the United States. This individual, Martin Manzo, quickly became one of the all-time biggest distributors of cocaine in the country. As a result, Manzo became one of the targets of the overall investigation, which took us up and down the eastern seaboard and even into high-speed boat chases in the Caribbean.

An FBI confidential informant told Manzo that he knew a guy—me—who was a highly respected and trustworthy money launderer. I could turn any amount of cash into a legitimate wire transfer, in just five or six business days. Would Manzo like to meet me?

Yes, he did. So a meeting was arranged, a sit-down in Washington Heights, a drug-infested neighborhood at the northern tip of Manhattan Island. On the appointed day, I drove up to a restaurant there in an expensive, late-model Mercedes. As far as Manzo knew, I was alone. He couldn't have known that the guy sitting a few tables away from me, quietly eating his lunch, was an FBI agent, that the drunk guy weaving erratically on the sidewalk drinking from a paper bag was another FBI agent, drinking soda and not beer, and that other FBI agents and New York City police officers were within a block or two of the restaurant, listening to our conversation over a transmitter on my body. As far as Manzo knew, I was the real deal—a wealthy, successful money launderer. Think about it. If I roll up in a dangerous neighborhood in an expensive car, park it right outside the restaurant, walk out of the car in fine clothing, a solid gold Rolex, gold jewelry, Santeria beads, the whole look, and I'm exuding an air of confidence and insouciance, what is Manzo, or any doper, going to think? My undercover mantra has always been "Think big, be big! Think small, be small!"

Most dopers think that anyone they meet is going to be a tough guy, so my M.O. is to disarm them with my affable, outgoing personality. I entered the restaurant with a bounce in my step, as if I owned the place. I made a comment about the weather: "Man, this heat is killing me! How you doin'? How you feelin' today? What kind of food they serve here, anyway?"

The dopers, expecting someone mean, are invariably delighted to see that I am a nice guy, someone they can talk to. I loved to look these guys right in the eye. No one ever did. It was a way of establishing dominance over them from the start. So we begin our conversation, my invincible persona clearly established in Manzo's mind.

I knew what Manzo was thinking. "Who is this guy? He should be afraid, coming into my neighborhood like this with a car like that!" But I showed no sign of fear. I had plenty of protection around me, and I knew I could take care of myself if things went badly. I could tell that he had completely fallen for my act. Of course, if I needed to take it up a notch, I would have. If someone was being a jerk-off, I would be a bigger jerk-off. But I wouldn't start off being a bully. I want the bad guy to be my friend. I would never appear intimidated or impressed by these guys, no matter how big an organization they claimed to represent. After all, I had a rich Uncle backing me—my Uncle Sam.

"You're Cuban, right?" Manzo asked.

The Hispanic guys always ask me if I'm Cuban, and I always say yes. My accent gives me away every time. And that's perfectly fine with me—if I sounded Mexican, they'd immediately start backstopping me, asking me what part of Mexico I'm from, who I know, the whole thing. So it's actually a blessing to come from Cuba in these circumstances. Next I worked to establish trust, to emphasize the fact that I had our mutual friend vouching for me.

The role of the person who vouches for a money launderer cannot be underestimated. Think about it: A drug dealer, not a person who places trust in humanity, is giving half a million dollars or up to two million dollars in cash to a person who is, when you think about it, a perfect stranger. The expectation is that this stranger will keep the money over the next five to six business days, as much as a week or a week and a half in real time, and then magically transform it into a wire transfer. That's a very high degree of trust. What if I skipped? What if the doper never saw me again? They wouldn't just come looking for me. They'd come looking for the intermediary. So if someone is going to vouch for another individual, the person who is doing the vouching has to be very sure, indeed, of the bona fides of the individual for whom he is giving an assurance. His life is literally on the line.

"We have a mutual friend," I said, shifting the topic of conversation to business. "He says that you've got more cash than you can handle."

Manzo clearly liked me and wanted to do business with me.

"I have a guy on the inside who could launder the money for you," I told him quietly. "I just need to know how much you're looking to do."

I always like to start small with these guys, just to prove to them that I'm capable of doing what I say I can. Also, from a crime point of view, the FBI doesn't want to be laundering more money than necessary! We have to perform a certain amount of facilitation of crime in order to put the bad guys away, but money laundering isn't our stock-in-trade. So we never want to start off too quickly.

Another time, when I was playing the part of a money launderer, I met an individual in the Queens Mall who gave me what he thought was a million dollars. I took it back to the office, and we counted it up. It turned out to be three million! We knew the guy was out there probably having a heart attack as soon as he realized what he had done. Sure enough, he called me fifteen minutes later, begging on his life for me to return the money. No way, I told him. I didn't tell him that we were the FBI and that there was no way we would allow two million of his three million dollars to go back into circulation in the drug world. I told him that the money had already gone into the system, that he had nothing to worry about, and that the transfer would take place. Give me a phone number and I'll call you as soon as everything's handled.

Well, the guy gave me the phone number, and now we were able to go up on a Title III wiretap on that phone number. We were thus able to trace his movements, everyone with whom he came into contact, and the locations of his drug operations. We were able to take him and his organization down, and by the end of the operation, we had seized well over three million dollars in drug proceeds. Since we were working with the New York City Police on that case, they got 10 or 20 percent of the money—that's the way it works.

Incidentally, when we're talking with these guys, you never discuss dollar figures on the phone. Instead, hundreds of thousands of dollars become "invitations" or "tickets." As in "I've got some invitations to the party."

"Oh, yeah? How many people are coming to the party?"

"Three hundred people."

That means the guy wants to move three hundred thousand dollars. Or he might have said he had three hundred tickets for the game.

Now that Manzo and I had agreed to do business, we had to work out the percentage I would take as a fee for my services. I always start high—around 8 percent. Then we usually work our way down to 5 or 6 percent, which is fairly standard as a fee for money laundering of drug money. Now the only remaining question on Manzo's part was whether he could have some references—some former customers of mine with whom I had done business, so that he could check further into my bona fides!

I looked at him as if he were an idiot. "References?" I snarled. "You want references . . . from *me*? Don't you know who you're dealing with? And let me ask you something. Let's say tomorrow morning I sit down with another dealer and *he* wants references. What am I supposed to do, give him your name? Is that what you want?"

Manzo realized his error and dropped the request. Instead, we moved on to the next topic—my team members. I always explain to drug dealers, when I'm posing as a money launderer, that I never touch the money or drugs. I never want to do anything that's going to put me at risk for arrest. Also, I want to enhance my status in the eyes of the drug dealer as the number-one guy in the organization.

"See that guy over there?" I said, motioning to FBI undercover agent Diego Rodriguez, sitting a few tables from us. This was my first indication to Manzo that I knew Diego.

"He'll be handling the transaction for me. He'll meet either you or someone in your organization at a location you choose to pick up the cash on my behalf."

Now, in the drug world, people don't have specific job descriptions. For all Manzo knew, Diego might have been not just a courier, or mule, for me but also a hit man in his own right. Diego certainly had a fearsome way about him in these situations. Manzo's respect level for me definitely went up a notch when he saw Diego sitting across the restaurant. He understood that I was not a man to be trifled with, if I had people like Diego working under me.

"What about the bar in the Ramada Inn in New Rochelle?" Manzo asked. "Tomorrow night? I'll send my man Tony."

Ironically, the hotel he picked happened to be the location of the FBI field office that handles Westchester County. How perfect is that?

"That's fine," I said.

We nodded our good-byes. I threw a hundred-dollar bill down on the table to pay for two coffees and I departed.

But things don't always go the way they should.

The next evening right on time, Diego spotted Manzo's man Tony in the bar of the Ramada Inn. They made contact, and Diego explained to him that he, Diego, would be providing Tony with a car with secret compartments to pick up the cash. It sounded good to Tony, so Diego handed Tony the keys to an FBI Volkswagen Jetta equipped not just with secret hidden panels but also with a GPS monitoring system and a kill switch that would allow us to stop the car from a distance of a hundred feet.

We put a tail on Tony as soon as he left the hotel driving the FBI Jetta, a new car on which the Bureau had spent about seventeen thousand dollars. Unfortunately for us, Tony made the surveillance almost immediately after leaving the hotel. He took us on a looping trail through Westchester County and the Bronx, circling repeatedly around Co-op City and City Island. He disappeared into a bodega and picked up some beer, and that's when we started to get nervous. What if this guy was drinking and driving an FBI car and then he mowed down an innocent citizen? On top of that, we wanted our car back! We had just spent seventeen thousand dollars on it, and we didn't want to just give it up to a doper!

So we began chasing him, and it was almost pathetic. There must have been ten cars—FBI and the NYPD—on his tail. And then Murphy's Law kicked in yet again—the GPS system failed, so we lost him for a period of time. Then we thought that maybe he felt that he had lost the tail and was heading to pick up the money for Diego. After a while, we spotted Tony again in the Bronx, heading back in toward the hotel where Diego was waiting for him.

We decided, "Okay, we've got the kill switch, let's force the car to a stop."

We wanted to do a police traffic stop and seize the money before it got to Diego. So we hit the button on the kill switch . . . and nothing happened.

The kill switch had failed.

The car just kept going, like the Energizer bunny. Tony passed the hotel and kept going north toward Connecticut. We figured we had to take him off the road—again, a guy drinking behind the wheel of an FBI car isn't a recipe for success. So we pulled him over on a random traffic stop. At that point, we told him there was something wrong with the registration of the car and it had to be impounded. He just walked away, alongside the exit ramp and into the woods, never to be seen again. The deal failed. All our hard work setting up Manzo was for naught.

At least for the moment.

We hit on the strategy of blaming Manzo for the *cola,* Spanish for "tail"—we told him that *he* must have triggered the tail, not us. As mentioned, that's how dopers react to situations. They always point the finger at everybody else. We must have seemed credible to Manzo, because before long, he was ready to do business with us again.

We were then able to "go up on," or arrange for wiretaps, on Manzo's phone. Within a few weeks, we seized two million dollars concealed in a tractor-trailer heading south to Mexico, which we picked up on Manzo's wire. We assumed that was the money we were supposed to have laundered, because it was the same amount that we had agreed on initially. So now the case was moving again.

Soon other subjects sought my services as a money launderer and drug dealer, on Manzo's vouch. At the end of the operation, Manzo was arrested, convicted, and sentenced to prison. He cooperated with the FBI and gave us some very good information that led to the arrest and conviction of others in his drug cartel. As a result, his sentence was reduced to eleven years. But just as I was writing these words, I saw on the news that Manzo had been rearrested on drug charges, tried, and found guilty yet again. You just can't stop these guys. It's not just a business to them; it's a way of life.

In these drug cases, I dealt with numerous subjects either as a money launderer or transporter, and we were very successful in seizing large amounts of both dope and money. The beauty of working with dopers is that although my appearance is very distinctive, they never caught on because the drug cartels are all compartmentalized. At the end of the day, Operation Reciprocity had thirty-five Title III wiretaps in ten different cities. It targeted the U.S. cell of the massive drug organization run by Amado Carrillo Fuentes. We seized $11 million in cash, 7.4 tons of cocaine, and 2,400 pounds of marijuana. In all, fifty-three subjects were arrested. This operation severely disrupted Carrillo Fuentes's drug-trafficking activity and was a major factor in forcing him to alter his appearance with plastic surgery. As a drug baron, he couldn't travel to the United States for his surgery, so he went with Mexican doctors who may not have had the requisite training or experience. Amado Carrillo Fuentes, who had survived numerous bloody turf wars to ascend to the top of a powerful drug cartel, actually died on the operating table.*

These investigations were instrumental in temporarily disrupting and dismantling the drug flow in

---

* Soon after, all of the doctors involved in the surgery were murdered; their bodies were found on a dirt road.

New York. Between our undercover work and the many Title III wiretaps we were able to procure, this investigation became a model in the law enforcement community as a method of working major narcotics trafficking organizations. And then I got involved in a case in South Florida that helped put an end to an even bigger narcotics ring. All experience that would help me play a credible mobster when it came time to meet Greg DePalma.

CHAPTER SEVEN

"Remember *Pulp Fiction*? I'm Wolf!"

During my first few years in New York, I also became involved in an investigation based out of Miami. Occasionally one field office in the Bureau would "borrow" an undercover agent from another office to work a case. It involved two drug kingpins, Willy Falcon and Sal Magluta, *Los Muchachos*, Spanish for "the Boys." They were the most successful, violent drug dealers in the history of South Florida, and that's really saying something.

They were Cuban immigrants and best friends who had met at Miami High School and dropped out to enter—and then dominate—Miami's drug trade. According to law enforcement, Willy and Sal used their talents as champion power-boat racers to move more than 75 tons of cocaine worth as much as $2 billion into Miami. Their wealth and their narcotics empire, it is said, inspired the opening segment of the 1980s TV hit *Miami Vice*. They lived like kings, with Miami Beach mansions and all the trappings of vast wealth, and in Miami they were treated like folk heroes. Of course, they were also treated as persons under investigation, and federal prosecutors in Miami had built a seemingly airtight case against the pair.

There was only one problem. The most celebrated drug dealers in the history of South Florida, in the most closely watched jury trial in the history of the region, walked. The jury found them not guilty, despite mounds of evidence that were practically as large as the mountains of cocaine and other drugs they moved. The reactions from the various participants in the trial were remarkable.

The chief prosecutor was so despondent that he went from the courthouse to a nearby strip club, where he ran up a $900 tab and got into trouble for allegedly biting the ear of one of the dancers.

Willy and Sal threw a celebration party where the entertainment included the Bee Gees and Miami Sound Machine.

The defense attorneys confessed surprise. Roy Black headed up a pre–O.J. Simpson "dream team" of top-dollar defense attorneys including Albert Krieger, who had unsuccessfully represented John Gotti, Martin Weinberg, and Frank Rubino, who would go on to represent former Panamanian strongman Manuel Noriega. Black never imagined that his clients would have been found not guilty, but it wasn't the defense team's courtroom heroics that kept Willy and Sal from the pen.

No one in or out of law enforcement understood how the jury could have examined the evidence against the pair and set them free. It didn't help that some of the witnesses scheduled to appear in the trial started showing up dead around Miami. Some narrowly escaped death as their cars were firebombed or their workplaces were destroyed. And that's when one of the jurors, a courageous Gulf War veteran, first voiced suspicions to the prosecutors that the jury's decision was bought and paid for . . . by Willy and Sal.

An FBI investigation ensued. The Drug Enforcement Administration was not interested in working the case, because it had lost the case the first time and felt embarrassed about the defeat. So FBI Special Agents Mario Tariche and Michael Anderson, along with an IRS agent, Dennis Donnell, went to work. The targets quickly became the jury foreman, a Miami International Airport worker named Miguel Moya, who at the time earned $36,000 a year as a ramp driver, and two other jurors whose personal histories included sudden jumps in spending.

Why was Moya the lead suspect?

Maybe it was the beautiful new home he bought in the Florida Keys.

Or the season tickets to the skybox for the Florida Marlins.

Maybe it was the trips to Vegas, where he blew tons of money gambling.

Perhaps the new Rolex watch he was sporting.

All on a salary of $36,000 a year.

It was evident that Moya had been reached and that he sold his vote on the jury for a sum of money which we eventually estimated at between half a million and a million dollars. Amazingly, he was just one of *three* jurors whom the Willy and Sal organization corrupted. Law enforcement discovered Moya had invited two other jurors, both Hispanic women, to sell their votes for a promise of a million dollars each. One received close to that amount; the other, just twenty thousand. It turned out that Willy and Sal had been as ruthlessly efficient at poisoning the jury as they were at running their drug operation.

Just how tough were Willy and Sal? An emblematic story from their careers as drug dealers should suffice. An attorney had done something to displease the pair, so they sent a team of Colombian hit men to kill him. Naturally, his secretary was in the office when they burst in, and she witnessed her boss's murder. As she watched, stunned, the killers then debated whether they should kill her or not. Ultimately, they decided that they had no reason to kill her, since they hadn't been paid to do so. Instead, they took her driver's license and told her, "We know where you live and we know where you work. If you ever say anything, we'll kill you next."

That's the kind of people Willy and Sal were. Reaching out to three members of a jury was all in a day's work.

Incidentally, the secretary who witnessed the murder later had the chance to testify against the Willy and Sal organization. One of the gunmen, arrested for another crime, flipped and admitted what he had done. The prosecutors asked the secretary to corroborate the story that the killer turned informant had told them, but she wanted no part of it. She didn't see anything, she didn't know anything, she didn't want anything to do with it.

She probably made the right choice.

With regard to Moya, the prosecutors' dilemma was this: They had financial records that indicated Moya was spending far more money than he possibly could have earned in his mundane job at Miami International. The question for us was how to get him to admit that he had actually taken money from Willy and Sal, when a confession was either a ticket to many years in federal prison or murder by the Willy and Sal organization, or both.

The FBI and the prosecutors in South Florida hit on an ingenious idea: They would send an agent, operating undercover, to meet Moya after he finished his shift at the airport. Instead of confronting him and seeking an admission, which for Moya would be the equivalent of signing his own death sentence, they would approach him in a different way. The agent would claim to be a member of Willy and Sal's organization. He would say that he possessed a purloined document from the prosecutors' office indicating that Moya was about to be indicted for the crime of jury tampering and accepting a bribe.

In other words, the undercover's message wouldn't be, "Why did you do it?" The agent instead would be saying, "Look, Miguel. We know you're in trouble, and we at the Willy and Sal organization are here to help. Whatever you need, just tell us, and we'll help you out. We're not going to abandon you in your time of need."

The hope was that with a setup like that, Moya would admit that he had taken bribe money. So now the question arose: Which agent fit the bill?

One of the Miami agents working the case, Mario Tariche, had a brother in the New York field office, Rey Tariche. Mario told Rey about the case and asked if he knew of anyone suitable. I was the right age—in my mid-forties and Cuban, just like Willy and Sal—and, of course, I looked nothing like law enforcement. So I traveled to Miami and was briefed on the case. We hatched a plan. I would rent a Cadillac and drive it to the parking structure where Moya parked his car for work so as to meet him. Early in the morning, an FBI van would pull in a few cars away from Moya's car. Another FBI van would take another space nearby, which he would vacate in time for me to pull in just before Moya quit work. The van would contain FBI agents with a camera and recording gear, and I would be carrying an audio recorder as well.

Well, the day came. That morning Moya pulled into a parking space, the FBI vehicles pulled in alongside, and all was looking right with the world. (Of course, I'm a believer in Murphy's Law.) Just before Moya's shift ended, I drove to the garage and I pulled my rented Cadillac (complete with a video camera and recording device, in case Moya wanted to get out of the Miami heat and sit in a comfortable, air-conditioned car for the conversation) into the newly vacated space reserved for me. Then I waited for Moya to get off work.

Only one problem: No Moya.

Where was he? Had he been tipped? Nobody knew. We were all going bananas—he always left his post at the same time, always traveled to the parking lot by shuttle at the same time, and so on. And yet none of us could get a visual on him.

My greatest fear as an undercover agent—aside from getting killed, of course—is that my recording device won't work. So even though I hadn't seen him yet, I turned it on and hoped for the best.

A short time later, as if he had materialized from nowhere, there stood Miguel Moya, about to get into his car.

I quickly intercepted him and engaged him in conversation.

"You don't know who I am," I told him in Spanish. "I'm from Willy and Sal's organization. I have inside information about an indictment being prepared against you."

I showed him the document we had created back at the office, which purported to be a summary of the indictment coming down against him.

Naturally, he was stunned. I continued with the script we had prepared.

"Willy and Sal are on your side," I assured him. "We will not sit idly by as this unfortunate indictment comes down. Whatever we can do to help you, we will be there for you."

Moya must have wondered who this hulking man was, delivering him this shocking news. Obviously, he thought he had gotten away with the crime, and he was devastated to learn that prosecutors were on to him. But I still had to get him to acknowledge what he had done with the money, because, in so doing, I would be getting his admission that he had in fact taken the bribe.

"Do you remember the movie *Pulp Fiction*?" I asked him. "Well, I'm Wolf. I fix things so I need to know everything. What did you do with the money? Did you give it to your wife?"

As it happened, Moya's wife left him shortly after the bribery incident and subsequently got herself a job as a dispatcher for, of all things, the City of Miami Police Department.

"I gave the money to my family," he said.

We had him. As long as my tape recorder was working.

The conversation quickly ended.

After Moya peeled out of the garage, I headed over to my car, my recording device in my hand, my heart pounding. If that little tape recorder was on the fritz, the whole plan would have cratered. I looked at the device, and I saw that beautiful little red light. I knew we had our case.

Moya gave enough of a clear indication in our conversation that he had taken the bribe from Willy and Sal that we were able to prosecute him, and eventually the other jurors, for what they had done. Willy and Sal were later charged for tampering with the jury. Moya and his attorneys sought to have the admission I had gained thrown out of court on the grounds that I was so big and scary that he had been intimidated. We played the video and the audio for the court, and the jurors were plainly able to see and hear that, far from intimidating him, I had repeatedly offered my help to him as a member of the Willy and Sal organization.

Moya's defense: He claimed he earned that money as a drug dealer six years earlier, conveniently one year prior to the expiration of the statute of limitations on such crimes. He was indeed a slippery character, and his first trial ended in a hung jury. He was retried, and this time he changed his story and said that the money came from gambling, again during a period after which the statute of limitations had tolled. The jury didn't buy it. He was convicted and sentenced to seventeen and a half years in prison.

What happened next to Willy and Sal? I spent several days on the stand in a new trial of Sal Magluta, for the criminal activities they both had undertaken with regard to fixing the jury in their original drug case. The jurors in this new trial were sequestered, under heavy police guard, for four months, and had the courage to bring back a guilty verdict. He was essentially sentenced to life in prison. After that, Willy copped a plea.

Not long after we put Willy and Sal away, the Bureau got a call from the owner of a strip club in the Bronx in need of law enforcement protection. As a result of that call, I would soon have the opportunity to infiltrate the Gambinos.

CHAPTER EiGHT

A Cry for Help from the Bronx

The most famous strip club in New York City is called Scores. If you've ever listened to Howard Stern, then you know all about it—the prestigious Midtown location, the luxurious appointments, the high-end clientele, the beautiful girls. The people who own Scores mostly cater to business guys with company credit cards, groups that think nothing of dropping thousands of dollars a night at the club, simply because it isn't their money. But if you think the people who go to Scores have a great time, meet the people who really have fun there.

The Mob.

Like any strip club, Scores offered La Cosa Nostra an endless sea of opportunity for making money, from the admission fee to the booze and food, and even from charging the girls for the right to take off their clothing in front of strangers. And when it came to food and drink, wiseguys scored twice: They got paid off by the alcohol and food suppliers, and then they collected a piece of what the customers paid.

The Mafia had its hooks into Scores from the start. The owners of the club were being shaken down by various members of the Gambino crime family: John Gotti, Jr., Mikey "Scars" DiLeonardo, and, most important for our purposes, a Mafia father-and-son combination, Greg DePalma and his son, Craig. Greg in particular, a capo in the Gambino family, was making thousands of dollars a night from the club. He was making money in every conceivable direction. The place was rocking—every night it was packed. The Mob didn't own the club, but they constantly shook it down for every penny they could. In the winter, without exaggeration, the coat check booth alone brought in thousands of dollars a night, money that Greg and the Gambino family controlled.

The dancers would do anything to work there because of the money they could make. Customers would buy scrip, or funny money, with their personal or corporate credit cards, in hundred-dollar increments; $110 buys $100, which guys would then distribute to the dancers in exchange for lap dances. The dancers would have to kick 10 to 20 percent of the funny money they received back to the club, as additional payment for converting the funny money into cash. The club was a gold mine for the DePalmas and the Gambino family, although you would never have heard any mention of that on Howard Stern.

Not everybody can afford a place like Scores, Greg DePalma understood, so he got his greedy hooks into a similar strip club up in the Bronx—the same high-end furniture and fixtures, the same huge space, the same layout, with bars, private rooms, and a big dance floor. The clientele was different, though—the working-class men of the Bronx who didn't have corporate credit cards to squander, merely their own hard-earned money. They flocked to the club, the Naked Truth,* along with the stray executive on his way home to Greenwich who would pull off 95 to unwind after a hard day's work on Wall Street.

Men who go to these clubs crave contact with beautiful women, but there's one thing they crave even more: anonymity. The last thing they ever want is to see their names in the paper or, worse, be present at the time of a raid or a fight. So clubs typically paid thousands of dollars a week in protection money to organized crime groups, in order to avoid any embarrassing violence that would have a chilling effect on the clientele and, of course, the business.

In the late 1990s, both Greg and Craig DePalma went to prison for shaking down Scores. That club remained open, but the Naked Truth eventually closed. In 2002, a Bronx businessman, who we'll call Jerry Spogliari, decided to remodel and reopen the place. He hired everyone who used to own, work at, or was otherwise associated with the Naked Truth

---

* The name of the club has been changed.

and got the club open again. After all, it had been very successful.

Spogliari was minding his business, using the appropriate Mafia-related purveyors of food and beverages and otherwise being an upstanding citizen, when one night he ran into serious trouble. One of the up-and-coming ethnic organized crime groups in New York, the Albanians, had targeted his club for a shakedown. No less than thirty members of the Albanian gang showed up to tear the club apart and beat up everyone they could get their hands on. Obviously, this is not something that the Greenwich executive or the Fordham Road auto mechanic is going to suffer lightly. Unless Spogliari made an accommodation with the Albanians, who were seeking to muscle in on the business, there would *be* no business. Spogliari had two choices: start handing over large wads of cash every week to the Albanians, or come to us.

Very quietly and very reluctantly, he came to see us at the FBI.

"I don't want to pay them protection money, but I need protection," he reasoned. "I'm just a businessman. I'm just trying to make a dollar. I don't want to lose my business because of these guys."

The FBI initially saw this case as an opportunity to take down the Albanian thugs. But while Spogliari was talking with the FBI, he was approached by a crew from the Gambino crime family different from the one that had shaken down Scores and the Naked Truth in years gone by. This new set of Gambinos was offering

protection from the Albanians. They assured Spogliari
that they would make the Albanian problem go away,
for a weekly payment of protection money. Of course,
nothing in the earliest stages of this case hinted at
the possibility of inserting an agent as an undercover
operative into the heart of the Gambino crime family,
although that's what it later became. At the time, it
looked like a very simple undercover operation: Put an
agent in, and take out some Albanians and Gambino
soldiers. And that was how it began.

The New York field office needed an undercover
agent who could play the role of Jerry Spogliari's new
partner, the guy who was investing in the club, maybe
paying for the upgrades, the guy who would make the
payoffs to the Mob and/or the Albanians.

In other words, me.

There was just one hitch.

Throughout my career, I had been working undercover with individuals or networks of drug dealers,
money launderers, extortion artists, or other bad guys
who acted either on their own or on behalf of drug
cartels. I was always playing the role of an outsider
with these Colombians, Russians, Dominicans, Puerto
Ricans—whatever. I was always the heavy, the boss,
the man who reported to no one. I played a Cuban
drug dealer and I had even played the role of an Italian, to Asian, Russian, and Hispanic criminals, always
to great success. But now I would be entering a world
entirely new to me: the world of organized crime, the
world of the Mafia, and specifically, the world of the

Gambino crime family of New York. I would be playing an Italian among Italians. That's a different—and vastly more dangerous—game.

Let's take a brief step back, because I know there are still people out there who don't believe in the existence of the Mafia. Stop doubting. It's for real, and it's as powerful as ever. To review history briefly, wars among disparate American crime families of Sicilian origin essentially came to an end back in the 1930s, when a structure was established that endures to this day. At the top is the Commission, which comprises the "bosses," or godfathers, of the five crime families of New York: Gambino, Lucchese, Genovese, Bonanno, and Colombo. Each family is organized in this manner: the boss sets policy and resolves high-level disputes involving his own and other families. The underboss assists the boss. The consigliere (you remember Robert Duvall as Tom Hagen in *The Godfather*) provides advice. Below the top three are the capos, or captains, who run the crime crews, which consist of made men, full members of the Mafia (also called soldiers) and associates, who are seeking to move up to soldier status. How do you move up? Earn a lot of money for your family, kill enough people, or kill the people currently in positions above you.

Okay, that's how you rise up. But how do you get in, in the first place?

You've got to come from the neighborhoods where the wiseguys flourish. Henry Hill, the focus of the book *Wiseguy* and the movie *GoodFellas,* grew up in Brooklyn watching the mobsters at the cabstand down the block. They knew him from an early age. Sammy "the Bull" Gravano, John Gotti's underboss in the Gambino family, grew up in Bensonhurst, Brooklyn, a tightly knit Italian neighborhood where high-level mobsters knew him for his fighting prowess even before he was out of his teens.

I was born in Cuba. Nobody knew me.

How exactly was I to pass myself off as one of them? As a wiseguy? As an Italian? As a Mafioso?

I had been working on the joint FBI–NYPD Narcotics Task Force, the most wonderful squad a law enforcement agent could hope to join. I've never seen a squad with so many excellent, complex, long-term cases working at the same time, and I had the privilege and pleasure of working with just about all of them undercover. The agents working the strip club case in the Bronx clearly needed a quick-thinking, experienced undercover agent, and they didn't have to look very far, because I was right there, ready to go.

Except this time, I would be playing an Italian to the Italians for the first time in my career.

It made sense tactically to present the undercover agent in this case as an Italian, because we were trying to create a sense of trust with the Mob guys who were also attempting to shake down the club. The Bureau initially had doubts about choosing me, simply because I'm not Italian. What do I know from Italian food? My whole attitude toward eating is: Give me some *pastelitos* (flaky dough pastries with beef or guava or coconut) and some *ropa vieja con moros y maduros* (shredded beef, Cuban black beans and rice, and plantains) and I'm happy.

Actually, I like Italian food—I like every kind of food. At three hundred and plenty pounds, how could I not? But I knew very little about how Mafia guys comported themselves. For this operation, I would be attempting to infiltrate an ongoing organized crime operation, and not just any crew but the Gambinos themselves, one of the most feared and powerful of the Five Families of the New York Mafia. If the FBI were to use me as the undercover, then I would have to go to school in order to learn how to play the part.

Mob school.

And that's exactly what the FBI created for me.

The FBI essentially has three primary levels of bureaucracy. First comes the undercover agent actually working a given case. Above him or her is the "case agent," or handler, who manages the case day to day and has regular contact with the undercover agent or agents involved. And then above the case agent or handler are the supervisors, in the field office or in Washington, who maintain control over which cases are opened, which cases close, and everything else.

On the Naked Truth investigation, I was assigned to a highly experienced case agent named Nat Parisi. Nat had spent his entire career working organized crime and narcotics, in both the New York City and the White Plains FBI field offices. Nat set up an educational program that would transform me from an undercover agent with almost a hundred undercover cases under his belt to an individual whose bona fides would pass muster with the ever-suspicious La Cosa Nostra. Obviously this was no small task. Ever since "Donnie Brasco"—an FBI agent playing the role of a wiseguy—the Mob had become paranoid about the possibility of law enforcement infiltration. Getting into the Mafia now required a background check that most likely rivaled that of the Bureau. How could a total stranger convince wary, prison-hardened criminals that he was trustworthy? This was the challenge that Agent Parisi and I faced as Mob school began.

Frankly, the Mafia's paranoia regarding infiltrators is almost comical. Members of the Bonanno crime family were even having guys strip naked prior to sessions in which they would be "straightened out," or made—initiated as full-fledged members of the Mafia. Pardon me, but if you think there's any possibility that a guy might be wearing a wire to his own initiation ceremony, do you really want him in La Cosa Nostra?

One intelligent precaution the wiseguys had taken was to cease holding initiation ceremonies in the basements of private homes, as had been the tradition for decades. They knew that law enforcement could bug private homes. Now they hold their initiation ceremonies in hotel rooms, which they rent for the day, conduct their business, and then get out. But what did they do all day? Was their life like a *Sopranos* episode, or something different?

Mob school at the FBI, therefore, was about creating an identity, a background, and personal knowledge about how mobsters carry themselves, so that I would never be seriously questioned or suspected of being a law enforcement agent. Actually, the least of my worries was to be made as a Fed. Mobsters never kill FBI agents. They don't want the hassle. The real danger was being considered a rat. If they thought that I was a rat—a real bad guy who had changed sides and was informing on them to the FBI or any type of law enforcement—they would have killed me on the spot.

If the Colombians discover a rat—either an undercover officer or an informant—they'll give him the "Colombian necktie." They slash his throat and pull his tongue out through the wound, as a tribute to the fact that he was talking to authorities. The Mafia would put "two in the back of the head" or stuff money or a canary in the rat's mouth, and leave the body in the trunk of a stolen car in an airport long-term parking lot.

For me, Mob school began with the creation of a new identity. I couldn't just create a "legend" or "pedigree" on the spot and bullshit, as I'd done on previous busts. I needed a solid backstory that they could look into, because they almost certainly would try to examine my bona fides. We started with a new name, which meant we had to decide about my ethnicity. There were two ways to go—either I would be a full-blooded Italian, having grown up in Cuba during the Batista era, when Mafia-owned casinos dominated Havana, or I would be half Italian and half Cuban. We figured we would make that decision once I was inserted into the situation in the Bronx.

I had to choose a name. We settled on Falcone, which was the name of a courageous Sicilian judge who had been murdered by the Mafia along with his wife and three police bodyguards a few years earlier. Then FBI director Louis Freeh honored Judge Falcone with a bronze bust at the FBI Academy because of his fortitude in his fight against the Italian Mafia. As it turned out, some of the wiseguys I met heard my name and winced, wondering aloud if I was related to this despicable guy. But Jack Falcone would be my name inside the Mob.

I needed a Social Security number to go with my new identity and quickly found out how easy they are to obtain in the streets of New York. I got a fake number, and with that I was able to go to the Department of Motor Vehicles in White Plains and pick up a driver's license in my new name. I then applied for and received a credit card. I kept calling and calling to increase my credit line until I got an American Express gold card and ultimately a platinum one. I charged everyday items like gas or meals to build up my credit score in my new name.

Later, when I was working the case and the Mob guys asked me why I had an Amex card, I told them that my accountant told me I had to show expenses in order to justify my legitimate businesses, which I told them was real estate. They bought the explanation. They asked because wiseguys don't carry credit cards.

They generally carry a large wad of bills wrapped up with the kind of thick blue or green rubber band that supermarkets use to hold stalks of broccoli. That wad of bills is called a knot, like the knot on a wooden floor plank, and always with a "hunje" or a "beaner"—a hundred-dollar bill—on top. The bigger the knot, the more successful you are. You'll never see a self-respecting knockaround guy (another term for wiseguy) with a wallet. They all carry their money in big bundles, with those broccoli rubber bands around them. As for identification, they'll probably just have a driver's license, typically out of state and expired. I had to learn these things. The simplest slip-up would indicate my identity as an undercover, and the game would be over.

I needed a story to go along with all of my fake IDs. We created the story that I was a guy from Miami with a team of crazy Cuban Mariel boatlift guys that did home invasions for me to net jewelry and dope. There were a few Gambinos down in Florida, but for the most part, they had little or no contact with Cuban drug dealers. The Gambinos in New York wouldn't have been able to have their Florida brethren check me out. The Miami cover story made sense, since I had spent so much time there on various operations. I knew all the best clubs and restaurants, the whole lay of the land. I could spin a compelling and credible story about my experiences in the city.

As for family, my cover story was that I was an only child and both my parents were dead. My father had been an Italian working in a Havana casino in the 1950s, and my mother was going to be either Cuban or Italian—we would cross that bridge when we came to it. I was born in 1952, and when Castro took over in 1959, my family eventually moved to Miami. As a child, after having lost both parents, I fell in with the wrong crowd, was arrested several times for various crimes, but never went to prison. I created a fake "jacket," or a police record, for Jack Falcone, something that I could share with my new Gambino acquaintances, if I so desired, or if they found their way to it on their own. It was important that I *not* have a prison record. That's because wiseguys across the country do much of their networking behind prison walls. A Mafia family member might spend twenty years behind bars in federal penitentiaries all over the country. It would have been too easy for anyone checking into my past to determine that nobody knew a Jack Falcone inside a certain prison at a certain time. Or they would have known that a particular wiseguy had been in a prison at a time when I claimed to have been there, and they could have called me on it.

As good as the FBI was at supporting and helping me establish an identity, I knew I had to take it a step further. After all, my involvement was much deeper than theirs. If we slipped up and something in my fabricated history gave me away to the Gambinos, the people back at the office would get up the next day, have coffee, and go to work. Meanwhile, I'd be dead. On my own time, while on a vacation in Florida with my wife, I visited cemeteries until I found Falcones who had died at the same time that I was created. That way, if anyone in the Mob said, "Let's go for a trip down to Florida. Show me where your parents are buried," I would have been able to say, "No problem, let's go."

I needed every aspect of my story to check out.

So now Jack Falcone had a credit history, a criminal history, and a family history. But life in the Mafia isn't just about the past; it's about the here and now. For wiseguys, the here and now means hanging out in bars and restaurants. People who've seen *The Sopranos* and *GoodFellas* and *The Godfather* and all those other movies probably have the same idea that I did about the Mob—that they're very action-oriented, always shooting people and chopping them up. The reality is different. Sure, they do those things, but most of their waking moments revolve around eating and talking about future scores.

If I was going to be dining with wiseguys, I needed to know about the food, so the next aspect of Mob school focused on eating and drinking. I don't have to be called twice for dinner, so this was a part of the training that I particularly enjoyed. When it comes to food, the Mob guys know which restaurants to visit for which kinds of food. For example, if you want lobster arrabbiata—spicy lobster—you go to F. illi Ponte's on the West Side Highway. If you want meatballs, you visit Rao's in East Harlem. If you want a nice piece of veal, you go to Il Mulino's in the Village. It's not that other restaurants don't do a good job preparing dishes. It's just that Mob guys know who prepares everything the best. And if you don't have that information, then what kind of knockaround guy are you?

My handler, Nat, took me to Italian restaurants and taught me about food—how to order it, how to taste it, what to look for, how to pronounce things the proper wiseguy way. I learned to say prosciutt', not prosciutto; manicot', not manicotti. I learned about osso buco, braciole and that some people say gravy and others say sauce, depending on where in Italy they are from— everything. (By the way, we paid for these meals out of our own pockets—the Bureau wasn't paying for that aspect of my education!)

Once I got the hang of ordering like a true paisan, I supplemented my education by watching the Food Channel. I especially enjoyed watching *Molto Mario*, with Mario Batali; *Lidia's Family Table,* with Lidia Bastianich; and *Everyday Italian*, with Giada De Laurentiis. These shows are like porn for the stomach, they made me so hungry! I was concentrating not just on the preparation of the dishes but on the proper Italian pronunciation. I also took my wife and our friends out for meals to Italian restaurants, where I tried out my skills at ordering food. Again, for a guy like me, this was not exactly the toughest part of the job.

On top of that, a wiseguy never even looked at a menu. Instead, he bounces in like he owns the place, greets the waiter and maître d' like long-lost relatives, and says jovially, "Hey! What am I gonna eat today!"

The waiter might offer some suggestions, which the adroit wiseguy ignores.

He instead says, "Hey, you know what? I'll tell you what I'm gonna have. Make me a little of this and a little of that, some prosciutt' with parmegiano reggiano, a little antipast', and some polenta with Gorgonzola and sausage, then when I'm done with that bring me a little linguine with clam sauce. How's that?"

The waiters, they loved it!

I also learned about the process of earning "Italian war medals." That's what the wiseguys call it when you spill sauce or traces of Italian dishes on your shirt during one of the many food orgies the Mob assembles. It was not a sign of honor, however, because it took away from your distinctiveness and well-groomed appearance. Once you got your medal, though, they all knew the recipe for removing it. I always found that club soda was best, and then after the stain dried, I would add some talcum powder to pick up the grease.

There were rules for drinking too. A wiseguy never walks into a bar and says, "What kind of beer do you have on tap?" That's for losers. As I learned in Philly, a true wiseguy always establishes dominance and control, even when ordering drinks. "Hey, gimme a Johnnie Walker Black on the rocks. Or gimme a Ketel One on the rocks." A wiseguy knows who he is and what he drinks. He doesn't have time for nonsense. That's the impression that I was taught to convey. Mob guys are also extremely generous. Why shouldn't they be? It's not their money! They stole it!

This isn't to suggest that wiseguys are the easiest customers. They love to show off by breaking balls, by putting working people in their place. This behavior always disgusted me. I found it revolting and unnecessary when Mob guys addressed hard-working Hispanic waiters and busboys, family men who were just trying to make a buck, as if they were lower forms of life. "Hey, what are you, a Mexi*can* or a Mexi*can't?*" they might say when the busboy failed to bring them more bread or water when they had asked for it. Whenever I saw that happen, I'd motion the waiter or busboy over to me—of course when the Mob guys weren't watching—and hand him a ten, a twenty, or sometimes a hundred, and tell him not to worry about it, that my friend didn't mean it. Mafia guys could be generous but tough customers at the same time.

That generosity was evident toward other wiseguys at Christmastime. John Gotti, Sr., the former Gambino boss, was known to freely distribute a very special Rémy Martin cognac, Louis XIII, which cost fifteen hundred dollars a bottle. Of course, Gotti got it for free from some guy he shook down, or it "fell off the back of a truck." These were really nice bottles, Baccarat crystal and the best booze. Again, it's easy to be generous when it isn't your money.

Also, when the check comes at the end of a meal, somebody always grabs it. Mob guys never say, "Okay, let's see. You had the macaroni, and I had the chicken parmigiana." Instead, somebody makes a big gesture of picking up the check and when the others at the table fight to pay for it, you say, "Don't embarrass me. You get the next one." It was all about the appearance of being a wonderful, generous person.

The reality is that these people aren't wonderful and they aren't generous. Greg DePalma told me over and over again that for a made man, his crime family comes ahead of his blood family. He told me often that if your kid was on the operating table, and he had only ten minutes to live, and your boss called you in, you had to immediately leave the hospital and report to him. You could send flowers later to your kid's funeral. This same information appears in *Underboss,* Peter Maas's compelling account of the life of Gambino underboss Sammy "the Bull" Gravano. So either it was part of wiseguy lore handed down to DePalma, or maybe he read Gravano's book. Mobsters certainly pay a lot of attention to the way they are portrayed in popular culture. In the 1970s, they all watched *The Godfather.* More recently, they never missed episodes of *The Sopranos.* Very few crimes were committed between 9 and 10 P.M. on Sunday nights (except for the fact that most of the wiseguys were stealing their cable signal!).

They also kissed each other on the cheek a lot. That took me a while to get used to. Why can't wiseguys just shake hands? I could have lived without all that kissing.

For guys who care little about how much they weigh, they certainly put a great deal of emphasis on personal grooming. Mobsters are always heading off to have manicures and pedicures. They never put polish on their nails—buffing is the only thing allowed. The first time I went out with the fellas for a manicure, I had to get over the initial shock of doing something that is perceived as not masculine. Honestly, it really felt great! No wonder that women do this on a regular basis—and they like to keep it a secret from us guys. I even had a facial and massage a few times, and all I can say is *Marron!* What a beautiful thing!

I also had to get a regular haircut and shave, because mobsters and wannabes have to be clean-shaven and properly coiffed. Facial hair is not allowed because mobsters feel that they are men who have nothing to hide and nobody to hide from. They also feel that facial hair is grown to make you look tough or intimidating, something they do not need to portray as that is what they are supposed to be already. And maybe it's to distinguish themselves from their grandparents' generation of wiseguys, who were called Moustache Petes, because of their devotion to facial hair. So those are the rules of grooming for the wiseguy set.

Mob guys are well versed in the finer things of life. They're knowledgeable about jewelry. The brilliance and the cut of the diamonds in their obligatory pinkie rings give them status. They love every kind of fine jewelry: cuff links, ostentatious bracelets, thick solid gold necklaces, assorted name-brand watches, and tie-pins with diamonds. Earrings are not allowed—probably not manly enough, in their estimation.

They're also into fine tailoring and can spot a Brioni or a Zegna, compared to any lesser suit. They favor custom-made suits tailored from the best Italian fabrics, worn with a silk tie and matching handkerchief, to complete the on-the-town Mafioso look. "Italian tuxedos" were very popular with the guys. That's what they called a Fila or Sergio Tacchini warm-up suit, usually worn over a wife-beater T-shirt showing off a thick solid gold necklace and cross. Such an outfit would be completed with new top-of-the-line sneakers. The warm-up suits came in velour for everyday attire, silk for formal wear, and nylon/polyester for summer.

They had to have the right shoes too—Ferragamos, Bally's, or Gucci's. They had a particular fondness for alligator shoes, and it was a sign of status to own them in black, brown, and even blue. As for socks, either cashmere or nylon was acceptable. Looking sharp from head to toe mattered enormously, because a guy could be classified as a *morte d'fam*, a brokester, if he doesn't look the part. That would be a disaster. Wearing nice clothes, Rolexes, and the finer jewelry pieces is a sign of having made it, of being successful in the Mob.

Nat taught me that wiseguys were extremely conscious of the status that various aspects of fine clothing and jewelry bestow. As a result, they can look at a watch and know if it's real more rapidly than an expert at Tourneau Corner. They can identify a diamond more quickly than a gemologist at Cartier or Tiffany. They are as knowledgeable as experts in all of these fields. For that reason, I had to become an expert myself. I had to know not only the various makes and models of fine watches, but I had to be able to identify what makes a diamond valuable. I needed to recognize whether a piece of jewelry came from Jacob and Company or Harry Winston or any other top company. In addition to being able to recognize pieces, I had to know their price ranges: retail values, what they cost if they were hot or stolen, whether new or used, and how the absence of serial numbers and warranties in the case of fine watches affected the price.

I couldn't be fencing stolen watches and ask ten thousand for a watch that only sold for forty-five hundred or five thousand on the street. So I schooled myself in differences among the Audemars Piguets, the Chopards, the Patek Philippes, the Breitlings, and above all the Rolexes. It was one thing to have a nice stainless steel Rolex, but if you didn't have an eighteen-carat, solid gold Day-Date Rolex President, how seriously could you be taken?

Mob guys, incidentally, never buy retail. If they come by a nice piece of jewelry, it fell off the back of a truck, or came to them through extortion or as a gift. Maybe they heard from one of the guys in the neighborhood, "We scored some watches—do you want to come and see?" Or they might go on a shopping spree and bang out (spend the limit on) some civilian's credit card. But that old Woody Allen joke about the greatest sin in his family was to buy retail could easily be updated to include wiseguys.

I learned that it wasn't just about how I presented myself. Wiseguys are also deeply concerned about how and with whom they present themselves. Let's say you wanted to have a quiet evening out with your girlfriend, your *gumara* (pronounced *goo'mod*). You better bring a "beard" with you, a guy who tags along with you and your girl to the restaurant or club. That way, if someone who knew your wife saw you, or you wound up on an FBI surveillance tape that could later come back to haunt you, your buddy could claim that the girl was with him and not you.

The next issue we covered in Mob school related to my personal safety—who might have known me? Who in the wiseguy world of the Bronx might recognize me and create a problem? After all, this wasn't the Badlands in Philly, where I didn't know a soul. I grew up in the Bronx. I played high school football there. I was a bouncer at N.Y. nightclubs, the Second Floor, Pemoes, Glen Island Casino, and at some other hot spots. I figured that the best way to handle anyone who might come up to me at a restaurant thinking they knew me was to tell them they got the wrong guy. That they did not know what they were talking about and walk away. I fet confident that I could have pulled it off. Surprisingly, there are a lot of big guys who look like me, and many times I got mistaken for a Vinny or a Tony from Brooklyn. I guess everyone in this world has a double! But because I grew up in the Bronx, there were two wiseguys in particular whom I knew and who knew that I was in fact an FBI agent. I dreaded having any contact with them.

One guy was known as Gigi the Whale. I used to see him hanging out in bars in Manhattan. One time he came over to me and shook my hand.

"Not for anything," he said, "but you're the biggest agent I've ever seen."

"What do you mean?" I asked, amazed that he knew who I was. I knew who *he* was. But how had he made me?

It turned out that a mutual friend had pointed me out to him. Still, Gigi wanted to be my friend.

"Gigi," I told him disgustedly, "you push junk. You sell heroin. You're a drug dealer. You did twenty-four years in prison. That might make you a stand-up guy with some people, but you ain't got a good reputation with me. Just don't do your business in front of me and everything'll be okay between us. I catch you pushing junk and I am going to personally lock you up. Do we understand each other?"

And things were okay between us, but if Gigi the Whale ever caught sight of me with DePalma or any of the mobsters with whom I was in contact, it would have been game over. Gigi had been part of the Purple Gang, a ruthless band of heroin dealers from the Pleasant Avenue area in East Harlem. They got their name, it was commonly believed, from the fact that when meat spoils, it turns purple. Everybody I ever met in the Mafia loved and revered Gigi, who was seen at all the Mob functions. He died while I was undercover, and although our paths nearly crossed, fortunately they never did.

The second wiseguy who could have identified me as an FBI agent was named Randy Pizzolo. He thought he was a tough guy. He was on parole, but he was always smacking people around, men or women. Someone told Randy that I was an agent. Randy was a guy like John Gotti—always manicured, always in a beautiful double-breasted suit, driving a Mercedes S500, a beauty queen on his arm. One time he came into a restaurant where he saw me seated at a table with a group of people. This was well before my undercover work as Jack Falcone. He announced in front of everybody, "Buy everybody a drink except for the Fed!"

The waiter looked at me, unsure of what to do. I told Pizzolo to shove the drinks up his ass, and *I* instead bought drinks for my guys. I told Pizzolo, "You got a problem? Are you stupid or something? You're on parole, and I could violate you just for breaking your curfew! Don't ever embarrass me like that again in front of my friends!!"

I saw him in another restaurant not long after and he gave me his hand to shake.

"No hard feelings," he told me.

I still wasn't over the insulting way he had treated me in the bar.

"No hard feelings?" I said, refusing to shake his hand. "Watch yourself, Randy! One day your big mouth is gonna get you in a lot of trouble!"

That was the last piece of advice I gave him, but I guess he didn't take it. Eventually he was found dead, with four bullets in his head. He had been whacked by a capo in the Bonanno family because of his big mouth. But as I was entering the world of the Bronx

Mafia, these two men were still out there, doing their thing, and either one could have identified me.

Thanks to my progress in Mob school, I could now carry myself like a wiseguy and I had a good story to tell. I also had to learn how to speak like a mobster. It was all about convincing people that I had Italian roots. Let's say that I wanted to correct someone. You just don't go around telling your capo that he's made a mistake. There's a specific language for doing it. Nat taught me to say something like this: "Hey, listen, I don't mean any disrespect by this. You're my skipper and if you say it's like this, then it's like this for me. But I heard this other possibility."

Again, the antennae of the wiseguys were up, way up, because of Donnie Brasco. In truth, *omertà*, the code of silence, which might have been violated by a renegade like a Joe Valachi only once in a generation, was now a joke, a thing of the past. The Mafia was more like a bird sanctuary. Everybody was singing if they got into trouble. It was no longer about being a stand-up guy and doing your jail time, with the expectation that the family would take care of you. Instead, the Mafia had evolved into an organization where each man was out for himself. Don't tell me about honor among thieves. The Mafia even employs private investigators who are former law enforcement guys to do background checks on wannabes like me. How people could cross over from one side of the street to the other was beyond me, but enough of them did it every day that I had every reason to expect a serious background check.

I also had to learn how to handle delicate situations. Let's say I was in a basement somewhere with a couple of drug dealers holding a gun to my head, and they said, "You're a Fed—blast this cocaine or we'll kill you."

Well, my indignant response to the Bureau managers proposing this scenario was "Never mind what I would do. More important—how and why did I allow myself to get in a situation like this in the first place?"

If I can be smart about protecting myself, I would never find myself in these kinds of jams. Sometimes I got a little frustrated with a few of the Bureau higher-ups who worked on this case for not being a little more street smart with regard to the Mob. I always had one fallback position: In the event that we were going out on a hit or if I was expected to shoot someone, I decided I would feign a heart attack. I would collapse, clutching my chest and yelling, "Oh, shit! I'm having a heart attack!" They'd help me out, take me to a hospital, and reschedule the hit to another day, thus giving the FBI enough time to protect and hide the potential victim. But I may be wrong about this. After all, who is going to pick up a 390-pound man! These guys would have probably left me there to die! I guess I'll never know.

One thing was clear: I wouldn't have to kill someone as a prerequisite for induction into the Mob. In decades past, when the code of *omertà* held, you had to do "a piece of work"—kill someone for your higher-ups—to enter the Mafia. The theory was that if your hands were steeped in blood, you would never cross the line and become an informant for the police or the Feds. In reality, though, so many people had killed for the Mob and then turned informant that there was no longer anything to be gained by making the next-generation wiseguys shoot or strangle someone. I guess they had become resigned to the fact that a certain percentage of inductees ultimately would go over to the side of law enforcement. You still could be asked to kill someone or be present at a hit, but it wasn't an automatic thing anymore. It mattered less to them who you whacked than what you earned.

I supplemented my knowledge of Mob affairs by reading Jerry Capeci's "Gang Land" columns at his website, www.ganglandnews.com, and the www.AmericanMafia.com website created by Detective Rick Porello. These are treasure troves filled with facts and stories about the Mob.

Before long, I was starting to think like a wiseguy. I was almost ready to enter the world of the Naked Truth. When I had entered Nat Parisi's Mob school, I was a Cuban-born FBI agent. When I left, I was ready for the Gambinos. But would the Gambinos accept me as a Miami jewel thief and admit me into their world?

CHAPTER NiNE

The Payoff at the Naked Truth

My role as a new investor in the strip club turned out to be a great idea, because it helped me establish my bona fides and get acclimated with the Naked Truth's regulars, the dancers, and the staff. The dancers were very nice and had some pretty good stories. They were hustlers—always trying to get you to buy a lap dance. I would say, "Look, I'm in the business, no thanks." So then I'd get to know their real stories—money problems, problems at home. I was surprised to find that many of them were going to school. They looked at stripping as a way to make money for their families, nothing more. It was a tough job for them—there were a lot of lowlifes out there trying to take advantage of them. We threw out a couple of guys along the way who were a little too adventurous with them.

I decided we should also bring in another undercover, for added protection, in case the Albanians came back to destroy the club. I also wanted to be sure that we didn't have a problem with the wiseguys the day we made the protection payoff. FBI management agreed and wanted to assign a second agent to work under-cover with me as backup. Unfortunately, the guy they chose was so pitifully wrong for the part that I almost had to laugh. No offense, but this was an agent who actually resoled his shoes. He had a 1970s-style haircut and always wore white tube socks whenever he wore his polyester dark suits and pants. He also wore short sleeve shirts and striped ties that only a Sears appliance salesman should be authorized to wear. He had a hor-rible reputation in the office as a blowhard and hothead who earned the nickname "Tick Tick" because he was wound up so tight that he was ready to explode. He had a porn star mustache that made Ron Jeremy look like an altar boy. Can you imagine a self-respecting wiseguy resoling his shoes or taking seriously someone who did?

I couldn't believe they were trying to shove this loser down my throat. I needed somebody who, even if he lacked elegance, still had the ability to project himself as a credible bad guy. My choice was Jimmy Gagliano, a West Point graduate, an Army Ranger, and a member of the FBI's Elite Hostage Rescue Team. This guy had tattoos on his tattoos, a shaved head, and a very tough and intimidating way about him. He was very street smart and had extensive organized crime experience. He had worked for Supervisory Agent

Bruce Mouw's elite Gambino squad during the John Gotti, Jr. era. Jimmy was going to be my muscle, and I wanted him in on the case. He only lasted a short while, because it turned out that some of the targets of the investigation could have recognized him from previous cases. But he was great for me while he was there.

Jimmy and I started hanging out at the club. He played it off like he was my cousin. He was the perfect choice for the job, because he knew when to keep his mouth shut. Some guys work undercover and they just talk too much. Maybe they're nervous, or maybe they think they need to demonstrate that they know everything in order to garner respect. Not Jimmy. He knew and understood his role. He knew when to just stand there and look terrifying, which was exactly what I needed.

I didn't just meet Gambinos. Strip clubs are magnets for wiseguys of every family, so I met Genovese, Bonanno, and Colombo guys as well. I can't say I wasn't scared, because everything I had learned about the new Mafia, the post-Gotti brand of wiseguy, frankly terrified me. In the old days, the men were motivated by honor and greed, in that order. Their first loyalty was to the Mob itself. They respected the rules, including the rules of who could be killed when, why, and how. The old Mafia had a sense of teamwork, a sense of mission, a sense, if you will, of pride in itself. It was like the NFL—there might have been a lot of separate teams, but they operated with a "league think" mentality. They put the interests of the Mafia as a whole ahead of their own personal needs, because they knew that as long as everyone did so, they all benefited.

Not so the wiseguys of today. First of all, a lot of the wiseguys in today's Mafia use drugs. They're always blasting cocaine, which was never the case a generation ago. These guys are so fueled by dope that you never know what they'd do. They'll whack a guy as soon as look at him—they are much more violent and dangerous than their predecessors, which is saying something. Any bad deal could end up with guns blazing. That possibility certainly included this simple delivery of money at the club whenever we made the payoff. Even the rough-and-tough Jimmy Gagliano couldn't do much for me if the Albanians or wiseguys decided to hurt me. Nevertheless, my responsibilities were clear. I had to enter the club, have a meeting with Louis Filippelli's people, play my part as the new Florida-based investor in the club, and fork over the money. That was my job, and I was going to do it.

When the date of the extortion payment arrived, December 18, 2002, Jimmy and I made a plan to meet at an Italian restaurant, Spaghetti Western, near the Naked Truth. I went to the restaurant early, but Jimmy was already waiting. We waited for a heads-up call from the bartender at the Naked Truth to tell us when Louis Filippelli arrived at the club. Remember, wiseguy time and doper time isn't military time. If a guy says he's going to show up at five o'clock in the afternoon, he could just as easily come in at midnight or three in the morning. You just have to sit and wait. We both rushed to the restaurant to be there on time just to sit and wait.

Finally, we decided to go to the club and have a few cocktails. I always drank Bacardi and Coke, the appropriate beverage for a Florida guy. And I was always sure to specify my brand.

Before long, our patience was rewarded. The owner of the club came in with Chris Sucarato, one of Louis's closest guys in the Gambinos. To my surprise, Chris wasn't dressed up in the traditional garb of the successful mobster—no Brioni suit, no alligator shoes, no diamond pinkie ring. Instead, he looked like he had just come in from a construction site wearing a sweatshirt, jeans, and boots. He was very cordial, a nice enough fellow, who looked to be around thirty-seven or thirty-eight years old.

Chris was an associate in Alphonse "Funzi" Sisca's Gambino crew and a close friend of Gambino soldier Filippelli. Sisca was a trusted friend of Arnold Squitieri, the Gambino family boss. Sisca's crew included Filippelli and Chris. Because Squitieri was on parole for his previous drug conviction, he had to be extremely careful about being seen with other criminals. Consorting with known criminals would have earned the Gambino boss a quick trip back to the slammer. So he essentially ran the family through the triumverate of Funzi Sisca, Louis Filippelli, and Chris Sucarato. They were his eyes and ears on the street and enabled the Gambino boss to remain in the shadows.

Filippelli had never been arrested prior to being straightened out. In the eyes of some in the Gambino family, we later learned, he hadn't really paid his dues—he hadn't been through the crucible of an arrest, a trial, a prosecutor looking to flip you, and jail time. Some therefore considered him an unknown quantity. Others in the family probably envied his close ties to the boss, Squitieri.

The club owner Jerry Spogliari, my guy Jimmy, Chris, and I exchanged pleasantries, and then Chris and I went into the back room to talk. We sat facing each other, sitting on couches in the VIP room typically reserved for high rollers getting lap dances.

"You guys resolved the problem with the Albanians," I basically told him when we were alone. "We really appreciate you and Louis. We're giving you this money as a way of saying thank you."

I handed him an envelope with cash. After opening it, he gave me a confused, unhappy look because the envelope didn't contain the fifteen thousand dollars he expected. Instead, it held only five thousand.

I shrugged. "Look around this place," I said, gesturing. "Ever since the Albanians came in, we've been dead in the water. Nobody wants to come here. Not our regular clientele and not the executives going home to Greenwich. We can barely even get girls to dance here. Everybody's afraid they're going to get killed when the Albanians come back. We're just dying. I don't think it's hard for you to see that."

"I see your point," Chris said, nodding.

"This money's just the beginning," I said. "If you can make our problem with the Albanians go away, I'm sure the club will take off, especially as soon as people know it's going to be okay here. And at that point, they'll be plenty more for you and your guys."

I waited warily as Chris digested this plan. Was he going to buy it? Was I credible to him as a street guy? Or was he about to take out his gun and blow me away?

Chris fingered the money in the envelope I had given him. Finally he nodded.

"It's okay," he said. "I promise you there won't be any more problems with the Albanians."

I felt a wave of relief that I couldn't possibly let come to the surface. Instead, I grinned and we shook hands on the beginning of what we both hoped would be a beautiful—and lucrative—friendship. To Chris's credit, the Albanians never came back. It shows either that the Mob is strong enough to bully the Albanians or that the Albanians and the Italians were working together and had another fish on the hook, namely us. I really believe that's the way it went down. After all, if you run a strip club, or any other kind of business that generates a lot of cash, what can you do? Call the cops? They can't monitor strip clubs around the clock! If you're going to get protection, you're going to have to pay for it, and that means reaching out to organized criminals—or, more accurately, sitting back and waiting for them to reach out to you.

Now I had enough evidence to put Chris away, if

I wanted to—it's illegal to accept protection money. It's extortion. But we didn't want Chris. We wanted an in at the club, so that we could see who else might come our way. The joke of it is that when I got back to the office and told them what had happened, FBI Headquarters insisted that Chris and Louis Filippelli were not members of the Gambino family, and that Alphonse "Funzi" Sisca was only a low-level soldier and not a captain. After all, these guys weren't on the FBI's official chart of Mafiosi, and if something wasn't on the chart, it couldn't possibly exist.

I couldn't believe it. These guys were swearing up and down that their charts were the latest and the greatest, the only accurate source of information about the Gambino family that could possibly be trusted. Obviously, these guys had been believing their own headlines ever since they had taken Gotti down. The problem with their charts was that a lot of the information on it came from guys in jail. A chart is only as good as your intelligence on the street. But the Mob changes and adapts itself every day. Its members learn from their mistakes. Guys in jail may not know the half of what's going on, on the street. Wiseguys are like chameleons, constantly changing to blend into the background. So just because names aren't on a chart doesn't mean they aren't active in the Mob. I wanted to be the guy who could provide new, accurate information from the street, firsthand, so that we in the Bureau would really understand who and what we were up against.

Along these lines, it's worth noting that John Gotti single-handedly destroyed the Mafia in his day by insisting that they all show up at the Ravenite Social Club once a week to kiss him. He took something that was supposed to be private and made it public, and as a result, the FBI's Gambino Squad was able to draw up charts that truly reflected the power relationships and the identities of the various members of the crime family. But that was then and this is now. Now a bunch of guys who were not even on that chart were running things, and I had a front-row seat.

Little by little, I developed a reputation as Big Jack, the friendly guy from Florida who owned a piece of the club, someone you could always count on for a good time.

I enjoyed the company of the wiseguys, and soon I was not afraid to step out with them. The Mafia is all about food. These guys might or might not have been committing crimes three to five times a day, but they certainly were eating nicely three to five times a day. Every night they'd mention a different Italian restaurant somewhere in the tristate area they wanted to try. One night the wiseguys might say, "Let's go to Port Chester. There's a new joint over there that's owned by Joey Potsandpans and Vinnie Bagadonuts is his maître d'." "Have appetite, will travel" could have been their motto.

I socialized with the mobsters, had dinners, lived large, established friendships. I wasn't doing business. That would have been a little too premature. Our targets were still Louis, Chris, and Funzi. I was hanging out with their friends, hoping that conversation about me trickled back to them—that I was a stand-up guy with a little juice down in Florida.

Before long, I was accepted into their midst. I was no longer the new kid on the block. I was thought of as a stand-up individual, one who walked the walk and talked the talk. No one ever thought I was law enforcement. Instead, it was "Hey, Jackie, let's go out, come on!" And they'd introduce me to their friends. My circle of introductions within the wiseguy community grew and grew.

The partying was seven days a week—it was nonstop, and it went late into the night. It was actually very demanding to be out there, playing this role, with these individuals. Let's not forget for a minute what wiseguys did for a living. They were professional criminals and killers, and if they had suspected I was an informant, the end would have come quickly and it would not have been pretty. So it was emotionally and psychologically very demanding to be out with these guys. At the same time, I was supposed to check in with the office every single day and keep the people there aware of my activities. I also had a wife and daughter who were seeing less and less of me as the Gambino case wound on.

At first, I went to the office early, did all my paperwork, went home, took a nap, and then went to work at the club, in preparation for a night out on the town with the wiseguys. After a while, I was told to quit coming in. The joint FBI–NYPD Narcotics Task Force and the Gambino Squad were practically sharing a hallway. The processing center for bad guys was right next to our squad. I could have been made at any time by some unfortunate mobster who had been arrested the night before.

There was another reason for me not to go in, and that had to do with the general antipathy some FBI agents have toward agents who work undercover. Except for Joe Pistone and me, there simply is no such thing as an "FBI undercover agent." There are FBI agents who work undercover from time to time, but by and large, the Bureau does not have a category of agents who consistently work undercover. As a result, undercover agents are looked down on by the agent population. Undercovers are viewed as people who are scammers, living large, driving nice cars, eating good meals, while the "real agents" eat McDonald's and Burger King. These agents simply didn't realize that undercovers are on the front lines of crime and have just as much at stake every day as they do.

No matter. My world was about to change because of the release of a certain Gambino crime family member from prison.

His name was Greg DePalma.

INTERLUDE ONE

Royal Charm

While I was working the Mob case out of the Naked Truth, I was working on four other major cases and a variety of minor buy-bust operations for the drug squad. In a buy-bust, the undercover buys drugs from a suspect who is then busted on the spot. This is the story of the first of the other major cases in which I was involved while the Gambino investigation unfolded.

The FBI learned that a group of smugglers from Asia was bringing into the United States counterfeit cigarettes, counterfeit Louis Vuitton handbags, counterfeits of everything a person could name. On top of that, the smugglers had promised the FBI agents working as undercovers that they had access to weapons, thanks to a relative who was a military arms dealer. Stopping the inflow of the counterfeit goods was important. Halting the flow of weapons was paramount. If this relative was willing to sell arms to mobsters, to whom else around the world might he sell his wares?

So we were going after them.

We explained that we would be brokering weapons on behalf of Colombian freedom fighters, who would give us cocaine at a really good price. That's why we were aiding them in the illegal importation of counterfeit cigarettes into the United States—to nurture the relationships that would lead to the weapons deals.

Two undercover FBI agents out of the Newark office were involved. One was Lou Calverese, and the other, Tom Zyckowski, aka Z-Man. They were posing as mobsters with a connection at the seaport in Elizabeth, New Jersey. The connection was a dirty customs guy. Lou and Z-Man told our new Asian friends that their guy could flag containers arriving on ships so that those containers would not be searched and their records would not be scrutinized. Of course, there would be a hefty fee involved, but for the money, our guys would take the container, deliver it to a safe warehouse in South Jersey, and arrange for distribution of the items inside.

Just as things got under way, for bureaucratic reasons, Z-Man was taken off the case. Before he moved on, he introduced me to the primary suspects in the case, a petite Asian woman in her fifties we'll call Mei-Lin and her husband, Chris. Right away, Mei-Lin and

I clicked. After Z-man's departure from the case, Lou Calverese took over the primary undercover position while I became the secondary.

Here's how the deal worked. Mei-Lin and her husband were importing forty-foot containers holding almost a thousand master cartons of cigarettes, all counterfeit. Each master carton contains fifty regular cartons of cigarettes. We're talking about hundreds of thousands of dollars' worth of pure profit from counterfeit cigarettes in each container.

So we worked the case. The cigarettes came in, and FBI agents posing as mobsters' helpers brought the contraband to a warehouse. Once there, Mei-Lin's guys picked the stuff up. Sometimes we'd go to Jersey City or Philadelphia to drop off the cigarettes, but the scenario was always the same: We helped her bring the cigarettes in, and she paid us. But every time we asked about the weapons, Mei-Lin always had another story. The time wasn't right. She couldn't do it just then, but she would soon. It was really annoying.

At about this time, the original case agent who had pioneered the case, Jodi Petracci, passed away from cancer. The whole case had been her vision, and we were simply following the trail she had blazed. We were bringing in the cigarettes and encouraging Mei-Lin to talk more about the weapons, which were really the heart of the case for us.

The counterfeiting, though, was no small matter. In China, I learned, you'd have one factory making polo shirts for an American company with another factory next door making counterfeits of the same shirts. Suppliers dropped off the raw materials—the cloth, the thread, whatever it was—at the main factory, and then they dropped off more at the other factory. From my perspective in the FBI, counterfeiting was endemic throughout the Chinese economy. Mei-Lin told us that whatever on earth we could think of, she could get us counterfeit versions that discerning people could not tell from the real thing. The joke was that if you stood still near one of these counterfeiting plants long enough, the Chinese would create—and be ready to sell—six new copies of you!

Mei-Lin also wanted a West Coast connection for the importation of counterfeit cigarettes, and we provided her with an undercover FBI agent in Los Angeles, working out of the Port of Long Beach. Our operation was called Royal Charm, and the one in L.A. was called Smoking Dragon. (These were pretty good names, by FBI standards.) Now we were bringing in cigarettes to both coasts, but what we really wanted were the guns. Mei-Lin and her people were still dragging their feet on the weapons. They must have figured they had a great thing going—they were making a fortune from the fake cigarettes, so why complicate matters with the weapons?

We still wanted to meet the arms dealer—we wanted him to come to the United States to talk with us. No dice. He was afraid to come to the United States. So we called for a meeting with Mei-Lin and Chris.

"We're done with cigarettes," we told them. "If you're not gonna help us with the weapons, we're not gonna do any more cigarettes for you. We're wasting our time here."

Mei-Lin and Chris finally got the message.

At last, husband Chris introduced us to one of his associates he thought might be able to help us with weapons. Let's call this associate Ken. After smuggling containers of cigarettes for Ken, we finally broached the subject of weapons with him.

"What can you do for us?" we asked. "Mei-Lin's husband says you can do weapons."

"I can do weapons," Ken said coolly. "I can do fake Viagra. I can do anything. I can also make the introduction to the arms dealer, so you can start getting the weapons. But you'll have to travel to Thailand. He can't come to the United States."

"No problem," Lou said.

The meeting place was set for the resort area of Phuket, later hard hit by the tsunami of Christmas 2005.

Lou, the main undercover on the case, told me, "Jack, pack your bags. We're going to Thailand to meet a new weapons contact."

My eyes went wide. "*We?*" I asked. "What do you got, a mouse in your pocket? I'm not going to Thailand! A twenty-hour flight? No way!"

"Why wouldn't you go?" Lou asked, surprised by my vehement response.

"I can't be on a plane that long!" I exclaimed.

"Look at me! Where am I going to go to the bathroom? You'll need the Jaws of Life to get me out of an airplane bathroom!"

"You gotta come!" he implored.

"I'm not going!" I replied firmly.

We went back and forth like this for a while. After I convinced Lou that I wouldn't go, we agreed that he should take another agent with him for protection. The agent we picked, Melissa Shields, would also act in an undercover capacity. Lou and I decided it was a good move to take a woman. Thailand may well be the sex trade capital of the entire world. If one male undercover agent, or even two, went by themselves without a woman, the targets would almost certainly bring one girl or even six to your room, or God knows what, along with a video camera, to try to get you on tape with a prostitute. That would obviously be a disaster. So instead, to counter that, it was Lou and Melissa, a loving couple, traveling together for a romantic vacation on the coast of Thailand.

They went and did a great job. Lou met with Ken and his connection in Thailand, a man we'll call Johnny, while Melissa went "sightseeing." They came back all excited—not only were we going to get weapons, but we were also going to get ice: crystal meth, a drug that was increasing in popularity at the time. We said we were interested in the drugs, but that wasn't really what we wanted. The problem with drugs, of course, is that you can't let them hit the street. Drugs were of interest to us, but not nearly as much as shutting down an illicit weapons distributor with a dirty Asian connection. That we found *extremely* interesting.

And then the case took an even more startling turn.

While we were asking Ken about what other counterfeit items he could get us, we asked him, in passing, whether they could do money.

"Yeah, we can do money," Ken said. Then he started dropping hints—he had counterfeit bills coming from North Korea.

If you thought cigarettes and guns had our attention, counterfeit bills coming from North Korea? Believe me, we were fully engaged.

After Lou and Melissa came home, Ken met us in Atlantic City, where he gave us a sample hundred-dollar bill. Now, I've seen a lot of fake bills in my decades at the FBI, but I'd never seen anything that looked as real as this.

"Man, this is real!" I exclaimed.

"No, no," Ken assured us. "It's counterfeit!"

"This is very good!" I was delighted. "What are you looking to sell this for?"

We went back and forth and finally negotiated the deal down to thirty cents on the dollar. The only question was how much we wanted to take in an initial shipment.

Before we made a commitment to buy the counterfeit notes, we wanted to take the sample back to the office and have experts take a look. We sent the money down to the Secret Service, and it was a bull's-eye. These turned out to be the infamous Supernotes, fake bills printed in North Korea using the same ink and the same paper as the U.S. Treasury. In the eyes of the Secret Service, they were as good as real.

We did our own test, just to corroborate what the Secret Service told us. We took the bills to executives at the casinos and banks in Atlantic City. We figured they were about as well trained as anyone on the planet to spot counterfeit money. They did not recognize them as counterfeit.

Counterfeit money poses a greater threat than practically any other contraband when it comes to national security. If North Korea flooded the United States with these fake bills, it could take down the entire U.S. economy. These bills were that good. So we put in an order and paid thirty thousand dollars in cash to get a hundred thousand dollars' worth of the Supernotes.

Operation Royal Charm was financially self-sustaining—every time we brought in a load of counterfeit cigarettes on behalf of Mei-Lin and her people, we were charging them fifty thousand dollars to insure that the container would not be searched by U.S. Customs officials. So the thirty thousand for the Supernotes wasn't coming out of the taxpayers' pockets. Instead, it was coming out of money that we had "made" as we were helping Mei-Lin to bring the cigarettes into the country.

The money arrived in one of the containers in which they shipped counterfeit cigarettes. The bills were numbered sequentially, and they were perfect. We couldn't believe how good they were! Ken told us that Johnny, the Asian arms dealer whom Lou had met in Thailand, was coming to the United States to meet us. He had some questions and he had some issues, since we were moving forward with the money on a larger scale. I was delighted. If Johnny had any doubts about dealing with us, once he saw me, everything would be okay in his mind—because I just don't look like an FBI agent.

Johnny arrived and we put him up at a nice hotel casino in Atlantic City. The Asian criminals love to gamble. We practically had to peel them away from the casinos to have our meetings. We finally sat down. Johnny's English was not perfect, but he certainly spoke better English than we did Chinese.

"We're interested in the Supernotes," we told him. "But we want to be the sole distributor. We don't want guys on the East Coast or the West Coast and all over the country bringing these things in. We want exclusivity."

"No problem," he told us. "We can arrange that."

We negotiated for a while before we finally put in an order for a million dollars' worth of fake hundreds. He told us he'd be willing to throw a little more in. When the container came in with the cash, it was not just a million dollars in Supernotes—it was almost three million. We were all set to pay the three hundred thousand dollars, because now we had the opportunity to shut down the flow of Supernotes into the country. But now we turned our attention back to the weapons.

"Yes, we have access to weapons," he told us.

"We want surface-to-air missiles," we said.

"We can do that," Johnny said. "We can do anything you want."

He hinted that the weapons came from either China or North Korea.

Then, seeing that we were willing customers for just about anything he could offer, he asked, "What about heroin?"

Again he asked "What about it? I can do heroin, Ecstasy, cocaine, ice, whatever you want."

We realized they must have a network of Chinese heroin, which we could take down at the end of the case. Fake cigarettes were one thing, but we couldn't put illegal drugs on the street. If we brought heroin into the United States, we would have to shut down the investigation right then and there. We didn't want it until after we had pursued the Supernotes and the weapons.

"We can get the drugs to Italy," he told us. "We can move it through Europe."

"How you gonna do that?" I asked warily.

"Through our many foreign embassy friends who can easily use their diplomatic pouches to smuggle it in," he said, as if he were just talking about moving steel or copper pipes or flat-screen TVs or some other legitimate product. It was mind-blowing.

"How do I know what weapons you've got?" I asked. "You got a catalog?"

"Sure, we'll send you one."

We wrapped up our meeting and promised we'd get back to them quickly once we had a chance to figure out what we wanted to buy.

We never thought we'd see a catalog, but sure enough, a few weeks later in the mail, we got a book with all the different weapons Mei-Lin's people could procure for us. The catalog actually contained surface-to-air missiles, helicopters, bazookas, AK-47s, and M60s. Once we got that catalog with its abundance of lethal weapons, we thought, "Man, these are businessmen who'll sell you anything."

We created a strategy to buy the Supernotes ultimately to get the weapons. We put in an order for some weapons, but there was delay after delay in their arrival. They claimed that a terrorist attack in London had increased port security worldwide, and they were afraid that the weapons would never get through. Eventually we decided that the weapons were never going to show up. Johnny also had sent over three million dollars in Supernotes and some meth, all on consignment, as a goodwill gesture, but now he had begun to pressure us for payment. So the case agent and supervisor decided that we had to take the case down.

We had to figure out how to get all of the bad guys in one place at one time. Melissa hit on the idea of sending out wedding invitations to all of the suspects involved in the case that we wanted to arrest, both here in the United States and overseas. They all knew Lou and Melissa, the undercover agents, to be this lovey-dovey couple, so the next step for them was getting married.

And that's what we did: We printed beautiful wedding invitations announcing that Lou Calverese was marrying Melissa, and I was the best man. All of those people were invited to the wedding in Atlantic City—the ones who brought in the cigarettes, the ones who tried to sell us the dope, the people involved in the Supernotes, even the people involved in the weapons' transactions, which unfortunately never came to pass.

It wasn't going to be a simple little wedding. This was a whole weekend affair. We held a rehearsal dinner at Morton's Steakhouse in Caesar's Palace. We even brought Z-Man back into the case for the grand finale. And what a beautiful party it was. We were all sitting there in the room, everybody dressed up nicely, eating steak, drinking the finest wine, all financed by the proceeds of the counterfeit cigarette operation.

Everyone was having a great time. Lou and Melissa were the happy couple, and I was making the toast as best man. The bad guys gave Lou and Melissa two solid gold Rolexes as wedding presents, which to this day I'm sure were counterfeit. They gave me "Cuban" cigars. Now, I know all about Cuban cigars! No way these were Cuban! They were so-so, definitely not the real thing. Lou, Z-Man, and I were puffing on our cigars, looking out at the crowd of bad guys we would arrest the next day. We were thinking, These people have no idea, no idea at all, that this will be their last free night on earth, maybe for years or even decades. I looked at them enjoying the party, celebrating this sham of a wedding between Lou and Melissa, and not one of the subjects present had the slightest clue of what was about to happen. It was a Hollywood moment.

The next day we sent limousines to pick up the guests—the suspects—to escort them to the wedding reception, which would be aboard a nonexistent yacht in the Atlantic City harbor. It was a boat we called *Royal Charm,* which was, of course, the official FBI name for the entire case. The limos, however, did not take our guests to the harbor. Instead, they brought them to the FBI office in Atlantic City, where they were all arrested in their tuxedos and gowns. I'll never forget that sight—these people standing there in total shock, still holding their wedding gifts, asking, "But what about Lou and Melissa? Are they still getting married?"

The next day's headline in the Atlantic City newspaper was "Love, Honor, and Arrest." We seized over 30 million dollars' worth of counterfeit cigarettes and over $5 million in fake currency. All in all, a good piece of work for the FBI.

PART TWO
Building the Case

CHAPTER TEN

Meeting Grandpa Munster

On February 28, 2003, former Gambino capo Greg De-Palma was released from prison. At first, this news didn't provoke more than a ripple in our own investigation. Greg later became my primary target and my entrée into the world of organized crime, but none of us could have predicted it back then. As far as we knew, DePalma was a has-been. Sure, back in the day, he had been close with Paul Castellano and then John Gotti, legendary bosses of the Gambino family during the 1970s and '80s. DePalma also created and ran the Westchester Premier Theater in the 1970s. This was a venue modeled on Westbury Music Fair on Long Island that generated tens of millions of dollars for the mob during its financing, construction, and operation. DePalma is front and center in the famous photograph of Frank Sinatra with Carlo Gambino, Castellano, and other Mob bigwigs. It's a photo taken during the theater's heyday.

The photo came about when Sinatra sang at the theater when numerous leading members of La Cosa Nostra were in New York to resolve "family" issues around the country. Mafia leaders present included Jimmy "the Weasel" Fratianno of San Francisco, Mike Rizzitello of Los Angeles, Tony Spilotro of Las Vegas, Russell Bufalino of Scranton, and several associates of Philadelphia boss Angelo Bruno. They also wanted to "pay respect" to Aniello "Neil" Dellacroce and Carmine Galante, whom *Time* magazine in 1977 called "front runners to succeed Carlo Gambino as the Mafia's next boss of bosses."

At the Westchester Premier Theater, the scams were as ingenious as they were lucrative. For example, the box office sold entire blocks of seats for cash. These were seats that did not correspond to any known seating chart for the theater. The revenue from these seats was pure Mafia profit, and that income was never accounted for on the theater's books. Before the Westchester Premier Theater went bankrupt, it brought in more than $9 million for New York's organized crime members. DePalma was personally skimming hundreds of thousands of dollars from the theater.

Prior to his involvement in the theater, DePalma had had diverse criminal business interests. He was a fence, with an office on Canal Street, specializing in moving stolen jewelry. He was also a shylock, making extortionate loans to desperate businessmen and degenerate gamblers. And he had a hidden interest in a trendy discotheque in Westchester called Fudgie's. He brought a lot of celebrities to the clubs to add some luster and get publicity. When Greg had a "hidden interest" in the club, it really meant that he was shaking down the real owner in traditional Mafia style.

After the Westchester Premier Theater, DePalma's next visible and lucrative venture was in the Scores nightclub in Manhattan. He and his son Craig extorted millions of dollars from it. Greg DePalma, Craig DePalma, and John Gotti, Jr., eventually went to jail for their involvement in that case.

When DePalma emerged from prison, there was little reason to believe that his involvement in organized crime would continue. After all, he was more than seventy years old, his comatose son Craig needed round-the-clock care, his bosses and protectors in the Gambino family had long since passed away, and on top of that, there was the matter of Nicky LaSorsa.

LaSorsa was a wiseguy whom Greg had first proposed for membership in the Gambino family before deciding to kill him. As a result, DePalma had legitimate reason to fear for his own life after his release from prison: Some Gambinos wanted to kill him as payback for his nonsanctioned attempted hit on LaSorsa.

But Greg DePalma was in no mood to retire. Instead, he hit the ground running. He immediately reached out to Jerry Spogliari of the Naked Truth and said, "This used to be my club and I'm taking it back.

If you're going to pay protection, you're going to pay it to me."

Greg demanded an envelope of cash—a tribute—from Spogliari. FBI headquarters started to hear from informants that he wanted to regain his power base in the Bronx and Westchester County just north of the city. We figured that somebody would simply kill De-Palma, whether it was LaSorsa, the new generation of Gambinos who had taken over the club, the Albanians, or someone else altogether. Yet the tenacious DePalma kept showing up all over his old territory, reasserting his authority. Other informants reported that he was trying to ally himself with the new Gambino under-boss, Anthony Megale, known as "the Genius" and "Mac" (short for Machiavelli). We learned that Greg was trying to resolve his problems with the Gambino higher-ups, but there was still a contract on his name.

When law enforcement gets credible evidence of a death threat, even against a criminal, we have an obligation to go to that individual and share our information. And so we did. Nat Parisi went to talk to DePalma. This wasn't that hard to arrange, because DePalma was on parole, so Parisi reached out to De-Palma's parole officer.

"We've got information that some Gambino members want to kill you," Parisi told DePalma, "because of Nicky LaSorsa."

DePalma, now seventy-one, a stone-cold mobster, shook his head.

"I don't know anything about that," he told Parisi. "Thanks for the information. Have a nice day."

He practically told Nat not to let the door hit him on the way out.

We would have liked to hear DePalma say, "You're right. I've got a big problem. The Gambinos want to kill me. If you'll put me in the Witness Protection Program, I can give you a lot of information." But I have to admit that my admiration for Greg's stance was enormous—he was a true stand-up mobster. If he had a problem, he wanted to resolve it himself without resorting to "outside assistance" like us. I found his behavior commendable, in terms of the wiseguy code.

Throughout his career, Greg had been arrested twenty or thirty times. He almost always went to trial, he never ratted associates out, and he always did his time. He was a true gangster. He respected the Mob, he lived for the Mob, he always kicked money up to his bosses—in the world of the wiseguy, he was a true samurai. DePalma was so tenacious that it became clear he would come back to power. My handlers and I decided that I would meet DePalma and get my own sense about his future life in the Mafia.

Had I been in his shoes, I would have told everyone in the world, "I'm done. I'm seventy-one years old. I don't want to go back to prison again, I want to just take care of my son. You want to help me out with a few bucks, that'll be great. But my criminal days are behind me." But that wasn't DePalma's way. He wanted back into the life, and it seemed that before long he would have his way.

Anyone could have whacked Greg at any moment: the Gambinos, the Albanians, LaSorsa, or who knows who else might have borne a grudge against him for some other matter long forgotten by everyone else. But it was clear that DePalma was on the verge of becoming a force to be reckoned with yet again in the Gambino family. I *had* to meet him. The only question was when and where.

On March 4, 2003, six days after Greg DePalma was released from jail, we received a tip that he would be dining at the Spaghetti Western. He would be dining with a bunch of wiseguys from various crime families, some of whom I now knew. The meal would take place late in the evening, after the rest of the restaurant's patrons had gone home. We decided that I would attend that dinner.

"I'm wearing a wire, right?" I asked.

Nat shook his head.

"Why not?" I asked. "Why can't I?"

"DePalma's gone on record," Nat explained, "that he doesn't want to meet anybody new. He doesn't want to get pinched again."

"But I always wear a recorder," I insisted.

Nat was just as insistent. "No."

"But I might miss some great evidence!"

"Doesn't matter," Nat told me. "Absolutely not."

So I was wireless. I'll never forget the moment I entered the restaurant for a quick drink. I saw at the far end of the otherwise empty dining room a table of ten mobsters eating and drinking, at the head of which sat Greg DePalma. I recognized him immediately from photos, but I wasn't prepared for his new, bizarre hairstyle, which made him look like Grandpa on *The Munsters*.

I thought about what DePalma was rumored to do to people he suspected stole from him. Spogliari told me he saw DePalma apply a power drill to the head of a guy he believed had stolen from him at the Naked Truth; and on another occasion saw him use a cattle prod on a guy's scrotum (his "beanbag," as they say in the street). Greg also told me he had fired shots into the car of some poor guy who was sitting in his car—for no apparent reason, just to fuck with him. I even heard that last story from the actual guy himself.

As I first glanced at Greg, I also kept in mind that we had credible information that he was going to get whacked any day now. This restaurant was as likely a setting as any. On top of that, we had learned from our informants that he hated the FBI with an abiding passion, because the FBI had convicted him and then confiscated everything he owned, from his home to his cars to his money to his art collection: everything. So if he ever had the idea that I was FBI, he could have had me killed on the spot, regardless of the Mafia "code" against killing law enforcement officials. After all, I'm coming in out of the cold—who the hell am I? Who am I to sit down at a table with him, at a time in his life when he can't afford to take any further chances?

I stood at the entrance, surveying the scene, and I won't lie: There was a certain pucker factor involved. But I also loved it. I loved the thrill of danger that this situation represented. I went in even more confident, because I knew that I could handle any situation. And if these guys patted me down, they'd find nothing. Maybe Nat was right, I thought. All of this increased my confidence as I made my way to the table. I felt an extra rush of certainty as I approached.

Greg's loud, whiskey voice echoed through the empty restaurant. He went on and on about how much he needed to make money, how he was trying to earn again, and how hard things were for him. I knew half the guys at the table because of my nights on the town. I saw a couple of guys I knew, including Jerry Spogliari, the owner of the Naked Truth. I gave the men I recognized a kiss on the cheek, and they kissed me. All that relationship building had paid off. I didn't even acknowledge Greg or glance at him, but I sensed—I knew—that he was looking at me, that he was wondering, "Who the fuck is this guy?"

I fell into loud conversation with the guys I knew, who dragged over a chair from another table and squeezed me into their midst. Out of the corner of my eye, I glanced at DePalma, who was smoking unfiltered Camels as if he were going to the chair in the morning. He truly looked like Grandpa Munster, with his sparse hair combed from the back to the front. He was a diabetic, he had suffered throat cancer, and I knew he had about half a lung left. Despite these and other health problems, he held court. In fact, he looked better, stronger, and more confident than I did!

His conversation turned to his hatred for the FBI.

"The Feds are a bunch of pricks," he rasped. "They took my jewelry, my art, everything. Sons of bitches. Cocksuckers."

I sat opposite from him and talked to the Lucchese and Genovese guys I knew, as well as Spogliari. Others stopped by, dropping off envelopes for DePalma, tribute money. When a connected guy comes out of prison, everybody in his Mafia family is obligated to give him some cash as a way of helping him get back on his feet. DePalma talked incessantly of how much he needed the money: He needed to go to the dentist, he wanted to buy a car, he wanted to get set up again in business. I sat with my guys, careful not to seem overeager to meet DePalma. Such a display could give me away.

DePalma fired up yet another cigarette. One of the guys nearby said, with great emotion, "Greg, why are you lighting up again? That stuff could kill you!"

"Fuck that!" DePalma rasped. "I'll smoke if I want to smoke!"

He then went on a rant about the high cost of cigarettes. Thanks to heavy taxation, a pack of cigarettes cost eight bucks at the time. For DePalma, this was the government's final insult. Not only had they taken away everything from him, but now they were making money on his favorite vice.

DePalma's right-hand man and driver, a weasely looking guy in his early forties named Joe Moray, made his way around the table to talk with me and check me out, on Greg's behalf.

I saw an opening.

"I can get you counterfeit cigarettes," I told Moray.

"Yeah?" he asked, eyeing me suspiciously.

I nodded. "It's not my business, but I can get hold of counterfeit cigarettes for four hundred bucks a master carton. There's fifty cartons in a master carton, so you'd be paying just eight dollars a carton."

Moray blinked rapidly.

"Eight dollars a carton?" he asked suspiciously. "We're paying eight dollars a pack!"

I nodded. "I got some in the car," I said nonchalantly. "I could bring them in."

Moray thought for a moment, glanced at DePalma, who glanced at me. It seemed as if everyone at the table went silent.

"Go ahead," Moray told me quietly.

I stood, and DePalma watched me rise to my full bulk. I headed out of the restaurant, thinking, I hope I haven't pushed the envelope too far. I knew they had to be talking about me as I left the table.

As it happened, I really did have counterfeit cigarettes in my car, because I was working the Royal Charm case in Atlantic City. I grabbed a pack each of Marlboro Lights and Marlboro Reds from my trunk and brought them back into the restaurant. No human being could tell the difference between my Chinese counterfeit cigarettes and the real thing. Maybe someone could tell by the taste, but not by the appearance. My cartons didn't contain the government license stamps, but aside from that, they were absolutely indistinguishable from what you might buy at the 7-Eleven.

I went back into the restaurant and tossed the two packs toward Moray who had moved and was now sitting next to Greg. We still hadn't said a word to each other, and this was the first eye contact the two of us had. He studied me, took one of the packs, opened it, shook out a cigarette, took the filter off, and stuck the rest in his mouth, tasting the tobacco as if he were a connoisseur in Virginia tobacco country. Then he lit it and inhaled.

"They're not bad," he told me, as the entire table waited for his verdict. "Can you get me Camels?"

"I can ask," I said nonchalantly, but inside I was feeling anything but calm. I had put a hook into De-Palma in the most innocuous way. And I rode the relationship that developed as a result of that hook for the next two and a half years.

Eventually, the dinner ended and we all got up. Greg didn't say good-bye to me. After all, why should he?

I made it through the meal without anyone suspecting me of being an FBI agent. It was a pretty good score for a single day. I now had a mission: to get De-Palma Camels.

And in that way, a friendship was born.

CHAPTER ELEVEN

Greg Lights Up

The next day I was hanging around the Naked Truth as usual when a guy I'd seen at dinner the night before came up to me and said, "Moray wants to see you."

Moray and DePalma were inseparable and remained that way until some sort of beef between the two of them caused a rift. Most likely it was over money. To the FBI's knowledge, they never spoke again.

I was excited—the impromptu ruse that I set up with the cigarettes started a conversation. That's what I wanted. I didn't want to appear excited, so I told the guy that I was on my way out to dinner.

"Where is Moray?" I asked.

"He's on his way. He'll be here in half an hour."

"He better be," I said nonchalantly. "Otherwise I'm outta here."

The guy went and made a phone call, and he came back, nervous.

"Moray will be here in five minutes," he said.

"I'll stick around," I said.

Moray arrived promptly and asked if we could talk. We headed to the VIP room.

"The Old Man's interested in the cigarettes," Moray told me.

"That's fine," I said. "I'll do you a solid. I'll help you guys out."

Moray tried to negotiate me down on the price.

"Money's really tight for the Old Man," he told me. "By the way, never say the name Greg DePalma anywhere—on the street, in a phone call, at any time. Instead, I want you to use the code 'the Old Man.' Okay?"

"That's fine," I said. What brain surgeons, I thought. What a dopey and obvious nickname.

We negotiated back and forth. I wanted their business—and I wanted them to know they were getting a great deal. I got my negotiating skills from my training in the dope world.

"I'm not making any money on this deal," I said. "I could let you have them at $390. Do the math—each master carton contains fifty cartons of cigarettes. You can sell them for, what, twenty dollars a carton, when the going retail rate is forty dollars a carton. Twenty times fifty is what, a thousand dollars! You're making good money! You're making $610 a master carton! It's a no-brainer."

I could tell he was a little slow doing the math, but he was definitely interested.

"Can you get more of these?" he asked.

"Sure," I said, "but this is not a business I want to undertake on a regular basis. I'll do it from time to time as opportunity permits. Here, just take the cartons."

I gave him a carton of Marlboro Lights and one of Marlboro Reds. Even though the cigarettes didn't have stamps on them, there was no doubt that they could have been moved easily. He could easily unload them at bars and bodegas. Moray told me he'd get back to me, and he was on his way.

Meanwhile, we received more corroboration from informants that DePalma was successfully ingratiating himself back into the good graces of the Gambino family. He was getting involved in construction jobs. He was getting involved in all types of criminal activity, in this thing over here, in that thing over there. He was everywhere. Wherever we looked, there was DePalma, on the move. On March 18, two things happened. First, word came down from the top of the Gambino family: "Greg is what he was." This was a way of letting the world know that DePalma had regained his stripes, his rank as a capo or high-level captain in the Gambino family. To DePalma's credit, in less than three weeks, he moved from an unwanted, washed-up brokester to a force to be reckoned with.

The second event that took place on that day was word from Moray—DePalma wanted to meet me in two days.

Now my FBI handlers and I had a dilemma. Do we stick with the trio of Louis, Chris, and Funzi? Or do we align ourselves with DePalma? DePalma wanted a piece of the Naked Truth, as he was trying to regain his power in the areas he had controlled before his arrest and conviction in the Scores case. He had been a part owner, along with his son Craig, in the Naked Truth. So he felt entitled to a stake of the strip club, no matter who owned it, no matter how much money had been poured into it in his absence. We had to make a decision: Who got the protection money, Fillipelli and his associates, or DePalma? The Old Man hadn't been shelved, or forced to the sidelines. He had forced himself right back into the middle of the action, and now we needed to decide what we were going to do as a result. We figured that a meeting with DePalma might give us the answer to our dilemma.

The following Thursday, I headed back to the Spaghetti Western in Bronxville for another meeting with DePalma. One of the guys at the Naked Truth tipped me off that Moray and DePalma would be at the restaurant, but when we got there, no one had arrived yet, so I hung around the bar area talking with the owners while I waited.

I went to the restaurant with an idea. Instead of looking to do business with DePalma, I decided that I would have a gift for him, ten master cartons of cigarettes. This would be my welcome-home-from-jail gift. I told my FBI handler, Nat Parisi, that we knew he liked the cigarettes, so let's make a power move. Everyone was giving the Old Man envelopes now that he was out of prison, and I would be giving him the cigarettes. I also spoke to Jerry Spogliari prior to this meeting with Greg. Jerry and I agreed that these cigarettes would be DePalma's welcome-home gift from the club.

The restaurant started filling up with some connected guys from the club, and we decided to get a large table at the back of the restaurant. Before long, Moray and DePalma arrived. I pulled Moray over.

"I want to give the Old Man a welcome-home gift," I explained quietly. "The ten master cartons of cigarettes are worth four thousand dollars to me. I could sell them for ten times that, but I'm not in that business. Instead, I want to give the cigarettes to Greg as a tribute and as a sign of my respect."

Moray studied me. Was I sincere? Who the fuck was I, anyway?

I had heard that DePalma was anxious to buy a car, a Chrysler PT Cruiser, to be specific. This in particular amazed me. DePalma had driven Mercedes and Jaguars all of his life—what the hell did he want with a Chrysler PT Cruiser? But that was the car he had his mind made up about, so that was the end of that.

Joe Moray considered the offer and extended his hand to me in gratitude.

"That would be wonderful," he told me, and then he whispered in Greg's ear.

Greg looked at me. "I appreciate your generosity," he said with a serious expression on his face.

"My pleasure," I said. "I'll arrange the delivery to Moray."

Then Greg suddenly changed and became jovial. He started to talk with the Genovese guys at the table. The meeting went from this tense affair to something like a college reunion. Instead of colleges, of course, these guys had all been away to prison. They chatted about their days in Lewisburg, Fort Dix, Allentown, and other places where they had been incarcerated. They started reminiscing about their friends in prison: "Yeah, I was with Joey Potsandpans in Fort Dix! How's he doing?"

I thought the scene was amazing. Prison was *their* Mob school! I didn't pretend to have a criminal record, as I've mentioned earlier, for the simple reason that it would have been too easy for them to check out my bona fides. I kept my mouth shut and listened in awe as Greg talked about how he was able to get free Broadway tickets and meals for corrupt prison guards while he was in jail in exchange for some contraband.

Greg went into a long soliloquy about what a privilege it was for him to take care of John Gotti while Gotti was a federal prisoner and wasting away from cancer. Every night DePalma made him special Italian meals—whatever Gotti wanted. He managed to get Gotti and himself into the prison hospital areas, where there was better food, microwave ovens, and cooking tools. He fed and took care of Gotti, even bathed him. If Gotti wanted angel hair pasta, DePalma got it. If he wanted chicken capriella, DePalma made it for him. Nursing Gotti meant the world to him, because Gotti was his boss and in his eyes Gotti was a stand-up mobster. It was fascinating to me.

Another successful dinner drew to a close, and I could tell that DePalma was feeling warm and fuzzy toward me. After all, I was a total stranger whose criminal bona fides were unproven. But now I spoke the language that he loved best: money. Money was everything to him, and the fact that I gave him money made me, in his eyes, the real deal, a knockaround guy who knew the significance of kicking up to his boss.

The evening was a smashing success.

A few days later Joe Moray reported back that his guy was having a hard time unloading the cigarettes because of the supposed harshness of the taste. What do I know about how cigarettes taste? So we dropped the cigarettes as a tribute and instead, at my third meeting with DePalma, also at Spaghetti Western, I handed him an envelope thick with fifty-dollar bills.

"We sold the cigarettes for you," I told him, "and I wasn't able to get much, but there's three large in here [in Mobspeak, $3,000]."

DePalma looked at me gratefully. He saw with his own eyes that I was involved in criminal activity. I demonstrated from the start that I wasn't a wannabe, a groupie, or a beanshooter.

"You did time for me," I respectfully told Greg. "You were in jail thirty years of your life. I did a lot of bad things, but I was never pinched. So you did my time! That means I'm indebted to you. Some other guy would have folded like a deck of cards."

DePalma's eyes practically welled with tears as I gave him this highest of Mob encomiums.

My seduction of Greg DePalma had begun.

CHAPTER TWELVE

The Seduction of Greg DePalma

A man wants to get to know a woman. He treats her nicely. He buys her flowers. He happens to turn up "accidentally on purpose" where he knows she'll be. I was doing the same thing to Greg DePalma. I wanted him to like me.

I knew that he didn't want anyone new in his life. He was keeping a low profile—he was on parole and could easily have been picked up had he been seen consorting with known wiseguys. Meeting new people was dangerous for someone in DePalma's position. He knew that the Feds were targeting him, and he had every reason to believe—accurately, as it turned out—that the FBI would still be following him, even as he entered his eighth decade of life. So my job was to become a person of interest to him without setting off alarm bells.

I had to tread a fine line, not coming on too strong as a big-shot knockaround guy, which would raise his suspicions. He might wonder, "Why haven't I ever seen or heard of this guy Jack Falcone before?" The other extreme was to present myself as someone who had nothing at all to offer him. If I didn't have a way of making him money, or if I didn't look the part of a successful mobster, he'd look at me and say, "Who's this brokester? He's a broken-down valise, a garbage can, a beanshooter, he's no good! He's got nothing to offer me!"

The Mob is interested in someone only if he has something lucrative to offer. The key question that DePalma would ask himself: Am I in a position to make money with this guy? That's because once they get the claws in, they'll suck you dry. They'll go into business with you and kill the business, take everything for themselves and leave nothing for you. Wiseguys only think of themselves and the families to which they belong. Again, it's not all about shooting people. It's about making money. Shootings happen only when people aren't paying or doing the right thing for the family.

I found it challenging to adapt to an entirely different routine. Actually, it was stressful for me to play the role of a somewhat obsequious bad guy. Typically, I was always the controller, the bigwig, the head guy. If I was involved in a dope deal, I was either a big-time transporter who was going to move a lot of weight, or I was the dealer and I was going to buy or sell a lot of kilos. Here I had to be much quieter in the beginning. I wasn't going to the table with power. There was a pecking order, and I couldn't go in cocky. That would be dangerous. So I had to be humble.

The offer of the counterfeit cigarettes and the three thousand dollars of welcome-home money enabled me to become part of the crew. We all chipped in to buy him a car. The gift definitely increased his gratitude toward me.

This courtship, however, had to be two-way. I wanted to make myself a nice, attractive package—I looked the part, I talked the part, and I was accepted by the other wiseguys and associates. But it had to progress to the point where I was no longer the hunter but the hunted. He had to want to come after me; that was the way this seduction would go down. If he had seen me as a mark, he would have taken advantage of me. I didn't want that. Instead, I wanted him to wonder who I was and how he could get closer to me.

Thanks to our surveillance, we knew where he was practically all day long and we knew with whom he was meeting. And from the guys at the club, I started to hear that DePalma was checking into me. Other guys were asking around on Greg's behalf—"Who is this guy from Florida? What's he do?" That pleased me. I saw that he was assessing how much he could get out of me—that he was asking the critical wiseguy questions: "Who is this new guy, and how can I suck things out of him?"

A typical day during this courtship phase would

begin with a call to the office. I'd ask my handler, Nat, "Where is DePalma now?"

He would tell me that he's at this restaurant or another, or he's gone to Manhattan for a meeting, or whatever. So I would get dressed and, looking the part of the Miami knockaround guy that I wanted him to believe me to be, I would accidentally on purpose turn up at whatever restaurant he was frequenting that day. I wouldn't do it every day, of course, but I did it just often enough so that he would continue to develop an interest in me. I wanted to be on his mind constantly.

If it wasn't a day for running into DePalma, I'd just call the guys, the other connected individuals I had come to know through the club. I'd ask them where they were going, what restaurant, what time, and I would show up.

I would arrive at the restaurant and have a meal. Again, it's insulting to go to a restaurant and not have something. I would go in and they'd say, "Order a little something. Order some soup. Have some soup! The pasta e fagioli here is fucking unbelievable! Don't embarrass me here, order something!"

For me, this was perfect, because you don't have to call me twice to show up for a meal. And with these guys, it would be breakfast, lunch, dinner, to the club, and then at 2 A.M. somebody would say, "Let's go to that place on City Island, I'm starving—let's get something to eat!" So you'd be having a big dinner at 2 A.M., and then the next day, you'd start the whole thing all over again.

While I was working on hooking Greg, we learned from informants that he was trying to get off a hook of his own. Greg, we heard, was spending a lot of time meeting with Anthony "the Genius" Megale, the underboss of the Gambino family, trying to resolve the issue of the hit he had taken out on LaSorsa.

Trouble first arose between LaSorsa and DePalma when Greg was in prison because of the Scores case. Greg had sponsored Nicky for membership in the Gambino family. But now that Greg was behind bars, Nicky demanded that a businessman he had previously shaken down on DePalma's behalf pay $2,500 to him and him alone.

Greg DePalma's worst enemy . . . was Greg De-Palma. Over a prison telephone, he issued threats that were, of course, recorded and passed along to law enforcement officials. When he heard that another mobster was taking over his rackets, apparently that was the last straw. He said, "I hope it ain't Nicky. I'm gonna stop him." He described in particularly grue-some details what he would do to LaSorsa's genitalia, once he got hold of him. DePalma then concocted a truly bizarre plot to kill LaSorsa, a hit he later claimed was authorized by John Gotti, although that seems more like fabrication and CYA (cover your ass) than an actual fact.

DePalma, who was not in the best of shape, turned to another ailing, wheelchair-bound mobster behind bars and ordered the hit on Nicky. The problem is that a Mafia rule states firmly that a made guy can order a hit against another only with the approval of the bosses, unless he's brazen enough to get a "sneak tip"—an unsanctioned murder. This led to Nicky placing a hit on DePalma in retaliation. LaSorsa, an automobile dealer as well as a mobster, had little to fear from DePalma's comical plot. The Old Man, however, had everything to fear from the enraged LaSorsa. Incidentally, the guy in the wheelchair pled guilty to his involvement in the planned hit. DePalma stood trial for it, like the stand-up mob guy he was, and somehow beat the charges. He was more surprised than anyone when the not guilty verdict came in!

Now, with DePalma back on the street having regained his stripes as a capo, it was sit-down after sit-down among the Gambinos' higher echelons, trying to resolve the unsanctioned hit. Joe Moray left Greg's "employ," so I began to take Greg to meetings, and I constantly heard from Nat reports from our informants of other meetings Greg was attending. Topic one in those meetings was always the resolution of the hit against LaSorsa, who by then was an acting capo in the Gambino family in his own right.

While seeking to resolve the LaSorsa matter, Greg went about regaining his own power and also helping the Gambino family recover from the excesses of John Gotti's reign. Greg was shrewd—as much as he loved John Gotti, he recognized that Gotti's taste for the limelight had cost the family dearly, in terms of income and the privacy organized crime requires in order to do its dirty work. So Greg organized the soldiers under him into separate cells, almost like little individual terrorist units. One group never knew what the other group was doing, or even who was in the other group. Only Greg knew everything, and he kept it all in his head. That way he maintained his value to the leadership—you could call it anti-getting-whacked insurance. Greg DePalma had done the unimaginable in the Mafia. He had unshelved himself. He had the power. And although I didn't know it at the time, his plans for his Mafia future . . . included me.

CHAPTER THiRTEEN

On the Books

By now people were saying "Big Jack, the new guy on the block—he's a good guy. He's in Greg DePalma's crew." Even though Greg hadn't put me on record—hadn't made our relationship official—people in the criminal world were beginning to associate the two of us. Actually, I knew I had him. Once I gave him the money, supposedly from the cigarettes, my power move had changed the focus. I had moved from being the hunter to the hunted. I knew it and could taste it. It was just a matter of time. I was an object of curiosity to him.

In late April 2003 we were back at the Spaghetti Western for lunch. Out of the blue, Greg asked, "Hey, Jackie boy, you want health insurance? Are you covered, or what?"

This is actually a big thing in the Mob. Since very few of the guys actually do any legitimate work, getting high-quality, inexpensive medical coverage for themselves and their families is important. Greg told me there was a union guy I could go see who would get me coverage.

"I'm interested," I allowed. "You have some way I can get it?"

"Don't worry about it," he told me. "I'll set it up for you soon."

I spent the next few weeks continuing to ingratiate myself with the wiseguys, both at the Naked Truth and at restaurants throughout the New York area, wherever the action was that day. I also traveled to Atlantic City, Miami, and other cities in pursuit of the cases I described in other chapters as well as some dope deals and other smaller matters.

I started telling some people whom Greg trusted that I had some stolen watches that I needed to fence for a good price. Sure enough he bit, and on May 17, I got a call. During this call, we didn't talk openly on the phone about jewelry. I just told Greg that I had come back from Miami with more than a tan.

We met two days later at a restaurant in Westchester County called La Villeta. I showed Greg the watches and a diamond ring. If he was interested, maybe he could unload them and make some money. He was definitely interested. In all, I showed Greg seven pieces of jewelry—six watches and one diamond ring, all of which I represented as stolen goods coming from Florida. The watches were Rolex Presidents, Corums, Piagets, all solid gold, beautiful pieces. In fact,

May 1980, at the FBI Academy in Quantico.

After the sixteen-week training course, I graduate from the Academy.

Greg DePalma and Anthony "The Genius" Megale, underboss of the Gambinos.

Greg and his acting capo, Robert Vaccaro.

Megale and DePalma coming out of Pasta Per Voi restaurant.

Vaccaro and DePalma, outside the nursing home; I was behind the tree.
Surveillance was asked not to photograph me because I was working
other cases.

But sometimes I would get in the shot. I am on the right, with Greg DePalma and Robert Vaccaro.

Yet another meet in a parking lot, me, Vaccaro, and DePalma.

A PT Cruiser and me, not a good fit.

Vaccaro with Alphonse "Funzi" Sisca, a captain in the Gambino crime family.

Vaccaro, on a pay phone outside Patsy's restaurant, distrusted
cell phones.

Tommy "Sneakers" Cacciopoli and Vaccaro.

Vaccaro, DePalma, and Nicky LaSorsa.

Sandro Rudivic, aka Alex Rudaj, outside Jimbo's Bar.

Louis Filippelli, acting capo
for the Gambinos.

Pasquale "Scop" DeLuca, acting
street boss of the Genovese.

Arnold Squitieri, Gambino boss.

Nicky LaSorsa, acting capo
for the Gambinos.

Tommy Cacciopoli, a Gambino capo.

Leonardo Colotti, an acting capo.

they were virtually new property seized by the FBI in other investigations. Greg asked me what I wanted for the pieces and I said I wanted a quarter, or twenty-five thousand dollars, for the works. Naturally, Greg had to negotiate me down.

"Marron!" Greg exclaimed, looking at the jewelry. "That's a lot of money! These are old pieces!"

"What, are you kidding?" I asked disdainfully. I had to show that I knew what I was talking about, or he would have seen me as a mark, someone he could roll over.

"These are solid gold!" I protested. "Beautiful, almost new!"

"I don't think so," Greg said dismissively.

"Look," I told him. "I've got a possible buyer for the goods, but I wanted to see if you could sell it at a higher price and make some *fazools* [money] along the way. If you're interested, ask around and see what price you can get."

I wanted to tease him a little bit, to see if he would take the bait.

The next day he called me.

"Jackie boy," he began excitedly. "I set up a meeting with that union guy for health insurance."

"No kidding?" I replied, delighted. He really was taking the bait.

"And in the meantime I want to see those 'things' again."

"Whatever you need, Greg," I told him.

He had me meet him at a tailor shop in Westchester.

This particular tailor might have been great back in the day, because his office was decorated with photographs of Joe DiMaggio and other celebrities from past generations wearing his suits. But visiting his store was like going back in time. The suits he made featured bright colors and outdated styles. They weren't for me. He also had a little section with new styles and decent suits. In the past, Greg had bought twenty suits from him, and Greg wanted me to have one.

I didn't want a suit, for several reasons. First, I was wearing a wire, so I didn't want to be fitted. In addition, I didn't want to have Greg get the tailor to make a suit for me, because I knew that Greg would stiff him, and I didn't want that.

Greg was insistent. "Come on, get fitted," he told me. "It's my treat."

"Don't take it personal," I told him, "but I've got enough suits, and I don't like his style. Maybe he was a great suit maker a few years ago, but time hurt him a little bit. I've got a guy who makes suits for me so, you know what, thanks anyway, Greg."

In reality, I wanted Greg to know that I didn't want anything from him and that I didn't want to be beholden to him in any way. If he had pushed, of course, I would have gone along. But the reality is that as Jack Falcone, knockaround guy from Miami, I could certainly afford my own suits. He told me to meet him the next day to get my health insurance.

Greg and I met with the president of a Mob-controlled labor union, an individual we'll call Teddy.

Teddy told me to put my name, Social Security number, and date of birth down on a form, and I would get medical and dental coverage, eye care, prescription drug insurance, and even a union pension. Ironically, the meeting took place in a restaurant/catering hall, right next to the union shop, where I had worked briefly as a valet while in college. My best friend was married there. And now here I was, a wiseguy outfitted with health insurance from a corrupt union official.

I put down Jack Falcone as my name and I also put down my fake Social Security number, along with my date of birth and all of my alias information. I gave him a check, and bingo—I was insured! Who says the Mafia doesn't have its privileges? At one point, I turned to Greg and asked him if the whole thing was legal.

"Don't worry about it, Jackie boy!" He laughed. "Of course this is legal! It's pretty good medical coverage too! You'll be very happy!"

I think the real reason Greg had me insured was not because he cared about whether I could afford new eyeglasses or a physical. I think he wanted to have a legitimate excuse for getting my Social Security number, my date of birth, and other personal information, so that he could continue checking into my identity. It was a pretty shrewd move on Greg's part. I'm almost certain that he had me checked out. Since we spent enough time at the Bureau making sure that I had all the right elements in my background, I knew I would pass any check with flying colors.

Two days later, I "ran into" Greg at the Raceway Diner in Yonkers. From his perspective, it was a fluke thing, just me being in the right place at the right time. I found him in a state of frustration.

"What's wrong?" I asked, sitting down and grabbing the menu.

"Moray isn't around," Greg groused. "I need to go to the city."

He paused for a moment and then asked, "Would you mind driving me down there?"

"No problem, Greg," I told him. "I'll be happy to."

That's exactly why I happened to show up at the diner. Greg directed me to an office building on Madison Avenue in the 30s. He went in, and I just sat in the car like some loser. I was always the big boss when I did undercover work. Being treated like a limo driver took a lot of getting used to for me. Later, at the Bureau, we ran the address of the meeting, checked out the tenants of that building, and determined that he had met with a Mob-related lawyer.

An hour later Greg emerged from the building. We headed out of the city and I didn't say a word. Again, it would not have been prudent—or in character—for a low-level guy to ask a capo what happened at a meeting. But for a guy as talkative as Greg, silence was a burden he couldn't handle. On the way back he opened up a little bit.

"They brought me down there to try to resolve the thing with Nicky," he told me. "And there's gonna be some new rules in the family. Gambino family business."

"Oh, yeah?" I said, keeping my eyes on the road.

I didn't ask any more questions, because it wouldn't have been smart for me. I was very cautious about asking any questions; real wiseguys didn't ask questions. I didn't want to raise any suspicions with him—he'd be asking me, and rightly so, "Why do you care who the fuck I see?"

Our next meeting was on June 3. We went out to dinner, and by now his level of trust in me was much higher. He must have had my Social Security number run, and he must have seen good results. He said right in front of me that he talked, yet again, with "the number two and the number three"—the underboss and the consigliere of the family (Anthony Megale and Joseph "JoJo" Corozzo)—to resolve the LaSorsa situation.

"It's out of control," he said, and he rambled on about what a cocksucker LaSorsa was.

I ate and listened, and at the same time I thought, He's still the target of a hit from Nicky LaSorsa—that's why all the bosses are trying to resolve this. Nicky could get the clearance to take out DePalma any day, and if he did, he'd be taking me out too. There's a famous photograph of Carmine Galante, a Mafia boss, who was gunned down in the courtyard of an Italian restaurant with his teeth still clamped firmly around his cigar. The people who were dining with him fared no better. I didn't want to be a trivia question in the photo of the crime scene where DePalma got taken out, but that's the risk I was willing to run. The good news from my perspective was that the more often we saw him meeting with the bosses, the more likely it was that he was going to be in the clear.

By now Greg and I were getting closer and closer. I was talking with Nat Parisi, my handler and case agent back at the FBI, five to ten times a day. We agreed that I had to be an "earner"—I had to be doing something that increased my credibility as a knockaround guy, and at the same time I had to afford Greg an opportunity to make money. So we decided that I'd bring Greg more and more forfeited and seized jewelry, telling him I got the stuff from a score. We had appraisals done, so I knew exactly what kind of diamonds we had and what everything was worth. Whenever I brought new pieces, Greg would take out his jeweler's loupe—the guy carried a jeweler's loupe with him for just these kinds of situations—and would tell me how he used to run a jewelry business on Canal Street.

"You don't know how much swag I moved out of there," he bragged.

Whatever the quality of the diamond I showed him, he always said it was imperfect, horrible, messed up—he was always trying to hustle me. Or I would bring him a Rolex President and tell him all I wanted for it was forty-five hundred dollars, knowing that he could sell it to someone else for six thousand. That's the nature of the mobster, making money every day. It didn't matter to Greg or anyone else whether they were making money selling jewelry, bread, Cheez Doodles, DVDs, beating up a guy, loan sharking—they'll do it all, if there's money in it.

"Where do you get this stuff?" Greg asked, putting down his loupe and eyeing me.

"I got guys who rip off drug dealers and businessmen in Miami," I told him. "I have a fence down there, but some of the stuff is so hot that my guy doesn't want to take it. But if you want, Greg, you could take it and unload it for me here in New York."

Greg nodded—the explanation satisfied him. He asked no further questions.

The jewelry was a smash hit with Greg. He was as relentless as could be in his demands for jewelry and watches to sell. We were now making money together, I had health insurance, and our personal friendship was deepening.

A few days later we met again at the Spaghetti Western, and DePalma said the most ominous words that one wiseguy can say to another: "Listen to me, we're going to take a ride."

Take a ride? I got a little concerned! What the hell does that mean? Had something gone wrong? Had they figured out who I was or what I really did for a living? Or were they going to test me? I had no idea. But what choice did I have? I got in the car.

They wanted me in the front seat, but I'm too big to fit in the front seat of a PT Cruiser. So Joe Moray drove, Greg sat in the passenger seat, and I squeezed in the back. I wasn't happy about this at all, because I was not in control. Wherever we were going, we could run into someone I might have arrested or even someone with whom I went to high school. I could easily be compromised. On top of that, maybe they were just taking me off to some desolate place to do me in. There's no way of knowing. I didn't have a gun, but I did have a recorder on me. If anything, that would have made it worse if they were to find it. Would they kill me because they thought I was a rat instead of an undercover agent? You could say the pucker factor was in full force.

We left Bronxville and drove, making small talk all the way. The destination turned out to be some jeweler in Westchester. DePalma got out of the car, went inside, and came back with a big, gaudy diamond-encrusted pinkie ring.

It was for me.

"You never belonged with any wiseguys, did you?" DePalma asked.

"No, only with Cuban guys," I said.

I had no idea where he was going.

"Well, I put you on record with me and my family," he said.

I was elated, but I tried hard not to show it. This meant that whatever test he had held for me, I had passed. Greg was now claiming me for his own. I was working with him, and no other wiseguy could make a claim on my time, my income, or my loyalties. I was Greg's man.

"Okay," I said cautiously, not wanting to betray the excitement and emotion I felt.

"You know what that means, right?" he asked.

"Yeah," I replied, in a manner that implied that I didn't know but was too proud to admit as much. I wanted him to say it, and I wanted to capture the words on tape, which we did.

Greg spelled it out for me. "Nobody can bother you, nobody can come near you. No wiseguys, nothing. I don't care if they're the boss, the underboss of another crew. I didn't even know your last name until last week! Falcone, right?"

"I appreciate that!" I said, deeply moved by the trust he had placed in me.

"Of course!" Greg said, smiling. "You gotta be kidding me! You are now under our umbrella." He showed me the ring.

"This is a token of my friendship. I've put you on the books with me. No other wiseguy can claim you. Nobody can fuck with you." It was on the record—now I was a connected guy. I was on record with the Gambino family. I was an official associate of La Cosa Nostra.

INTERLUDE TWO

Atlantic City—Friends in High Places

While working Royal Charm out of the Atlantic City field office of the FBI, I ran into Jim Eckel and Ed Corrigan, two agents I have known for many years. FBI offices are divided up into squads based on the violations that are most prevalent in a particular area. I was working out of the organized crime squad, and they were working out of the public corruption squad.

"What are you doing here?" Jim asked, surprised to see me.

"Working on Royal Charm," I replied.

"I just had an idea!" he exclaimed, excited. "Got a minute? Let's go into the conference room!"

"What's your schedule like, big guy?" they asked.

"Oh, I've got a full plate," I said, seeing where this was going.

"We know," Jim said, "but maybe you've got a few minutes to hear a story."

"I've always got time to hear a good story," and they certainly had one for me.

"We've got a guy in construction, a great cooperating witness," Jim began, "a very, very good source. A black male. He knows this other contractor who's a hustler here in Atlantic City—he's out there doing this and that and the other thing. We know this other guy pays off city council members and politicians. We thought about using a black undercover agent to get to know this guy. But we started thinking about you instead. Suppose you were some kind of Miami/New York–based Cuban drug dealer looking for ways to legitimize your money?"

"How would this work?" I asked, intrigued.

"You'll befriend him and after some time passes you'll create a business with him, and maybe he'll take you into his confidence," Jim said. "Together, you'll pay off politicians to procure contracts in Atlantic City. He just got his minority contractor's license so we know he's going to be rocking and rolling."

The states and the federal government have programs that permit members of minority groups to receive special preferences in the awarding of government contracts. In order to receive such preferences, the company must receive government certification that it is indeed minority-owned. Our guy had just gotten that certification.

I always have a hard time saying no.

"Listen," I said. "For you, Jim, I'll do it. I'll have to sneak it in, though. I've got an undercover meeting on Royal Charm tonight."

"How about tomorrow?" they asked.

"Okay," I said, and suddenly I had a new case with which to contend, on top of all my other cases.

The following morning, I met the cooperating witness, a real nice guy, who instantly took a liking to me. We agreed to meet the next morning to have breakfast, so he could introduce me to the bad guy, whom we'll call Speed. I would be introduced as Manny, a retired Cuban drug dealer with a lot of cash to launder. In the scenario we concocted, I was not connected with the Mob, but instead moved a lot of dope in New York and Florida. Now that I had retired from the dope trade, I was looking to make some investments and possibly create a business in Atlantic City that would legitimize me.

The next morning the three of us met at Denny's. Speed was a tall, muscular black man—about as tall as I am. I could tell by his actions that he was a hustler, a hard-charger. At the same time, he was smart and cautious. He was personable and well liked in the African-American community in Atlantic City. Later on, when we drove around together, people would wave to him as if he were a local celebrity, calling out, "Hey, Speed, what's up!'"

We checked each other out at this breakfast. I didn't put my résumé out there.

"I'm being vouched for by this guy here," I said, pointing to our source, "who's also vouching for you."

"What are you looking to do?" Speed asked.

"To be honest, I'm looking to eventually settle down. Do some legitimate investing. My real problem is that I need some money to be cleaned."

"How do you want it to happen?" Speed wanted to know.

"I need cash," I explained, "sent through banks to a special account that I created in Los Angeles and New York without raising any suspicion. I also need cash to be turned into certified checks."

Speed lit up. "Well, I can do that!"

We knew that was one of the things he did. So we started negotiating.

"What kind of fee?" I asked.

"Five points," he said, meaning that for every hundred dollars of money he laundered, he kept five dollars. That was fair, so I said, "Okay, I've got no problem with that."

"How much do you want to do?" he asked.

Again, it's never wise to jump too quickly with these guys.

"I don't know you, you don't know me," I said. "Let's start slow. I've got another guy who cleans my money now, but I always like to have several. I don't want to have one guy knowing my whole business, and I like to have an alternate source. I've also got to use a particular launderer when I'm dealing with my Colombian friends. But if I find another guy for them that they can trust, then they'll be happy, then I'll look good. I'll come out ahead financially, 'cause I'm paying eight points to the Colombians' guy, and you charge me five."

Speed liked everything I was saying. I explained to him that I had recently made some money from a good score, selling several keys of cocaine. Now I needed to send payment to my Colombian suppliers. Jim had established a bank account so that we could have Speed ship money into it. We started with fifty thousand dollars.

"I'll give you the money," I told Speed, and then I pointed to our source. "This guy's vouching for you. I've been around the block a few times. I don't want anything bad to happen to my money. Do we understand one another?"

"Listen, man," Speed assured me, "I'm established here. I'm established in the business community."

"How long is this going to take you?"

"A week at the most," he said. "I'm gonna do it piecemeal."

This was great, as far as I was concerned. The violation is laundering money derived from illegal proceeds. So now we'd have him.

The next morning I gave him a suitcase full of cash outside the parking lot of Denny's. I told him that if he didn't arrive on time, I wouldn't wait—I'd be gone and I wouldn't be coming back. I was exerting my authority, my control—my dominance, if you will—from the start.

Everything worked out great. The money I gave him came back into the account, minus his 5 percent. Also, some of the money came in the form of a check from a source we didn't recognize. Naturally, we wanted to know who it was. I explained to Speed at another meeting that I wasn't too comfortable with a third party involved with our business and I wanted to meet this guy. It turned out to be a wannabe wiseguy associated with an organized crime family in Philadelphia, not a made guy. We met him, and shortly thereafter, I gave Speed a hundred thousand dollars to launder.

The purpose of this investigation was not to take down Speed for money laundering. The real mission was to get to the allegedly corrupt city officials who, we heard, were taking bribes from Speed. Speed became very high maintenance—he began calling me practically around the clock wanting to do more money laundering. I'd be in the car with Greg and the phone would ring, and it would be Speed, looking to launder more cash for me. I'd hang up on him.

"Who's that?" Greg would ask.

"Some asshole," I'd reply. "I keep telling him never to call me."

That's what I'd tell Greg when the caller was another agent looking for me, by the way!

We didn't need Speed to launder more cash for us—we already had him for money-laundering violations. The trick was to start reaching out to the corrupt officials. So Speed and I were at cross purposes: I was trying to set up a construction business with him so that we could put in bids for city projects and bribe city councilmen or who knows who. He was fixated on making money by laundering it for me.

And then he came up with a new idea—he would start a transportation business. He would transport drugs in specially concealed compartments of cars and trucks (*caletas* and *clavos*, as we used to call them in the Badlands).

Speed knew that although I wanted to retire from the drug trade, I still had a hand in selling drugs, and he wanted in on transportation. He also thought that if I could make money by selling drugs, he could create a niche for himself in transporting my drugs and then laundering my proceeds. He was looking to double-bang me, in the language of the street, or collect on both ends of the same deal. I tried to get it into his head that selling drugs was the worst thing in the world. I was almost retired, I told him, and I didn't want to get back in the business.

I couldn't tell him the real reason—that, as I learned in the Badlands, drugs can't walk. If he started transporting drugs, he would want a few kilos for himself as his fee. We could have staged fake packages of drugs for him to transport, paying him in cash instead of kilos. But that would have taken him out of our true mission—to reach the corrupt politicians. If he started selling drugs, we would have to scoop him up for that, and our investigation of the elected officials of Atlantic City would end. He was pestering me for money laundering, I was getting nowhere trying to convince him to start a construction business with me, and now he had this brilliant idea to transport drugs.

Speed was nothing if not stubborn. One day he came to me and delivered the news that I truly didn't want to hear: He was going down to Florida to do a test run transporting dope. He was going to bring a small amount, just a few keys, in a specially equipped truck from Florida back to Atlantic City. I thought, What, does he want me to be happy for him? He was about to blow our whole investigation. But there was nothing I could do.

"Speed, you don't want to do this," I told him as earnestly as I could. "Trust me. Don't get involved."

Here I was, a drug dealer, trying to talk a guy out of going into the drug business, because once you mix drugs into the equation, your case turns to shit. I'll say it again, drugs can never walk!

He went to Florida, with his newly modified truck, and stuck some dope into it. And it looked like all the hard work that the FBI put into this case was about to go up in smoke—or blow, in this instance.

Well, he was as stubborn as ever, and called me every couple of hours to tell me where he was.

"I'm in North Carolina—it's going great!"

Now the agents on the case held a powwow. "If this freakin' powder comes in," we concluded, "we gotta take him down." So we rallied to do this.

A few hours later, the phone rang again.

"I'm in Virginia!"

He was getting closer and closer, and our case was ·

on the verge of vanishing . . . when, instead, Speed vanished.

We were all staring at each other in the office, thinking, "Where the fuck is Speed?"

I had told him to call me when he got to New Jersey so that I would know everything was okay. Finally, we couldn't stand it any more, and we sent agents to his house. And to our surprise, we discovered that Speed had been arrested . . . by the New Jersey State Police and the DEA! They had been on him from the start.

I thought, This stupid fuck! This should have been our arrest and seizure, because then we could have kept the Atlantic City politicians case alive. We started scrambling, like, Now what are we gonna do?

So Agent Jim Eckel approached the New Jersey State Police and the DEA. "Hey, guys," he said, "we've been working this case. Can you defer the prosecution—can we work something out here? We're trying to get to the politicians in Atlantic City, and he can do this for us."

We also learned how the DEA discovered that Speed was going to run drugs. It had a snitch who knew about the modified compartments in Speed's truck and that Speed was going to bring a large amount of dope, about five hundred keys, for a guy named Manny. Of course, Speed was on his test run with five keys when he was arrested—he didn't have anything near five hundred kilos! DEA deferred to us because they were disappointed with the five-key seizure. Since the seizure was so small, their attitude was, if the FBI wants to prosecute Speed, have a good time.

So Jim went to the jail where Speed was held and pitched him on the idea of cooperating. He quickly agreed.

"I'm ashamed of myself," he told Jim. "I shouldn't have done it. I'll cooperate, but the only thing I ask is, you gotta protect me from Manny! He's a big drug lord—he's Cuban—he's gonna kill me when he finds out what happened! I'll cooperate, I'll give you what you guys want. But please . . . protect me from Manny!"

At this point, Jim laughed. "You know who Manny works for?" he asked.

"A Colombian cartel?"

Jim shook his head. "Team America!" he told him. "He's an FBI undercover agent!" Speed exclaimed, "Oh, shit! No fucking way!"

He had to be relieved. He wasn't afraid of jail time, the state police, the DEA, or the FBI. He was afraid of me! So now we had Speed right where we wanted him. If he wanted to help himself, he had to help us. It's poetic justice. As much as he hounded me to have him launder more money, I should have gotten an Oscar for all my acting. I came up with story after story—I'm going to Florida, my cat died, my kid's sick, my Aunt Maria needs a new hip—whatever. But now that he crossed over to Team America, we changed the whole scenario.

That's why it's so important for me that I never come across as a blowhard tough guy when I'm an undercover. Obviously you've got to be feared and respected. What I aim for is to be respected . . . and liked. When they like me, the fear just comes along naturally. You start low key and kick it up when necessary. You can't start tough and then become mild. I always used to tell the dopers, "Never mistake my kindness as a sign of weakness!"

Now we came up with a new scenario. Speed was assigned to Jim Eckel as his new cooperating witness. Speed was going to introduce me to the politicians of Atlantic City as Manny, a big dope dealer with a lot of money to invest. I recommended that we introduce another agent, Michael Grimm, aka Mikey Suits, who would come along as my money launderer and close associate. Mikey would be a Wall Street investor who consorted with the Mob and with bad guys like me. Speed promptly started setting up meetings with city council members in the casinos of Atlantic City.

First, we went out socially with the City Council President. We put on a spectacular show. We went to the Old Homestead restaurant at the Borgata Hotel, had a good time, relaxed, and just hung out and shot the breeze about finance, politics, girls, sports, whatever. At the next meeting, Mikey Suits pulled the city officials aside. "I have a lot of selective clients," he told them, "including big Manny over here."

I just nodded. Mike's my front guy—he does all the talking for me.

"We want to invest in Bader Field," Mikey told them, and they started nodding in understanding.

Bader Field is an old airstrip in Atlantic City, a very hot property about to be redeveloped.

"My problem is that Manny here doesn't know anybody in this town," Mikey explained. "He wants to get involved. He wants to have friends in city hall who can make sure that his bids are always viewed with a high level of regard. This is what we want."

Everybody understood what Mikey was talking about. I disappeared for a little bit, and Mikey Suits made payments to Craig Callaway, a member of the Atlantic City council and an official in Camden, New Jersey, and Ramón Rosario, a Camden councilman. Throughout the case, I always excused myself while Mikey Suits made the payments, and then we all would go to dinner together. I became close with Ramón— he's Dominican, I was playing a Cuban, so it was all good.

Before long, we explained to Craig what was going on, that this was an FBI sting, and he agreed to cooperate and wear a wire in meetings with other people. This way Mikey Suits and I went further into the City Council, and we picked up a few more officials who were breaking the laws they were elected to uphold.

Callaway proved to be a very difficult and hard-to-manage cooperator. At one point unbeknownst to us, he engineered the creation of a sex tape ensnaring a fellow city councilman. He went to the trouble of renting a motel room, setting up a hidden video camera, and hiring a young woman to entice the other councilman to the motel, where she had oral sex with him, in full view of the hidden camera. According to the other councilman's attorney, the purpose of the tape and threats to make it public was to force him to resign from the city council.

This beautiful case was all teed up and ready to go. Except for one sudden shock: pressure from the U.S. Attorney's Office to shut things down. My understanding was that they told the Bureau, "It's enough. You've reached the end of your rope."

We were telling them "No! Instead of taking the case down, we could flip some others—and get more guys."

One thing about Jim Eckel—he was such an outstanding agent, he could flip suspects into cooperating like a short order cook can flip pancakes. But for whatever reason, the U.S. Attorney's Office had had enough. Maybe they wanted to get some headlines by getting convictions for the people we had already implicated. Or maybe it was just politics and bureaucracy as usual. Who knows? In any event, the case was done.

The result of the case: All of those indicted took guilty pleas, and they went to prison. The thing that sticks out in my mind is not just the fact that they were corrupt but that they were so brazen about it. We weren't having furtive meetings outside warehouses in the dead of night. The corrupt politicians with whom Mikey Suits and I were involved met us in plain sight at places like the Borgata Hotel, where anyone and everyone could see the city's top politicians breaking bread with people who could be nothing other than gangsters.

Look, we weren't just going after a few bad politicians. We were trying to shake up the criminal culture that existed in Atlantic City. A few bad guys went to prison during that time, and we changed the political landscape in Atlantic City.

CHAPTER FOURTEEN

"If It Was Raining Tits, We'd Get Hit over the Head with a Cock"

With the gift of the pinkie ring and the information that I was now on record with the Old Man, I was suddenly a connected guy in the Mafia. Some people live to experience something like that. It's like the beginning of the movie *GoodFellas*. Henry Hill was a kid growing up in Brooklyn, and he saw all the wiseguys dressed beautifully, driving fantastic cars, having tons of money, and never having to do anything that even resembled work. When he was an adolescent, Henry's wildest dream was to be in with those guys, and that's what happened for him. Hill isn't the only one. Countless people who grow up in that world dream of the moment when one day they will be put on record, when one day they will be part of the Mob.

It's really like hitting the lottery. If you mess up or steal something that belongs to some other wiseguy, no one is supposed to whack you or even beat you up. You can say, "I'm with Greg DePalma." This means that DePalma will have a sit-down on your behalf—the result of which will be that as long as everybody makes money, no matter what you did wrong, it can almost always be fixed!

Had I been a real wiseguy, I would have been able to feel safe as I perpetrated my criminal acts. Let's say I steal a truck and it turns out it belongs to a trucking company under the umbrella of Vinny Bagadonuts, a skipper in the Lucchese family. Okay, I fucked up. But instead of getting beaten up or killed, a sit-down happens between Greg and Vinny. The result: I can split the load or the proceeds with Vinny or give it all back. Of course, Greg would take a piece of it because he's my skipper. And if the truck contained a hundred thousand dollars' worth of stolen merchandise, we would have told him that we sold it for a smaller amount and pocketed the rest. Who wants to argue over shit like that? It's not like we can go to small claims court or turn up on *Judge Judy* to work it out.

I always remember what Greg told me, "Wiseguys don't sue other wiseguys, wiseguys kill other wiseguys!" Everybody gets what they can. Thieves are thieves, especially to each other. That's why the system of sit-downs is so important to the Mob—it created a means of resolving problems that they could not take to the police. For example, if a guy didn't pay what he owed, or a guy didn't pay the vig—the inflated interest—on some loan shark money, or somebody overstepped his bounds in his criminal activity, the skippers could sit down to resolve things amicably so they can coexist . . . and make money. And there's no such thing as honor among thieves. If one wiseguy said, "He sold it for twenty thousand dollars," you can count on the fact that he sold it for fifty thousand. And the other wiseguy knows it's a lie too. It doesn't matter. Everybody'll get a taste.

From a law enforcement perspective, the beautiful thing about becoming connected was that I moved from posing as an extortion victim of the Mafia to becoming a part of the crew. Instead of sitting around the club and waiting for things to happen, I could experience firsthand what DePalma and his associates were doing. My undercover status allowed me to identify made members of the Mafia who had yet to turn up on any of the FBI's wall charts. I could tell the Bureau who the skippers and crew members were, who talked to whom, what they talked about. In this way, we began to build cases against the mobsters I was meeting and the ones they were talking about on wiretapped conversations.

I want to make clear, of course, that I never took part in the commission of an actual crime, nor was I ever present when someone got killed, or dismembered, or any of that Hollywood horseshit. I never crossed that line in the Gambino case or in any of the undercover cases in which I worked during my decades in the Bureau.

Now that I was on the inside, we could also order up wiretaps, which allowed us to monitor the movement of these criminals as never before. This way the Bureau was able to tell whether I was in any danger, and that was a huge advantage. We bugged DePalma's table at Pasta Per Voi, a restaurant in Port Chester, New York, close to the Connecticut border, where Greg often met with Anthony Megale, the Gambino underboss. The restaurant was owned by Joe Fornino, a longtime Gambino associate and someone Greg was considering putting up for membership in the Mafia. He was also called "Joe Machines" because he put a lot of gambling machines into restaurants throughout the New York area. While Greg was in prison, Joe provided ingredients and even full meals for Greg to bring to John Gotti or the corrupt guards who bent the rules for the incarcerated Mafiosi. By eating at Joe's restaurant, he not only kept things "all in the family," but he never had to pay for lunch either.

The recordings we made at Pasta Per Voi were very bad because, like all good mobsters, they blasted stereos anytime they needed to talk about anything important, so as to render the recording unintelligible.

That didn't keep us from planting a bug in DePalma's phone. The court gave us limited access to his calls—we were only allowed to listen in on the calls related to criminal activity. Personal calls were not within the scope of the wiretap. This shows the court system bending over backward to protect the rights of a person who had spent his whole life in criminal activity and was still consorting with known criminals. Contrary to newspaper reports, we never wired his son's room at the nursing home.

Some days were terrific—we captured great conversations: we were hearing about loan sharking, leg breaking, and all sorts of criminal activities. Then other days we failed to capture a conversation because Greg and company left the phone in the car when they went outside to talk. That's law enforcement—"Some days you eat the bear, other days the bear eats you." One of the other agents on the case used to say, "We had so much bad luck today, that if it was raining tits, we'd get hit over the head with a cock." But we persevered. We intercepted many calls from Greg's phone, and now we had access to much more of his schedule.

While the bugging device in Greg's phone gave us a great advantage, there was one little hitch: Greg was an angry and violent man who kept smashing his phone every time he heard something he didn't want to hear. Each time this happened, it became my responsibility to make sure that we replaced Greg's cell phone with a newly bugged one. By the end of the case, I was on a first-name basis with the cell phone salesman.

Nat and I worked on new angles to exploit our relationship with the wiseguys. For example, everyone in New York knows that there's huge bid-rigging in the construction industry. In fact, not a drop of concrete gets poured anywhere in the city, not a nail is hammered into a wall, without the Mafia taking control . . . and taking a piece of the action. We wanted to set up a construction company so as to build bid-rigging cases against the wiseguys. But the supervisors—the layer of FBI bureaucracy above the case agent or handler—told us that the answer was no. The liability was too great.

"Liability?" I asked, amazed. "What kind of liability are you talking about?"

Here's the answer that came back: "What if your cement truck hits a school bus and there's an explosion and everybody dies? In that case, the Bureau would be responsible."

"Did I hear that right?" I asked. "What are the chances of a cement truck hitting a school bus? What if a meteorite hit a school bus? I don't see the FBI worried about that!"

"Well, what if your cement is below par, and there are lawsuits, or somebody gets hurt or killed?"

In New York, they call cement Italian gold. The Mafia never cuts corners on cement, because that would only bring the heat onto them. Has it happened that some inferior cement made it to a job site? Of course it's happened. In the history of the world, everything happens! But that's something we can use informants and undercovers for, so that we can keep an eye on it. Running a stoplight and hitting a school bus? Inferior cement? Come on, guys! Why don't you just tell me no, and get it over with?

Despite the fact that we wouldn't be establishing a construction company anytime soon, my life was getting really complicated. To depict the insanity of my life during this period, on one particular day I met and had lunch with Greg in Westchester. Then I drove down to Atlantic City for a series of meetings on the Royal Charm case. While there, I also worked on the Steal Pier case—the corrupt politicians I described in the previous chapter. I then received a call from Miami regarding a case involving some renegade cops on the Hollywood, Florida, police force, and I booked a flight out of Newark Liberty Airport, where I left my car. After a few days in Hollywood, I booked my trip back to Kennedy, where I normally landed. When I arrived, I realized that I had left my car at Newark! I took a car service home. The next day my wife drove me to Newark to retrieve my car, giving me a rash of shit about why I should retire from this whole crazy business.

"Look what you're doing!" she told me. "You're killing yourself! You don't even know where your car is! You don't even know who you are on any given day!"

She was right. I was juggling all of these identities for all of these different cases, and away from her and my daughter half the time, always in harm's way. A lot of guys do undercover work during their career—but no one had ever done this, working multiple cases at the same time. That's why I say that the agents are great, but the real heroes are the spouses and children. They're the ones who sacrifice the most.

It's ironic—I'm always very cautious and prepared before I go into a case. I learn all about the people I'm working with, understand exactly what the situation is, who I'm going to be meeting, and how I'm to portray myself. The only time I forgot to make up a good cover story for myself was in real life. People asked me, "What do you do for a living?"

Well, when I told people I was an FBI agent, they would all roll their eyes and say "Yeah, right!" At the same time, I didn't want everybody on the planet to know that I was in the FBI, because I don't know who their friends were or who they might tell. So I just created stories. I told one neighbor I was in construction. Another that I was in real estate. A third that I owned a restaurant. I made up stuff off the top of my head.

And then my wife got on my case: "I just met a woman when I was dropping our daughter off at school—you told her one thing, and now I don't know what to tell her. You told her you were Italian, but you told her husband that you're Cuban! You gotta get your story straight!"

At the same time, my daughter wanted me to go to school and explain to her class what I did for a living, like all the other daddies did. It really broke her heart because there was no way on earth I could do that. On top of that, until she was six, she never even knew my real name. She'd hear me on the phone. I'd be Hector, Antonio, José, Manny, whatever—all she knew was I was Daddy. As much energy as I put into my undercover role, I should have put some into creating a role for myself in real life. When we lived in Manhattan, the only time our neighbors knew I was in the FBI was when my wife and infant daughter were assaulted by a homeless guy near the United Nations. Here in the suburbs where we now lived, I was afraid that my neighbors would say to somebody "He's in the FBI."

But my neighbors must have been saying "This guy's the biggest bullshit artist on the face of the earth!" They also thought that I was in the Witness Protection Program because of the way I looked and acted as well as the hours I kept. I was like Steve Martin in *My Blue Heaven*—I just didn't fit in. They now say to my wife, "We always thought there was something a little strange with your husband—one day he's Italian, the next day he's Cuban, the day after that he's half Italian, half Cuban."

I couldn't worry about any of that, because when DePalma put me on record, the nature of the case changed. The initial thrust of the case had simply been to see what kind of wiseguys were coming through the strip club and maybe to find out what we could do in terms of arresting some of them for various crimes. But now it took on an entirely new dimension. If I was DePalma's associate, I would be privy to some, but definitely not all, of his conversations with regard to the Gambino family criminal enterprises. I heard all kinds of Mob-related information, and there was literally no end to where things could go. At the FBI, our question was this: How do we make this even bigger?

At this time, I was not an official "made" member of the Mob. An "associate" can serve his entire life without ever being made. Or if he is loyal and lucrative enough, he can be proposed for membership. I know this is Mafia 101, but I bring this up because Greg DePalma could now introduce me to other wise-guys as "a friend of mine." This was a step up from the wary cordiality that had denoted our relationship to this point, but it still wasn't the same thing as being made. If I was a made member of the Mafia, Greg could introduce me to other made men as "a friend of *ours*" (*amico nostro*). The difference between "a friend of mine" and "a friend of ours" was enormous, because one made guy could speak freely to another in the presence of a third. I had not yet attained that level. In truth, I never expected that I would be proposed for membership. I had no illusions or expectations that I might be the second law enforcement officer, after Joe Pistone, to be proposed for membership into La Cosa Nostra.

Being a part of Greg's crew changed my schedule. He felt a responsibility to check on his guys every day. Greg always wanted to know where we were the night before, always afraid that we had been scooped up by the Feds and that we were cooperating with them, which would put him and the entire Gambino family in danger. He knew that if he could reach out to his boys every night, he'd feel secure.

My contacts with Greg became more frequent, and we spoke at least daily. It became increasingly stress-ful, because Greg was so hungry for jewelry to move. On the phone, he referred to jewelry as "trophies."

"Jackie boy," he'd say, "I need more trophies! When the fuck are you gonna get me more trophies?"

It drove me totally insane.

The Naked Truth was the perfect foundation for my role in the case, because it gave me the opportunity to rub shoulders with mobsters from all of the five families, not just the Gambinos. It was a great backdrop for other criminal cases the Bureau was pursuing. For example, in order to capitalize on the opportunity that my relationship with Greg presented, my handlers and I wanted to insert another agent into the case. That agent was Mike Grimm, aka Mikey Suits, who also played a role in the Atlantic City investigation of the corrupt city officials. Mike looks like a male fashion model, a total Wall Street guy, from his Armani suits to his Ferragamo shoes. He's always manicured and barbered perfectly. Women love this guy. He's a great undercover. I knew he could enhance my case, while it would bolster his image in the eyes of the targets of an investigation he was pursuing if he could be seen in the company of Gambino guys like Greg DePalma and Jack Falcone. At the time, Mikey was the undercover on Operation Wooden Nickel, an extensive investigation into corruption in the foreign currency trading market on Wall Street.

So I told DePalma, "I've got this guy, he's a knock-around kid, a good guy. You gotta meet him. He's got a lot of friends. They could come up here and drop a lot of money at the club."

"So let's meet him!" DePalma said. "Bring him up here!"

Mikey Suits brought twenty or thirty Wall Street

foreign exchange traders in limos to the club in the Bronx. He told them all to look good.

"You're going to be meeting some people connected with the Gambinos," Mikey told his targets. "Girls, booze—whatever you want, you'll get it. But listen, you guys are not in New York City! You're in the Bronx! This is a connected joint, so don't be disrespecting anyone. You'll see a lot of crooked noses in there. Behave, or somebody could get hurt."

Greg was elated, because they were going to spend a lot of money at the club. The guys were thrilled, because they were getting to experience the excitement of being on the "inside" with the Mob. Little did they know that they were on the inside with the FBI. They spent money left and right, and DePalma was absolutely delighted with me.

"Great job, Jackie!" he told me.

I introduced him to Mike.

I said, "Mike, here's Greg DePalma."

Mike showed him his due respect, thanked Greg for accommodating his party, and went back to his guys. He played it perfectly. As a result, Mikey looked good. The "field trip" of Mike's Wall Street guys enhanced his investigation and certainly had a positive effect on mine.

Before long, I had become Greg's confidant. His unexplained split from Moray left him with a void to fill—driver, business partner, best friend—and I took on all of those roles. Some of the tasks were relatively easy. In the early going, he tried to arrange for a free trip to Las Vegas for the Mafia bosses. He also sent me down to look at a club he wanted to shake down. Only then came the first bit of real trouble. He sent me to shoot someone in the kneecaps because the guy hadn't paid back Greg's money quickly enough.

The order to kneecap a guy occurred when I visited Greg one day at the nursing home where his son lay in a coma.

The hardest thing for me to handle during my two and a half years with the Gambinos was doing business in front of the comatose Craig DePalma. As a teenager, Craig belonged to the Tanglewood Boys, essentially a Mob farm team, a group of sons of wiseguys who grew up together north of New York City. These kids committed all sorts of crimes and mayhem and eventually became made men in their own right. Some of the mobsters I knew said that Craig was not a naturally tough guy like the others and needed the backing of either the Tanglewood Boys or the Mafia to make him feared. Craig was like a kid who followed his father into the family business without really having a feel for it the way his Old Man did.

John Gotti proposed Craig DePalma for his button in the late 1980s. Craig was probably made shortly after the induction of Mikey "Scars" DiLeonardo, John Gotti, Jr., "Skinny" Dominick Pizzonia, and Nicky LaSorsa—who were part of the same "entering class." A funny thing happened during the ceremony marking Craig's new life in La Cosa Nostra. The tradition is that when you go to get your button, they always ask you,

"Do you know why you're here?" Mob etiquette demands that you say "No." Well, John Gotti asked Craig DePalma the fateful question and Craig just looked at him and said, "Yeah! I'm here to get my button!"

Greg always laughed about it, like Ha-ha, my son, what a card!

Gotti and the others were shaking their heads, like What's wrong with this guy?

In 1999, Craig DePalma, his father, Greg DePalma, and John "Junior" Gotti pleaded guilty to racketeering and extortion and were sentenced to federal prison. In 2002, Craig agreed to cooperate with the government then backed out at the last minute. Once his father found out about his cooperation in prison, Greg somehow got word to Craig to the effect that Craig had brought terrible shame on the Gambino family, that he hadn't lived up to the oath he had sworn when he was straightened out, and so on and so forth. Craig, who had no business being in the Mafia to begin with, was so ashamed of himself for letting down his father that he tried to hang himself in his prison cell. He barely survived the suicide attempt, slipping into an irreversible coma, as a result of which he lay unconscious in an Atlanta prison hospital.

Greg spent months and months calling in favors, trying to get Craig released on a compassionate care basis. Six months after I began my work on the Gambino case, Greg, tenacious as always, succeeded. He then had the problem of figuring out where to put Craig. The world is not exactly awash in long-term-care facilities willing to accept mobsters and sons of mobsters. Greg considered a variety of places in New York and Florida and finally set his sights on the United Hebrew Geriatric Center in New Rochelle. The management there did not want to accept Craig, but Greg persisted.

"I don't want anything to do with mobsters!" the director of the center told Greg.

"We're not like that anymore," Greg assured him in a voice that oozed fake sincerity and regret. "I've been out of the criminal life ever since this happened to my son. I promise you, we'll be model citizens. We'll never disturb anyone."

"I don't want mobsters trooping through my place!" the director insisted. "We have elderly people here, and they don't want to be disturbed!"

"I have nothing to do with criminals anymore," Greg assured him soberly. "The only visitors will be my wife and myself. We will never cause you the slightest trouble. I give you my word."

Well, the director relented, to his everlasting regret. Before long, Greg was holding court for as many as eight or nine wiseguys at a time. We met and did business right in front of Craig's body. Or we would have him placed on a gurney so we could take him to the "garden" out back and get him some fresh air. Craig's room became Greg's office—it's where he met everyone from Squitieri and Megale, the Gambino boss and underboss, to members of his own crew including Louis Filippelli, Robert Vaccaro, and me.

Squitieri, who never met anyone in public, came to the home one time wearing a baseball cap and glasses. We got a surveillance photo of him nevertheless. This was the most distasteful and disquieting part of my job. I couldn't stand going to the home, but I had to do it almost every day.

Greg received many of the payoffs from construction company owners and others at the home. They conducted business right in front of the comatose Craig. Greg veered between ordering violence and demonstrating compassion for his son. He'd say, "Son, boy, listen, are you comfortable? Do you want me to put this video on? You see big Jackie here? He's gonna be one of us soon."

I looked around and thought to myself, What kind of life is this? Here's Craig DePalma, made by John Gotti himself, a guy who had been in John Gotti, Jr.'s crew—and yet none of the wiseguys ever came to visit him? They only came to do business with Greg. Where is that bond of closeness that the Mafia pretends to have? It goes only as far as sitting down in a restaurant and pouring back the Chianti and feasting on the veal. After that, everyone is on his own. It was really horrible to go to the center and watch Greg do business there. I'd see the old people who were ill, in horrific states, but it didn't matter to Greg.

Why would any bad guy want to expose his son to a life of crime? Greg should have kept his son out. Instead, he ensured that Craig became a made guy. People could say, "What a good father! He visits his son every day." But a really good father would have never let that happen in the first place.

Greg's wife blamed Greg for getting their son involved with the Mob. "You put him in the life!" she told him, in front of me and many other people. The implication was that if Greg had not done so, their son wouldn't be lying in a coma in the United Hebrew Geriatric Center. Whenever I saw Greg in a tender moment with his son, I wondered if he was doing it because Craig was his son or because Craig was a made man.

At any rate, on this particular visit to the home, I could tell that Greg was fuming. Even as I went down the hall toward Craig's room, I could hear Greg's voice "cocksucker this, motherfucker that."

I walked into the room and found Greg standing with Neil Delieto, a Gambino associate who owned a construction company.

"Hey, Greg, you all right?" I asked, approaching Greg and giving him a kiss, as always.

"That cocksucker Joe Blow owes me money," Greg said.

Greg had a construction deal of some sort with "Joe." Joe had to pay money to Neil, and Greg would get a piece of it. I didn't know the details because that wasn't a question associates asked their higher-ups.

"Jack, I want you to go shoot that motherfucker in the kneecaps," Greg rasped.

I knew he was upset—whenever you saw him like that, in a tirade, you knew somebody was going to get hurt.

"Greg, what are you saying?" I asked, trying to hide my alarm. I was scared, but at the same time, I recall how pleased I was that he trusted me enough to give me a job like that. This was a different subculture from the rest of the world—if the skipper gives an order, it's got to be for a fucking reason. Think of Luca Brazi in *The Godfather*—he just nodded and went and killed whoever he was supposed to kill.

In my role as an associate in Greg's crew, the two things I would never do were hurt or kill people. But if I turned down or talked my way out of too many of these errands, it would have looked very bad for me, and it might have had a negative impact on the entire investigation.

"I want you to shoot that motherfucking Joe Blow in the fucking kneecaps!" Greg reiterated. "He fucking owes us money!"

I knew who Joe Blow was. I'd met him before. He was just a young businessman, a harmless guy. A civilian.

"Okay, Greg," I said. "Whatever you need."

I delayed this until finally I had to go see the guy. It turned out that Joe's company did *not* owe money to the construction guy named Neil Delieto, who operated under Greg's umbrella. Greg followed this Mob logic: Since Joe didn't cut Neil in on some subcontracting work, Joe owed Neil the $30,000 Neil would have made had he been the subcontractor. This was the nature of Joe's "debt."

I found out one day from the guys at the strip club

that he ate lunch at a particular restaurant in Yonkers. I couldn't shoot him or slap him around. I had to find a way to resolve this without violence . . . and without raising Greg's suspicions.

When Joe saw me enter the restaurant, he knew exactly why I was there. People knew I was with Greg. He blanched. Imagine having me come to shoot you or even just break your leg. Even a Mob guy could lose his appetite over the sight of me coming toward him with a malicious look on my face!

But instead of hitting him or shooting him in the knees, I told him, "Hey, listen, we got a problem here. How are we going to resolve this with Greg? He's got a pebble in his shoe about this. I like you. I know you're not involved. I know you're not that kind of guy."

Joe, relieved to be still breathing, replied, "I don't owe Delieto any money."

"Well," I replied, "Greg believes that you do. So what are we gonna do to make this problem go away?"

"I didn't recommend Delieto because my partner doesn't like him. By the way, my partner's brother is an FBI agent."

That was all I needed to hear. That was a great "out" for me. If you had a connection with law enforcement, you were all but untouchable in the world of the Mob.

"Just watch yourself," I warned him. "It is what it is. I'm gonna tell Greg about this and try to calm him down."

I went back to DePalma.

"You talk to that cocksucker Joe Blow?" he asked.

I nodded. "Turns out his partner has an FBI agent in his family."

"He's full of shit," Greg replied dismissively.

"You want to take a chance with the FBI?" I asked. Of course, he was taking a chance with the FBI just by hanging around with me, although he didn't know it at the time!

Greg said nothing further to me about the matter, which came as a great relief to me. But six months later, Greg happily told me that his goons gave a serious beating to Joe Blow at a construction site. "They tuned up that motherfucker pretty good," Greg told me with great satisfaction.

Another time Greg told me to come with him to smack around "this fucking guy who's bad-mouthing me about an insurance claim."

So Greg and I went down to pay this guy a visit at the car dealership where he worked. This was trouble— Greg wanted to smack him, and I would have to stop the beating. As an FBI agent, I can't have an assault happen in front of me. This could have ended the case. As luck would have it, the guy wasn't there, but his son was. Divine intervention, in my opinion. Greg yelled at the son for a while, but at least he wouldn't smack him.

"Make sure you tell your father to apologize to Greg," I told the young man in my most fearsome manner.

And that, thank God, was that.

On another occasion, Greg told me to take a baseball bat to a particular individual who was not cooperating in a manner that pleased the Gambino captain.

"Jack," Greg said, "here's the kind of car he drives, here's the gym where he works out at, here's how he gets to work. Take a baseball bat and go after him."

Somehow I prevented that beating from happening too. Was I being tested? Or were they simply giving me errands to do, now that I was on their team? I'll never know. In these situations, I would always tell Greg that the guy wasn't there, or was on the lam, or I just missed him. Somehow Greg never pursued these things any further.

Like everyone in the Mob, Greg was hypocritical about drugs. At one point, he said to me, "Jack, you have to promise me you're not involved in pushing junk. Whatever you do, you can't do that. That goes against the code. That's going to get you and me killed, you understand, if you fuck with that shit. Are you dealing dope?"

"I used to do that, Greg, but—"

"I don't give a shit about what you used to do," he interrupted. "It's about what you do now."

I promised him I had retired from that business a long time ago and that I had nothing to do with drugs now, but we both knew that I was lying. How else could I possibly make the money that I appeared to be making without selling dope? Bunch of bullshitters.

Another issue that arose was whether Greg would

be offered a "promotion" from capo to underboss. The underboss, Megale, had been arrested on drug charges in a related investigation run out of the FBI's Bridgeport, Connecticut, office. Once that happened, Greg talked repeatedly about the possibility that he might become the family underboss.

Greg was torn. All his life, he never advanced past the rank of capo, and here he was, seventy-three years old. As underboss, he would make a lot more money, because many more people would be kicking up to him: all the twenty-six capos in the Gambino family (just twenty-one, if you trusted the FBI's chart), all the soldiers, and all the associates. On the other hand, he feared that accepting the position put him on a road straight back to prison.

"They don't have that many experienced guys," Greg told me, explaining that there were very few other contenders for the position, "but I don't want to do it. That's too visible a position. I don't want to go back to jail. I'm toying with the idea because of the garbage cans they are making now."

In other words, the low quality of the modern mobster so upset Greg that he considered putting himself at risk of imprisonment simply to improve the caliber of newly minted wiseguys.

Meanwhile, the recorded conversations to which I was a party, along with the wiretaps we were able to order because of my role as undercover, allowed us to build case after case against Gambino family members, from Squitieri and Megale down to the capos, the soldiers, and the associates. We had my recorded conversations with Greg and the other mobsters, we had wiretaps at various locations where they congregated, and we had wiretaps on their cell phones. It was a treasure trove of incriminating statements and gatherings. The case was becoming so big that Nat brought in a second handler, Chris Munger, a tireless case agent who had investigated the Tanglewood Boys, to work alongside him. Chris did a sensational job here as well. Nat and Chris worked tirelessly with the U.S. Attorney's Office to turn the raw material of the recordings we were making into cases against the wiseguys.

The list of Mob guys we would eventually take down grew longer and longer. This was the best case I'd ever worked on—there was literally no end to the number of mobsters against whom we could build airtight cases. The only questions were whether the FBI had the courage to keep the case open long enough to maximize its value . . . and whether my identity could remain a secret long enough for me to survive in the community of wiseguys in which I now moved.

CHAPTER FiFTEEN

"If You've Got the Hole, You've Got the Gold"

How does the Mob make money? Let me count the ways.

One of their all-time favorites is construction. It's a corollary to Newton's First Law of Gravity: In the New York metropolitan area, whatever goes up, or comes down, happens only when wiseguys get paid.

Greg DePalma loved dirt. As a wiseguy and a businessman, Greg understood that money was to be made in dirt. In construction, you've got to take the dirt out and then put it somewhere else. If you're in the position to do both, you can make money on both ends. As a result, construction was a constant topic of conversation with Greg. He was always discussing big and small projects where he could dig up dirt, sell dirt, store dirt, put in his own people for no-show union jobs, sell material, or just simply charge the 2 percent Mafia tax. If anyone had overheard any of our lunch or dinner conversations, they'd have thought we were contractors, not criminals.

Greg's success in construction is what had led to his becoming capo. John Gotti, the notorious Gambino boss, promoted Greg to that level in the 1990s. Greg received this promotion as a reward for "putting on record," or bringing under the Gambino crime umbrella, the DeFoe Corporation, a major force in highway construction in the New York area. Greg frequently received envelopes full of cash from John Amicucci, the president of DeFoe, whom DePalma called "Daffy Duck." DeFoe had been associated with the Genovese family, but DePalma managed to persuade them to move over to the Gambino camp. For this, Greg was awarded capo status. Greg even reportedly offered Amicucci membership in the Gambino family, which Amicucci respectfully declined. Amicucci was charged for making illegal labor payments. In 2006 he was tried in Federal Court in Manhattan and acquitted of all charges by a jury after two days of deliberations.

One of the biggest projects on Greg's mental drawing board was at the Van Cortlandt golf course in the Bronx. (If you played it in the mid-1990s, you might remember the abandoned Buick to the left of the seventh fairway.) The city planned to build an underground water treatment plant there, which would require dismantling the golf course. The dirt would be shipped out, the plant would be built, and the dirt would be shipped back in. For Greg DePalma, it didn't get any better than that.

But bad luck kept striking: Community activists protested the project. The elderly complained that they didn't have five years to wait before the golf course reopened. It happened over and over in our time together—the project would be almost there, and then some community activist would kill or delay it. "Man, you have no idea how much money we're gonna make!" Greg would say gleefully, whenever it appeared that the on-again, off-again project was on again. That first-person plural pronoun—"we"—was always reserved for future projects, for things on his drawing board. The "we" disappeared whenever the project got real. Then it was all about Greg and the Gambino administration. The envelopes were always passed around, but there was nothing for the crew. That's how it was—those at the bottom of the food chain don't get anything.

Before going to prison in the Scores case, Greg lived like a king in his beautiful Scarsdale home. When released from prison, he got himself a two-bedroom, standard garden-style apartment in the town of Tuckahoe, New York. He had to justify his expenses whenever he met with his parole officer—rent receipts, the phone bill, the electric bill. That's part of the parole process. He couldn't even dress nicely at his parole hearings, because the question would have arisen: Where'd you get the money for those threads? So he was a great undercover agent himself—to the cops! Sometimes that attitude spilled over into the Mob world when he would cry poor mouth—that he was broke—even to me.

I liked to goof on him. I teased him for the Norwegian imported bottled water he favored and for the fact that he had sports memorabilia (fake) and artwork (stolen) covering practically every square inch of every wall in his home. His kitchen contained boxes and boxes of everything—water, sodas, all kinds of food, everything that had fallen off the back of whatever truck. He especially liked Voss water, a super-expensive brand of artesian well water from Norway that retailed for more than $43 a case of twenty-four.* Why did a guy who smoked like a chimney and ate like a pig insist on drinking such pure water? Because it was free.

Greg's home looked like a storage facility with all those boxes. One time his parole officer called his wife, who gave him Greg's cell phone number. Greg was deeply annoyed with her for that—he wasn't supposed to be able to afford a cell phone, not on the money he was earning at whatever job he told the parole officer he was working. He lived very simply for a man who was raking in a huge amount of money as a newly energized capo in the Gambino family.

How much money was he earning? When I think about all the envelopes I saw, all the scams he ran,

---

* Voss Artesian bottled water is taken from a virgin aquifer that "has been shielded for centuries under ice and rock in the untouched wilderness of central Norway. . . . Voss's stunning cylindrical package has quickly developed a superior image and significant market share in the ultra-premium bottled water segment," according to www.Voss.com.

the shakedowns, the illicit gambling, loan sharking, union activities, and everything else that he was up to, I would conservatively estimate that within six to nine months of his release from prison, Greg DePalma was taking down $25,000 tax-free each month. That adds up to over a quarter of a million dollars a year. This demonstrates Greg's tenaciousness, both at reclaiming his position in the Gambino hierarchy and at making money.

As a skipper, he reaped the rewards. Everybody who worked in construction under his umbrella paid him 2 percent, and 2 percent of a lot of New York construction projects adds up in a hurry. Law enforcement agencies estimated that the 2 percent Mob tax on construction projects in New York added more than $10 million to Gambino family coffers.

The more time I spent with DePalma, the more confident I grew in my role. I was accomplishing the unimaginable. I passed myself off as an associate, a Mob guy in training, among the *real* wiseguys. As a result, my true personality came out even more. I am by nature a gregarious, fun-loving, people-loving person. I think my nature was a large part of the reason why the Old Man took to me so quickly. I don't know if I was ever afraid of him. I certainly respected him for the seriousness with which he took his responsibilities as a Gambino capo. But as our friendship deepened, I could do things that really expressed my true nature. I hugged him, goofed around with him, and teased him a little bit. And I know he loved it. I know he loved *me*.

I was under his umbrella, in his circle, but even within our group, there was still the pecking order. Whenever he was on a conversation with a made guy, the guy would whisper directly to him so we could not listen in. Sometimes it looked like the guy was nuzzling him and whispering sweet nothings into his ear! Or they would go to another table or even step outside. The rest of us at the table who weren't invited along felt like the second string. We wanted so badly to be on the varsity! It's seductive. When we were left out of a conversation like that, we thought, I'm no different from those other mopes! Why are those guys so close to Greg, and not me? I thought I had a special bond with him! But it didn't matter. Until I was a made guy, certain conversations were off limits for me, and I had to accept that fact.

Greg was a master at manipulating people. He could cry, whisper, and whine about the state of his son, his lack of money, how the government had taken his beautiful house in Scarsdale—whatever it took to get his hooks into someone. Once he got them under his umbrella, it was game over. He sucked the guy dry. Watching him talk to a businessman or a contractor with whom he wanted to do business was like watching the quarterback of the football team ask a cheerleader out on a date. He was seductive, warm, and appealing. He was the man's man whom men wanted to hang out with. He could manipulate anybody out of anything, as I saw over and over again.

At the same time, he had one of the worst tempers

I've ever seen in a human being, and he flipped from seductive to sinister in a heartbeat. One moment he was sweet as sugar, and then someone mentioned the name of an individual who had given him a hard time or had failed to pay him quickly enough, and his demeanor would change like a storm coming in. He would go off on an expletive-filled tirade: "Fuck him, I'm going to own him soon!"

I started to learn how to manipulate Greg myself. I could tell when he needed stroking, and when I needed to back off. These were techniques I developed from the undercover roles I have had. Greg was aware of my sensitivity toward his moods, and it further cemented the bond between us.

The other constant theme in Greg's meetings with the administration was the poor quality of the new members that the Mob was proposing. Greg would go off on a tirade about these guys—he never liked any of the new members or the ones being proposed. "I saw a list of the guys they're gonna make," he would growl. "They're all brokesters, garbage cans." He felt that the guys weren't proven, that they hadn't been around long enough to deserve full membership. There wasn't enough documentation of them as stand-up guys doing the right thing, kicking money up. Maybe these people being proposed for membership had done some jail time, or maybe they had done just a few scams. Whatever the reason, Greg viewed them as unworthy successors to the kind of men of honor with whom he served for decades in the Mafia. Kids today.

In truth, I wanted to commiserate with him—I had the same problem with some of my inexperienced supervisors at the FBI! My handlers, Nat Parisi and Chris Munger, were great, but I was constantly having run-ins with the higher-ups, many of whom rarely laid eyes on a real, live criminal. There was even talk in the Bureau of shutting the entire investigation down. That kind of talk drove me crazy.

Greg could turn practically any situation to his own advantage. For example, he heard that Louis Filippelli was opening up a restaurant near Rao's. Rao's is located at Pleasant Avenue and 114th Street in East Harlem, a traditional Italian neighborhood, and is an all-time wiseguy favorite, where it is almost impossible to get a table. In fact the owner, Frankie "No" Pellegrino, got his name because whenever anyone asked him if they had any tables available or could make a reservation, the answer was always "no."

The idea of opening up another Italian restaurant in the vicinity of Rao's made sense from a business standpoint. Greg came up with a brilliant stratagem. He reached out to a guy we'll call Tommy who used to work at Scores. Greg had gotten to know Tommy back when he was shaking down that club. Tommy, in fact, was also arrested in the Scores case. Tommy was now in the radio business in New York, so Greg told him that he wanted a ton of free radio advertising for the new restaurant. This way Greg would be able to go back to Louis, who started the restaurant, and say, "Look what I did for you! I got you all this free advertising time!" It was pure Greg DePalma—the move would cost him nothing; somebody else would foot the bill; he would get credit for being generous; on top of that, he would feel entitled to eat for free in the restaurant whenever he chose; and it further empowered him with the Gambinos.

The only problem was that Tommy wanted no part of Greg, that restaurant, or doling out any free advertising. This infuriated Greg, who felt that he might look bad in front of Louis, to whom he had made the unsolicited offer of assistance.

"Go find this cocksucker Tommy," Greg told me, "and fuck him up with a baseball bat."

"You got it, Greg," I told him, swallowing hard. "Whatever you need."

I knew Tommy. He was a real nice guy, and Tommy knew who I was. We had mutual friends, so I couldn't possibly have gone near him. It would have ended the case on the spot if he told anyone that I was working undercover. I avoided him, although I told Greg over and over that I was hot on his trail.

Greg had plenty of people to perpetrate violence for him, but even in his seventies he wasn't afraid to reach out and slap somebody himself. The owner of a construction company ripped DePalma off in some transaction, and Greg was furious. One night Greg saw him at a diner. Greg went over to him and slapped him hard across the face. The guy practically cried: "Greg, please don't hurt me anymore!"

Greg dined out on that story for months!

"I cracked him one!" Greg would growl. "This guy here, he's gonna disrespect me? I told him that he was a piece of shit, that he was gonna pay!"

There was another individual, a former body-builder in his sixties with massive biceps who scared the pants off anybody he looked at the wrong way. The guy didn't faze Greg in the least. The guy was trying to move in on a strip club, but Greg shut him down in a New York minute.

As tough as Greg was, he lived with complete respect for Mafia traditions. One of those traditions is that whatever the boss wants, the boss gets. Greg often told me the story about how he had a beautiful Jaguar XJ12. One time he and John Gotti were in Pennsylvania together, and John saw the car. John was the boss of the Gambino family at the time, and Greg just a capo. Gotti told Greg how much he liked the car.

"Oh, no!" Greg would say as he retold the tale. "What am I gonna do? So I threw him the keys."

According to Greg, John Gotti said, "What's this?"

"It's my gift to you," DePalma said, choking back tears over the loss of his beloved car.

"No, I can't do this," Gotti replied, but he was just saying that. As Greg says, "What are you gonna do, charge the boss?"

With Greg, though, finances ran one way—up. Greg was always looking to kick up money to leadership. He was especially interested in kicking up money to them that wasn't his own. Guys would constantly come around Greg and give him an envelope. I was there on countless occasions when someone handed Greg an envelope bulging with cash, protection money, Greg's share of a score, Greg's piece of a loan-sharking or a bookmaking operation, whatever. I witnessed many such payments. Greg never took any money out and said, "Hey, Jackie boy, here, this is for you." Greg pocketed what he received less what he kicked up to the administration.

Very simply, the more money a member kicks up, the more valuable he is to the Mob. An earner has to do some serious shit—must really violate Mafia rules—in order to get whacked. Instead, because he generates cash, he sits closer to the throne. He becomes much more involved with his capo or boss and becomes a trusted confidant. The best analogy I can offer is college football—Ohio State's players have those little Buckeye symbols on their helmets. They play to get their helmets full of stickers. Why? Because a helmet full of stickers connotes respect. Well, capos like De-Palma are trying to get all the money they can and kick up, because they know that one day they may be up there and they want the money to be there for them. They want the power and the respect.

Knowing Greg DePalma was lucrative and valuable for a business. Most people think of businesses that have to pay protection money to the Mafia as victims, but they got their money's worth and more. First, they had no choice in the matter. What were they going to do? They could stop paying and call the police, but they weren't stupid. They knew they would rather align themselves with the Mafia. And then, once they had that alignment in place, cemented by those envelopes full of cash, they would be able to use those connections to increase the size and importance of their businesses.

"See that guy over there?" someone might say of a Gambino "victim." "He's a connected guy—he's with the Gambinos! Hey, we better give him the business—who knows what they'll do to us otherwise!"

Businessmen who paid Greg DePalma actually received plenty of benefits under his umbrella. Many companies were more than willing to pay the "Mob tax"—2 percent of a Mafia-generated contract is better than 100 percent of nothing. Greg made use of a particular minority coalition as a bargaining chip. If a business owner or contractor wasn't doing things Greg's way, wasn't bringing him enough money or bringing it fast enough, he threatened that he would send in the minority coalition to picket the stores or the job site. In construction, the last thing businesses want is the aggravation of picketers standing in front of the site wasting everybody's time. So Greg usually found a ready ear for his services as a person who could make job-site problems go away.

Of course, he created even more problems. When he got hold of a union contact for a work site, he piled in all the nonunion workers he could to do the actual work. He charged for union labor and pocketed the difference. The Mob got the money, and there would be no disruption from the guys who monitored union membership on the job site. They were on Greg's payroll. If the Mob became involved in a construction project, the company had access to workers, the union, the material, and bid-rigging. Greg thought that 2 percent was a bargain for all of these services. I was surprised the Mafia didn't ask for more.

No amount of money was enough for Greg. Mob guys are never satisfied. One particular dirt company paid him not only at Christmastime, but at other times of the year as well, and sometimes when Greg just needed a few extra bucks. Some companies paid every week, some every month. All were obligated to give Greg cash commensurate with what they earned. Otherwise, they would have been in trouble with him. Some wanted to pay annually instead of more often because they didn't want to get caught up in FBI surveillance.

Here's another scam Greg invented. I mentioned Rao's, the century-old Italian restaurant in the Pleasant Avenue section of East Harlem. The way the tables worked at Rao's was similar to leasing a luxury box at a stadium. A table that seats eight at Rao's must have eight people eating dinner—and paying for their dinner—every week at that same time. If they don't, they lose the table and the prestige that goes along with it. For many years, John Gotti had his own private table at Rao's. When he went to prison, Greg DePalma inherited it. Greg turned that table into a moneymaking venture. On nights when he couldn't use it, he called someone up and said, "Guess what? You can eat at John Gotti's table at Rao's! I've arranged it all for you!"

The victim or mark would be incredibly excited to have this prestigious experience, if you can imagine such a thing. It wasn't exactly Clinton renting out the Lincoln bedroom to big donors, but it was close. After Greg's victim, along with his seven closest friends, had enjoyed a meal at Rao's that undoubtedly cost a couple of thousand dollars, Greg would call, crying the blues.

"Hey, I'm out of money. I'm hurting for cash. I just set you up at Rao's. You gotta help me out with a few dollars here."

Greg DePalma had a way of making money out of absolutely anything.

As much as Greg loved restaurants as places to meet, receive tribute, and spend hours on end eating, he was not exactly the best of customers from the restaurant's point of view. We would stay for hours and hours; we might arrive for lunch and stay right through dinner. Greg would smoke in restaurants, which is against the law in New York State, making the owner nervous because it was also an annoyance to the other diners. Greg's presence—that loud, menacing, growling voice, along with the crew of mobsters surrounding him—detracted from the atmosphere in a restaurant. But everyone, including the restaurant owners, was afraid to tell Greg to quit smoking or talking loud. He was in his seventies, a wreck from a medical perspective, but still tall and tough looking—a terrifying figure on the criminal landscape.

Like any intelligent business, the Mafia outsourced certain functions to freelance workers. In particular, the Mob outsourced violent beatings and terrorizing functions, like hanging guys upside-down from the ceilings of their businesses. The freelancers to whom the Mafia turned to at such moments were a New York Albanian crime family, the same people who had busted up the Naked Truth and prompted this investigation. It used to be that the Mob's muscle was the Westies, a ruthless gang of Irish New Yorkers who grew up in Hell's Kitchen. After the Westies disbanded, the Albanians took over.

Well, when Greg went to jail, the Albanians also took over the table at Rao's that belonged first to Gotti and then to Greg and became an increasingly menacing force in the world of New York organized crime. Initially they were used as contract killers and performers of mayhem. On many occasions I heard Greg say, "If we have a problem, we'll just have the Albanians take care of it." But before long, the Albanians began thinking, How come we're the brawn and those guys are the brains? And after I got to see firsthand the limited mentality of some of the Mob guys, I realized it was actually a pretty good question.

The Albanians decided that they wanted to become a sixth organized crime family in New York, on a par with the other five. Naturally, this didn't sit well with the Sicilians. The Albanians went into Astoria— Lucchese family territory—and put Joker Poker machines into Lucchese-controlled establishments. They beat people up. They moved in on La Cosa Nostra territory by shaking down businesses.

The Albanians were fearless. In 1998 they went into Valbella's, a celebrity-studded restaurant in the elegant Connecticut suburb of Greenwich. The owner allegedly paid the Gambinos five thousand dollars a month in protection money . . . and all the food the Gambinos could eat. The wiseguys had a regular table at Valbella's, which was an absolute gold mine of a restaurant. The Albanians noticed this and said to themselves, Why aren't we getting that money? So they went into Valbella's and *hung the owner from the ceiling* until he agreed to pay them instead of the Gambinos. So now they had the table at Rao's, the protection money at Valbella's, and had made other incursions into sacred Gambino territory.

Greg was in jail so he couldn't resolve the matter himself. Instead, he sent Nicky LaSorsa to handle it, the same individual whom he had made and later ordered killed in a hit. Upon learning of the Albanian shakedown at Valbella's, LaSorsa said, "Wait a minute, fuck those guys!" So he went back to Valbella's on DePalma's behalf and arranged to end the payoffs to the Albanians and now the Gambinos could return to the restaurant and enjoy all they could eat. When Greg, still incarcerated, heard the news, he went ballistic. What good was an all-you-can-eat voucher at a restaurant when you were behind bars? Where's the money? After he got out of prison, Greg reclaimed the location for himself and made sure that the payoffs included cash and meals.

The Albanians were tough enough, bad enough, and didn't-give-a-shit enough to do whatever needed to be done, which is why they got the violent assignments from the Mafia wiseguys in the first place. They would murder guys and chop them up, do whatever it took. According to Greg, there was a story about a couple of made guys who had gone in to see the Albanians in the Bronx for a sit-down and had been stripped and thrown outside stark naked. The Mob didn't do anything about it. To Greg's mind, this was an absolute outrage.

Greg decided that he would go by himself to Café Dion, the principal hangout of the Albanians, to straighten things out.

"You want help?" I asked, impressed at his fearlessness. "I'll back you up."

"No, that's okay," Greg told me dismissively. He could handle his business without my assistance. I had to admit, he had balls. He played by Mob rules and he expected those guys to obey as well. He had no fear. Greg went to Café Dion and he resolved the issue of the table at Rao's and most of the other disputes between the Albanians and the Mob. I have to hand it to him—he had the courage to walk into the enemy camp and handle things the old-fashioned way.

The sit-down between Greg and the Albanians didn't resolve all of the issues, however, and relations between the two camps worsened. In late September 2005 things had deteriorated so thoroughly that the Gambinos decided to have a serious showdown with

the Albanians. Arnold Squitieri—the boss himself—
was present. In the minds of the Gambinos, the Albanians needed to be cut down . . . a lot.

The confrontation, Greg told me, took place at a
gas station in a rest area on the New Jersey Turnpike.
It may sound like urban legend, but it really happened.
Squitieri brought firepower with him—twenty guys, all
packing, all strapped. Meanwhile, regular citizens—
people with families—were pumping unleaded gas and
wondering what the hell was going on. The Albanians
were similarly armed. The conversation, never friendly
to begin with, rapidly escalated.

"You took what you took," Squitieri began, "and
you ain't takin' no more. Or there's going to be a problem . . . do you understand?"

The Albanians responded to this threat with a
burst of bravado straight out of James Cagney. The
leader turned to one of his men and said, "If they start
shooting at us, aim your shotguns at the gas tanks, and
we'll all go."

It was a Hollywood moment—the Albanians basically said, "We're tough guys, too. You wanna fuck
with us? We'll fuck with you!"

The confrontation could have gone either way, but
the Gambinos had twenty guys there and the Albanians
had only half a dozen. The Albanians had worked with
the Gambinos long enough to have respect for La Cosa
Nostra, and in the gas station, the Albanians blinked
first. Somehow, Greg told me, the Albanians listened
to reason . . . or at least to Squitieri's threats. They

were outnumbered at the gas station, and they must have finally realized that the Gambino family was too powerful to be fucked with.

Greg told me the Albanians were spanked, and they never evolved into that sixth organized crime family in New York.

Greg didn't spend all of his time threatening Albanians, of course. One of the doctors he somehow knew ran a foundation with an annual golf outing to help raise money for heart transplants for children. This was a big fund-raiser, and I don't know how the Old Man got involved, but he did. He was responsible for contributing a lot of sports memorabilia, which was offered in a silent auction at the event.

Greg didn't just donate the memorabilia—he also brought a full table of mobsters and connected businesspeople, at five hundred dollars a head. He took me a couple of times, and I have to say that it was one of the most perfectly organized and worthwhile events I've ever seen.

It took place at a beautiful country club in Westchester County, and it kicked off with a fantastic breakfast. Then there was a shotgun tournament (an appropriate format for wiseguys!). There was a different sponsor for every hole. On the par threes, if you got a hole in one, you would win a car from a nearby dealership, and so on. I'm not a golfer, so I just went for a ride on the golf cart with my foursome. Afterward, there was a dinner with celebrities, sports figures, and leading New York businesspeople. There was a silent auction with the sports memorabilia and a fashion show where someone could buy a fur coat. They had a comedian who was absolutely hilarious, and the dinner was out of this world. It was a perfect day . . . except for the company I was keeping.

The Old Man was all dressed up for the dinner. I sat next to him at our table. A steady stream of well-wishers approached all night long. All kinds of people—businessmen, politicians, you name it—stepped forward practically to kiss Greg's ring, just to have a few words with him. They treated him like some sort of celebrity instead of what he really was, a lifelong criminal. I couldn't believe it. I couldn't believe all these people would be willing to be publicly associated with a guy like Greg. It was even shocking to me that legitimate businesspeople were among those who had bought tickets at our table. These were people whom Greg was currently extorting, had extorted in the past, or were future marks he was setting up! Working this case, I learned that there is no shortage of lines of ass-kissers and people who want to be around wiseguys. It's amazing. The whole experience was "business development" for Greg, because he was lining up his next victims, and it showed him at his most charming.

I'm hoping that since I never saw a good side of him, this was it, but it's hard for me to believe that Greg wasn't benefiting financially in one or more ways from his annual appearances at these events. Did he keep some or all of the five hundred dollars a seat he charged the people at his table? Or was he simply generating goodwill for himself and meeting new people to shake down? Was he getting a piece of the money raised by the sale of the sports memorabilia in the silent auction? By the way, who knew just how legitimate that memorabilia was? Most likely he got it for nothing, donated it in exchange for a free table, and then proceeded to make five hundred bucks a head from each of us. In any event, as nice as the event was, we didn't belong there! We were freaking mobsters! But that didn't matter to Greg. Every year it was "Jackie boy, you gotta go to this! How many tickets do you want?"

The other thing about the Mafia, aside from eating and making money, was the absolute love and care they bestowed on their bodies. Obviously, we ate lot, so none of us looked like we were in training for a marathon. But anything we could do to make ourselves look nicer, we were there. At one point, somebody in Florida hooked Greg up with an excellent hairpiece, so he no longer had the Grandpa Munster look that he sported when we first met.

After months of meetings, Greg finally managed to resolve the matter of the mutual hits that he and Nicky LaSorsa had taken out on one another. The two men, first bound by the fact that Greg had made Nicky and now bound by their commitments to kill each other, finally agreed to sit down in a Bronx restaurant and kiss and make up. And since it's the Mafia, the kissing was literal. Greg ceased badmouthing Nicky at every opportunity—his favorite epithet for Nicky was "cocksucker," but that didn't mean much, because that was his favorite epithet for a lot of people. Now he was telling us what a great guy LaSorsa really was. This was an order from above, so as to avoid dissension.

As much as Greg loved money, there was one financial offer even he could not accept. Lenny Minuto was a sixty-four-year-old Gambino hanger-on who had been around the family for decades. He had made a fortune in Mob-protected bookmaking and shylocking operations. He had continually begged Paulie Castellano, the Gambino boss whom John Gotti eventually murdered and succeeded, to allow him to buy his way into the Mob.

Castellano refused to accept the $50,000 to $100,000 that Minuto offered, even though, according to rumor, a number of made guys had paid cash for their buttons. Everybody knew who they were, and no one respected them, because they had paid for membership instead of earning it. Yet Paulie kept passing Minuto by, as did Gotti and all of the bosses, up to and including Arnold Squitieri. According to Greg, Minuto was a "beanshooter" and a "jerk-off" who didn't have the nerve to be a full-blown soldier. By the time I was involved in the case, Minuto had upped his offer to a cool million—he was willing to pay seven figures to be inducted in the Mob.

Greg joked about the idea of taking his money and then just laughing at him but never did accept Minuto's cash, as far as I know. For once, Greg's Mob scruples outweighed his enormous greed. When the Gambino case ended, Lenny and his son were arrested and indicted for shooting at a witness's car. Minuto ended up cooperating with the government. Turned out Greg had been right about him all along. (His lawyer denied that the convicted gambler tried to buy his way into the Gambino family. "In listening to the tapes," said the lawyer, "the only conclusion I can come to is this is gossip, Mob gossip, and judging from the sources you must evaluate the information based on the persons making the statements.")

Greg was by far the most difficult person I ever encountered in my years of undercover work. It was a very difficult case for me to work. Merely being in his presence was a constant strain. It was a test of how much information I could get from him and how many connections I could make, while at the same time he was always trying to figure out how much money he could get from me. I never respected him as a person, but I give him his due as a mobster: He always played by the rules.

And he sensed the same thing about me. Even with my Social Security and background check complete, Greg was still very much in the business of getting me checked out. He wanted me to meet the bosses and have them also check me out.

Why? Because he wanted to have me made. He wanted to make me a full-fledged soldier in the Gambino family. Greg wanted me to be straightened out, to get my button, to become a soldier, a goodfella in the Mafia. A full-fledged *amico nostro*—a friend of ours.

INTERLUDE THREE

Going Hollywood

In December 2002, not long before I enrolled in Mob school with Nat, I got a call from FBI agent Kevin Luebke in Miami. He had heard about me—he knew my reputation for having handled some significant cases there.

"We have the possibility of introducing you into a case involving a fence," Kevin explained. "We heard from a guy who was looking for leniency that there was a jeweler where you could bring swag to sell. The owner of the store melts the pieces down and sells the precious metal."

"So what's the case?" I asked. "What makes this a matter for the FBI?"

"I was just getting to that," Kevin said. "The jewelry store owner employs a lot of cops. They fence stolen jewelry and are involved in everything from insurance scams to robbery."

It sounded good to me, so I grabbed a flight and joined the case. Ronnie was the guy sitting in jail giving us information, so my role was to be his uncle. Ronnie had gone to the jewelry store repeatedly, both as a customer to buy stolen jewelry and to sell stolen goods to the owner. In so doing, he became friendly with the many off-duty Hollywood police officers who moonlighted by providing protection at the showroom. The cops must have seen the owner fencing stolen goods. Ronnie even felt comfortable enough around the police to buy bulletproof vests and other police apparel from them so he could do stickups dressed as a cop. In so doing, Ronnie was not just fencing jewelry; he was actually stealing it. The cops even sold some of the jewelry themselves.

Eventually, the Feds arrested Ronnie for being part of a breaking-and-entering ring that specialized in stealing money, jewelry, and other valuables from private homes. That's when he decided to flip in exchange for leniency. He told the Feds about the dirty Hollywood cops who hung around the jewelry store, and this attracted the attention of the FBI. The Bureau needed an agent to work undercover on the case, befriend the jewelry storeowner, whom we'll call Freddy, and get in close with the dirty cops.

I decided to drop in cold, one hot summer day in Hollywood, and meet with Freddy. That day I went into the jewelry store dressed like a New York gangster vacationing in Miami—the silk guayabera, the nice pants, the expensive shoes, the solid gold Rolex President, and the obligatory mobster diamond pinkie ring, the whole look. I even drove a new Cadillac Escalade that I rented at the airport.

Delicacy is the hallmark of a successful undercover operation. Instead of trying to do a deal with Freddy right away or shake him down, I just said to him, "I'm Big Jack—Ronnie's uncle. I'm from New York. I heard great things about you from him, and I know you did certain deals with him. He's in jail, but he's doing well, and he just wanted me to say hello. He said you were one of the good guys down here."

It was apparent from his body language that Freddy's defenses were up. But I wasn't talking about stealing or dirty cops. I was just saying that I had come from New York and I heard he was a good stand-up guy and I wanted to introduce myself. Take it easy. That was my whole message. I never wanted to scare a guy when I was just doing hellos.

I went back to Freddy's store a couple of weeks later. By now I was immersed in the Naked Truth case and was also working the corrupt politicians and the Asian counterfeiters out of Atlantic City, not to mention the smaller buy-busts and some other cases too. So I had a pretty full plate as an undercover.

"Listen," I told Freddy, "something's come up. I'm looking to buy my girlfriend something. I'm just looking for a trinket, something nice."

As it happened, Freddy had something to fit my needs—a lovely piece of jewelry, which was undoubtedly stolen, that he offered to me for eight hundred dollars.

"That's a beautiful thing," I said. "You're bailing me out of a jam. Thank you."

"Don't worry about it," Freddy said. "By the way, we make jewelry too. Maybe we can make something up nice for your girlfriend sometime." I pulled out my broccoli-rubber-band knot and counted off eight one-hundred-dollar bills.

I said to him, "Yeah, maybe," and I left.

On my next trip to Miami, I went back to his store, this time not to buy anything but just to get to know him better, pay a social call. I invited him to get together and have a drink. I was courting him, and I could tell that he was feeling more relaxed around me. He dropped hints that he suspected I was a mobster from New York. He would say things like "You've gotta have friends down here—you must know this guy, so-and-so," and he would drop the name of some knockaround guy or other whom I truly didn't know.

"No," I would tell him, "I don't know him. In fact, I don't know anybody. I've got no friends. Nobody likes me. You're the only guy I know down here! That's how fucked up I am!"

That cracked him up. It didn't make sense to him that somebody as personable as the character he was getting to know could have no friends in a place like South Florida. He knew that this was something a mobster would say to have him not ask questions.

Normally, when I went into situations like this, I wore a wire. But this was a jewelry store with a metal detector—every time I entered the store or the adjacent factory, I'd have to pass through a magnetometer, which would have picked up my wire. Before long, Freddy didn't make me go through it—he thought I wasn't a threat. I wasn't just befriending Freddy. I was seeking to make an impression on his whole staff. I did little favors like buying a whole box of cannoli and bringing them to the staff.

"Hey, look what I got here!" I'd announce jovially, doing my whole song-and-dance.

This went on and on until the point when I felt I could walk in anytime and just talk to Freddy, friend to friend. And then there came the moment when I knew that I could essentially seduce him: cross the line from friendship into criminal activity. This moment is indefinable—it has to be left to the discretion of the undercover. It's just a sense that develops after years on the job. It comes from listening, having cocktails with the target, hanging around him. The main thing is that the guy has to like the undercover's personality.

The right moment had come, and I took him into my confidence.

"Listen," I said, "I've got a situation on my hands. Don't ask too many questions. I know you did some things with my nephew. I want to know if you can do something for me."

I could see it in his eyes—greed kicked in immediately.

"What do you got?" he asked.

This is the moment when people ask if we aren't entrapping ourselves. Here's the distinction. If the guy isn't interested, he'll say, "Get out of here! I'm not into that! Get away from me!"

That's what an honest person does. A person open to criminal activity will continue the conversation and pursue the subject. Entrapment would be where the target would say, "I've got no interest—get away," and I would pursue it over and over again: "You've got to do this with me. I need you to. Please. You've got to help me."

If you're trying to wear down an individual who has no interest in criminal activity, that's entrapment. But simply making someone an offer—that's legitimate law enforcement. If a person is predisposed to commit a crime and we offer the opportunity, that's not entrapment. If he is not predisposed and we push the opportunity over and over again, then it is. I didn't have to do any pushing with Freddy. He was on board from the start. I had him at "Listen."

I had with me a brown bag containing a bunch of jewelry that the FBI had seized during various investigations, mostly stuff forfeited by drug dealers. There was a solid gold ring with the word "SEXY" on it, big crucifixes, large names like "Foxy" emblazoned on necklaces—the gaudiest stuff you've ever seen, but it was solid gold.

"Oh, man, look at this shit!" Freddy exclaimed. "I can't move this stuff—I gotta melt it down."

"Look, I understand," I replied. "If you've gotta give me scrap value, that's fine."

When gold jewelry is too hard for a fence to move, the answer is to weigh it, melt it down, and sell it as scrap metal at the current gold market price. And that's what Freddy's intent was right now. He had the jeweler's scale and together we weighed the gold.

He offered me a price that I thought was ridiculously low. "You're killing me! That's all you're going to give me per pennyweight? I could get more from my guy in New York—but I wanted to move this stuff here in Florida because it was hot up north."

We went back and forth and finally settled on five thousand dollars for the lot. He told me that he only had a couple of thousand on him and asked me to come back the next day, when he gave me the rest of the money, all in hundreds. The weird thing was that he liked a chain that was part of the package. He put it on and always wore it for the rest of the time that I knew him.

"I appreciate this," I said.

"No, anytime you have a brown bag like this, let me know," he said.

Now, obviously, we could have scooped him up for fencing jewelry right then and there, but he wasn't the object of the case. The real object was the dirty cops he employed. And before long, sure enough, he started telling me about the dirty cops he worked with, the ones who helped him out. That is exactly what I wanted to hear about. So he was telling me these wild stories—

one time, he went to the Hollywood Police Department in order to take inventory of some seized property. He said he saw cops stealing jewelry out of the evidence locker, right in front of him. Now I had him right where I wanted him. I told him, "Listen. Once in a while, I may need some protection. I may have a tractor-trailer of hot stuff I'm moving north and the driver may need to get a few hours of shut-eye before driving up there. I don't want it to get pinched by the cops or other thieves while he sleeps."

"I got some guys," he said.

"Who do you got?" I asked.

"Come back tomorrow," he said. "Just keep in mind, these guys don't want to know and don't care what's inside the truck. They're just gonna watch it. So don't tell them anything and they won't ask you nothing!"

The "guys" to whom he was referring were the Hollywood Police Department cops. But it wasn't acceptable for me to have the cops not know what was in the truck. There's no crime in guarding a truck if you don't know that there's contraband in it.

"They've gotta know what's in there," I countered. "I can't have them finding religion at the last minute and having them arrest me and seizing my stuff!"

"No problem," Freddy assured me. "They won't, I know these guys. You tell me what time you want them here. They're not going to ask you for a manifest, a bill of lading or nothing."

So we made the agreement. The following week I

would arrive with a tractor-trailer. It would be empty, with a seal on it, so I would know if anybody had looked inside. If the cops opened it up, I would have said, "I didn't trust them, Freddy, and I was just testing them."

Sure enough, the next week I arrived with my tractor-trailer and parked it behind Freddy's business for twenty-four hours. Uniformed members of the Hollywood, Florida, Police Department watched my empty tractor-trailer truck for twenty-four hours. The rate of pay to which we had agreed was thirty dollars an hour, but the cops told me they wanted thirty-eight an hour—that way they could declare it as income and pay taxes on it. So, if something was to happen to them, they could get their benefits—they were entitled to work off duty. But for an obvious criminal like me?

When I arrived on the scene, I saw the cops, in uniform, watching my truck pull into the parking lot. I was in a black Cadillac Escalade. I was dressed like a criminal—a guayabera shirt, lots of jewelry. I had my hair greased back, a pinkie ring on, and a solid gold Rolex President! What the fuck! I was thinking, I walk like a mobster, I talk like a mobster—I must be a mobster! These cops weren't stupid. They knew what a criminal looked like, how he carried himself. The secrecy of guarding a truck in a desolate parking lot. Come on! And yet, they were treating me as if I were a legitimate businessman who needed their legitimate services.

The individual playing the driver of the tractor-trailer was another agent from the Miami office. He had long hair, and I asked him not to shave for three days. I brought him over to the cops and said, "This is my driver. I want him to get a good night's sleep, because he's got a big drive tomorrow. I want you to watch the truck so he can get some sleep."

Nobody asked for the manifest, the bill of lading, the license, or the registration. And this was the Hollywood Police Department! So I was hanging out with the cops, buying them coffee; I didn't say anything meaningful to them. My sixth sense told me not to take the step—it wasn't time yet. I was simply establishing my bona fides for future deals.

At the end of the twenty-four-hour period, the truck left for its journey "up north," and I paid off the guys.

Freddy's constant refrain was the cops didn't want to know that the goods in the truck were hot. And I kept saying, "I need them to know what it was, because I don't trust them." And that's how it went. Freddy wasn't in business by himself. He had a brother, a guy we'll call Stevie. Stevie was a player, slick as hell, a wannabe wiseguy. He was fascinated with criminals, but he was a punk. He'd always try to spar with me, to act as if he were my equal, like he was connected too. He was enamored of me, wanting to be like me, but wanting to impress me at the same time. I really felt like smacking this guy a couple of times, and then one day he walked in with a black eye. With an attitude like his, I wasn't surprised.

"I told you somebody would smack you around!" I chided him.

So there I was with Freddy and Stevie, and it was time to take another step forward.

"I got a problem," I told Freddy one day. "I've got a guy who owes me money. I want to bring someone in as a deterrent. What about a guy coming with me, in uniform? 'Cause these mopes might want to whack me, and I may have to crack this guy one."

"That's fine," Freddy said. "I know this guy, he's like you. His name is Kevin Companion. He's a detective with the Hollywood Police Department."

"That's great," I said. "Have him meet us at the Mamma Mia restaurant tomorrow at noon."

This was a good Italian joint not far from the jewelry store.

We set it up this way: We had another undercover agent, a Spanish guy, who looked like a doper, showing up at the bar. He was a very good undercover. "Do me a favor," I said. "When you come into the restaurant, go by the bar. I'm gonna approach you, get a little animated, smack the bar, yell at you a little bit."

He understood.

So the next day, at a quarter to twelve, I went to the jewelry store, and there was Kevin the cop, with the two brothers. The nice brother, Freddy, stayed behind, while the wannabe tough-guy brother, Stevie, came with us. Kevin was dressed in the Hollywood PD's summer uniform—a white polo shirt that said POLICE on the back, along with his badge and gun. I was dressed in a black shirt, black pants: the attire of a New York gangster.

"Okay, listen," I explained to Kevin. "I don't know if this is gonna get ugly, but with you here, it's gonna be okay. I just have to talk to this guy, the Spanish guy. When he comes in, we'll see if he gets out of line."

"I'll make sure you're protected," Kevin assured me.

We drove to the restaurant and sat in the front near the bar. Kevin was not hinked up in any way—he was not suspicious in the least. He acted like he was out on a lunch date. It was no big deal. And I couldn't have looked more like a wiseguy if I tried.

We sat at the bar, waiting for the other undercover to walk in, and guess who breezed into the restaurant: the chief of police and four or five captains. They walked into the freaking restaurant to have lunch! I didn't know any of those guys, because I was from New York. But Kevin did.

"Oh, shit!" Kevin exclaimed. "My chief is here!"

I thought the operation was over. Kevin was going to run like crazy. He couldn't be seen by his bosses in the presence of a wiseguy like me, could he? But what did Kevin do? He *introduced* me to the chief and the other police officials! I couldn't believe it! As if I were an acquaintance of Kevin's and we were going to have lunch!

The chief even said to Stevie, "I may come by and see you this week. I gotta buy a gift."

I couldn't believe it.

The chief took a table about twenty feet from ours, and I knew it was about to get interesting. I said to Kevin, "Listen, let's get the fuck outta here!"

"Don't worry about it!" he reassured me.

"Don't worry about it?" I repeated, incredulous.

"Yeah, everything's cool," Kevin said.

"How can you *not* be worried about it?" I asked, but before Kevin could reply, my undercover came in.

I threw a look to Kevin and Stevie indicating that this was the guy and they should stay at the table. I sauntered over to the undercover and glanced back at our table. Kevin was fixated on me. I had to admit, he was doing his job perfectly, keeping his eye on me.

I put my hands on the undercover's shoulders, like I was upset with him. We had an animated conversation—at least, I had an animated talk with him. To Kevin, and to anyone else who was watching, it looked as if I were saying "You better not fuck with me, pal!"

The undercover gave me an envelope and took off. I went back to the table with Kevin and Stevie and resumed eating.

Kevin was pleased—he hadn't needed to get involved. It all got handled. Well, of course he didn't need to get involved. The whole point of this was to hire him, in uniform, to baby-sit an obvious drug transaction. And it worked out just fine.

Here's the best part—when the bill came, I said, "Let me handle this."

"Make sure they give you a discount," Kevin said. "They always give us a twenty percent discount!"

"Damn, that's a good deal!" I marveled. In days gone by, cops ate free at every restaurant. That's just how it was, but today, police officers generally are not permitted to accept free meals or even discounts.

"Yeah, all the restaurants give us discounts," Kevin told me.

I paid, and Kevin said his good-byes to the Hollywood Police administration. Then we walked back to my car, which was parked in the street across from the restaurant. Stevie took off somewhere else. I drove Kevin back to the jewelry store and paid him the two hundred dollars to which we had agreed. Kevin looked about cautiously as he accepted the money. "Next time, give the money to Stevie. Just in case the Feds are taking pictures."

Now, from a law enforcement standpoint, we had a case against Kevin, right then and there: What could he possibly have thought he was protecting if not a drug deal? But this was only the beginning of the operation. We wanted to reach as deeply as possible into this apparent morass of corruption. We wanted to see where it led.

It was also the beginning of my friendship with Kevin. I've got to say that he was one of the most likable and funniest guys you'd ever want to meet. He could bust your balls and have you laughing out loud at the same time. He also had an undying fascination with organized crime. He just loved to talk about it. He loved knowing a guy like me. He could—and frequently did—recite entire scenes to me from *Scarface* and *The God-*

father. He had the dialogue of those movies cold, and he had the accents perfected as well. He'd say things like "I made him an offer he couldn't refuse!"

I would say to him, "Kevin, what the fuck do you do all day, just sit home and watch this shit?"

He'd laugh, and he'd put on that show all the time. Detective Companion loved all things Italian, to the point where he had an Italian flag on his car and used the voices of Dean Martin and Frank Sinatra on his cell phone, for voice mail messages. He even liked to tell people that he had driven to California to attend the funeral of his idol, Frank Sinatra.

So now Kevin and I were friends, and as far as investigating corruption in the department, the sky was the limit.

Until I got back to the office.

The SAC—the Special Agent in Charge of the Miami office at that time—got it into his head that this case was moving too slowly.

Suddenly, instead of fighting dirty cops, I was back to the tired old business of fighting bureaucrats.

"What do you mean, it's moving too slowly?" I asked, incredulous. "It's perfect! The corruption is systemic throughout the whole police department! We've heard from numerous sources just how corrupt these guys are. You can't just throw a rope around them all at once. Something like this takes time to develop."

The SAC couldn't be shaken. "It's moving too slowly," he said. "Unless you ask them to drive a drug load for you now, I'm gonna shut the whole case down!"

I tried to explain to him that you can only gain the trust of a bad guy very slowly . . . and with dirty cops even more slowly! Our arguments were not successful. The SAC closed the case. And yet, for the next year and a half, while I was hanging out with DePalma, I occasionally received voice mails and calls from Freddy— did I have any more jewelry to sell? Did I have any more jobs for the police? Kevin was asking for you! It was so incredibly frustrating. It was a perfect case, shut down by the bureaucracy within the FBI, which often allows people with little or no street experience to be in charge of critically important cases.

When a new SAC was appointed in Miami a year and a half later, he started a push for opening bigger and better cases. Special Agent Mario Tariche, the same guy who had been my case agent on the Willy Falcon and Sal Magluta case, became a supervisor. As good an agent as he was, he was equally as good as a supervisor. His first order of business was to reopen the case of the corrupt cops of Hollywood, Florida. Together Mario Tariche and Kevin Luebke called me asking whether I thought I could resuscitate the investigation and infiltrate the Hollywood PD. So I packed my bags and headed down to Hollywood, where I again met up with Freddy the jewelry dealer and Kevin Companion, the dirty cop. Before long, it was as if I had never left—we were talking about doing all kinds of criminal things together.

Because of my work schedule with the Gambino case, Royal Charm, Steal Pier, and a major drug case out of the New York office, I didn't have the time to devote to the Hollywood case. So I introduced as my "crew" FBI undercover agents, guys I trusted and had the utmost respect for: my friends and undercover partners Mikey "Suits" Grimm and FBI agents Dave and Joe. I told the bad guys that I had been promoted to capo in order to explain why I was handing off some of my responsibilities to these other supposed mobsters. I continued to appear for the important meetings, where we made payoffs or invited Kevin Companion to add another cop to the team.

As I expected, Companion, the rest of the Hollywood cops in his crew, and the guys who owned the jewelry store accepted these three undercover FBI agents completely. My guys gave the bad cops "stolen" diamonds, art, and securities, which the cops drove to Atlantic City. Our guys always told the cops that it was stolen—all contraband. This never bothered the cops, because they were making money with each trip.

We kept on doing more transportation runs, because with each new truckload, we had Kevin Companion add another cop to the scenario. We wanted to flush out all of the bad cops from the Hollywood PD. Entrapment? Of course not! What's a cop supposed to say when he's offered the opportunity to run stolen goods out of state? He's supposed to say "Fuck you, you're under arrest!" This wasn't entrapment. It's law enforcement.

One time I told Companion, "You've been very

helpful. If the books ever open up down the line, there's a chance that I could bring you in."

In other words, I was telling him that at some point, he could be proposed for membership in the Mafia. Where did I learn to sound like a Mob capo? From the master himself: from Greg DePalma. I was just repeating to Kevin the exact words that Greg had spoken to me.

"You never know," I told him.

"I would be honored," Companion practically gushed. "I'll do anything for you. I'll run your Florida crew from down here. I'll go up to New York and work for you up there."

He had no idea he was setting himself up for a decade in prison, not for his button in the Mob. One of the other dirty cops in the case, Tommy Simcox, who later agreed to cooperate with the FBI, showed us just how deeply Kevin believed that he would become a made member of the Mafia. Simcox told the FBI case agents that Kevin told him and the other bad cops that Jack was going to get Kevin straightened out. How insane was this police department! Not one of the cops apparently batted an eyelash at Kevin's remarkable news about his future in organized crime.

Kevin would say, "I've got plenty of guys who'll come on board, but they don't want to know what they're transporting and that it's stolen."

I would say, "That's not okay. I don't want guys suddenly getting religion on me. If they're in, they've got to be in all the way."

Kevin kept demanding to know why he wasn't making more money from what he and the other cops were doing.

"You want to make more money," I told him, "you gotta touch powder." That means, you've got to get involved with helping us run heroin from Florida to New York.

Kevin shook his head. "I'd rather not touch powder or be in the same car as it," he said. "If we get stopped and they find it in our vehicles, even our badges can't get us out of that."

"Who said anything about having it in your vehicles?" I replied. "You can just escort it."

All he had to do was provide security or protection for the load.

His eyes lit up. "Escort it? No problem! We could do that!"

And they did.

The dirty cops watched as undercover FBI agent Joe put suitcases containing ten kilos of heroin into the car of another FBI undercover agent playing the role of the Colombian supplier. Joe, Dave, and I then got into my rented Hummer H2 and watched the cops, driving in four rental cars, playing leapfrog up I-95 from North Miami to Hollywood, to the rear loading dock of a store there. Kevin had given us walkie-talkies. We recorded all their transmissions and kept in touch with them throughout the whole escort to Hollywood.

Having worked dope for twenty years, I can tell you that the way the cops operated was perfect from a tactical point of view. One cop pulled over on the highway to make sure that no one was following. They were acting like seasoned dope transporters. When I do drug cases, I'm usually involved just at the point of delivery of the dope, not along for the ride. This was bizarre to me, seeing cops playing the part of bad guys perfectly (while at the same time, we FBI agents were playing the part of bad guys too, but not for real).

When the cops went to a hotel in Hollywood to meet up with us and get paid, undercover agents Dave and Joe took them up to my room one at a time. I was there with stacks of hundred-dollar bills, and I paid off each of the officers . . . in view of a hidden video camera, which captured the entire scene. They all believed they had escorted ten keys of heroin. In keeping with the wishes of the Assistant U.S. Attorney prosecuting the case, we told them exactly what they were protecting, before and after the run, and not one of them raised a murmur of complaint.

Even more surprising, in the hotel room, I remember telling Kevin Companion, "We're giving this one cop eight thousand dollars." And he told me, "Nah, just give him six. Fuck him."

Again, we got all of the payoffs on video, and we had a solid case against the cops, but it was still a very depressing day for law enforcement. I mean, these were police officers . . . happily getting paid by "mobsters" to move real, live heroin! Heroin kills! We built a solid case . . . but it wasn't a pleasant experience.

Throughout the case, Kevin always talked about

getting straightened out and running a crew of dirty cops for me. As I've said, there's never a shortage of ass-kissers, wannabes, groupies—whatever you want to call them—who are fascinated with wiseguys. But these were *cops*! And these were the good guys that little kids want to grow up to be like?

Four Hollywood police officers were charged with the sale and interstate transport of stolen property, protecting a crooked high-stakes gambling enterprise, cargo theft, transportation of heroin, and the protection and transportation of stolen bearer bonds. Kevin Companion had been on the force for twenty years when he was indicted. The three other officers had fifteen years, twenty-four years, and eight years respectively on the force. The total amount of bribes paid to the Hollywood police officers fell just below $100,000 for all four men. The actual amounts: Kevin Companion, $42,000; Jeffry Courtney, $22,000; Thomas Simcox, $16,000; and Stephen Harrison, $12,000. For these relative pittances, each of the four men faced life in prison.

A coda to this case brought even more discredit to the Hollywood police (if that's even possible). The FBI brought word of this investigation to the chief of police in Hollywood—on a confidential basis, of course. Before we flipped Simcox, we set up a meeting with Kevin. We were actually scheduled to meet him to plan our next escort of contraband with the aid of additional cops, but he did not return our calls. Within days, we found out that they failed to return our calls because

Kevin Companion and Jeffry Courtney resigned from the department and filed their retirement papers in order to protect their pensions. Somebody had clearly gotten word to them about who we really were. There was an internal leak inside the Hollywood PD.

Thank God these cops were not cold-blooded killers, otherwise they might have kept the meeting and silenced our testimony by giving us two to the back of the head.

How did they find out about the case? The chief, we later learned, told no less than eight individuals, including the mayor, the city manager, and members of his staff, including a major in the department, about the FBI investigation. The major told a lieutenant, who told an officer . . . who told Courtney, who told Companion. Simcox was already cooperating with us, so Companion and Courtney left the fourth member of their enterprise, Stephen Harrison, out to dry. Those involved in the leak were demoted and suspended from the force for thirty days and could have been charged with obstruction of an investigation. The lieutenant, who was arrested for lying to FBI agents about his involvement in the leak, pleaded guilty.

CHAPTER SiXTEEN

I Could Die as Jack Falcone!

After all those breakfasts, lunches, and dinners with the Mob, my weight zoomed perilously close to the dreaded 450-pound mark. I knew that I was putting a lot of strain on my heart. At the FBI, we were required to take physicals every year, and they sent us to this exclusive place in Manhattan where we took a whole battery of medical tests. It was really first class. The only problem was that my birthday fell right around the end of the fiscal year, so every year for six or seven years running, the FBI had canceled my physical on the grounds that there was no money left in the budget for such things. This was actually a good thing for me, because if I had taken my physical, I would have gotten hassled all over again for my weight. My attitude was, I'm out here in the streets working, why should they care how much I weigh, or what I look like?

One day I mentioned to Greg that I was thinking of scheduling a physical examination. This was over a meal in mid-December 2003.

"I'm thinking about seeing a cardiologist," I told him.

"You've got insurance from the union," he reminded me. "Hey, I know a great cardiologist. Let's all go see him!"

And so it was decided—the whole crew would troop over to the office of the cardiologist, whom we'll call Dr. Medavoy, and we would all have our hearts checked out.

"We're all gonna go," Greg announced grandly. "Jackie boy, I want you around for a long time!"

And so I went for the test, courtesy of my union-provided health insurance. Dr. Medavoy turned out to be a nice man, very sharp. I went in and he checked me out, and boom—he found I had atrial fibrillation. It's a heart condition that requires taking medication. He gave me three different prescriptions, and I took them regularly, but I had reactions. I went back to the doctor and he told me that he wanted to give me a contrast echocardiogram, a stress test. The problem was that his machine could handle only those individuals who weighed three hundred pounds or less. So we set up an appointment with another cardiologist, this time at New York Hospital in Manhattan.

I went down there, still using my Jack Falcone identity and my union insurance. They shaved my chest, put on the electrocardiogram pieces, and ran the test. Suddenly all these doctors come in, all talking at once.

"Excuse me, Mr. Falcone?" one said. "You're aware that you have atrial fibrillation?"

I nodded.

"We can't give you this test! Your resting heartbeat is 220! The normal for a man your age is 80! You're going straight to the emergency room!"

That got my attention. "You got to be kidding me!" I exclaimed.

"Don't you feel it?" asked the doctor. "We're admitting you to the emergency room! We called Dr. Medavoy, and that's how it's going to be."

I was terrified. They took me downstairs to the emergency room in a wheelchair, and this was a New York City emergency room: there were people seriously wounded, bleeding, and all sorts of horrible things going on. Suddenly I was placed on a gurney, with IVs coming out of my arm, and I had so many nurses and doctors all around me poking and prodding me that I thought to myself, What's going on here? I've got monitors and needles everywhere—I'm a mess!

My wife didn't even know where I was, and I couldn't call her. I couldn't use a phone at that point, because I was tied up to all this medical equipment. And if you use a cell phone in a hospital, everybody goes bananas. I was certain that Dr. Medavoy called Greg DePalma, who would come over with other members of the crew. So I sneaked a call to the doctor. I told him what had happened and that my heart rate had dropped to a healthier range and that I was leaving the hospital. He told me to come see him the next morning. That was fine with me. I just didn't want him to tell Greg, because I didn't want Greg to tell me he wanted to scoop up my wife and kid and bring them to see me.

All of a sudden it dawned on me: I was lying there in the emergency room with an elevated heart rate, nobody knew where I was—not my wife, not anyone at FBI Headquarters. What if I die as Jack Falcone! I figured I'd just be there for an hour or so . . . but instead they kept me there for eight hours—eight long, long hours! It took that long for my heart rate to drop enough so I could leave.

This took place two days before Christmas. I had a lot of time to think while I lay on that gurney in the emergency room. I thought about my daughter. I thought about Christmas. I thought, Why the fuck am I doing this job? How did I let myself get so damn fat and out of shape! Am I fucking crazy over here? To die all alone in a hospital, unable to call my wife and daughter?

Finally they released me, but I knew that my troubles had only begun. I immediately called Nat Parisi and told him what happened.

I said, "Nat, you gotta promise me—I know how these fucking bosses are. As soon as they hear this, they're gonna pull me off this job."

"This *is* serious," Nat agreed. "The hell with the case! I'm worried about you!"

That was typical Nat, always looking out for me, a real stand-up guy!

"I want to make sure that you are okay and are going to seek medical attention," he said.

I promised him that I would.

Nat then said, "I'll see what I can do."

And then I made the call I dreaded making: I called my wife.

As I expected, when I told her about my heart problem, she went ballistic.

"That's it, you're done," she said. She was already mad at the Bureau because they never gave me the physicals. "For years they've been dodging you."

"I gotta get this resolved," I told her. "It's Greg's doctor. I've gotta go see him."

This really ticked my wife off. "You're gonna do *what*?" she shouted. "You're not gonna go see some Mafia cardiologist!"

"But what am I gonna do?" I implored. "Find a cardiologist in the Yellow Pages?"

"Well, why don't you?" my wife demanded.

"He's not a Mafia cardiologist," I tried to explain. "He is one of the best doctors in Westchester."

Perfect timing. At that moment, my two-way pager went off. It was Greg.

"You're not answering that call!" my wife said, already furious at the fact that she had nearly lost me not to an assassin's bullet but to the excess weight I was carrying around due to my constant socializing and dining with the wiseguys.

"I have to answer the call!" I replied. "Greg'll think I got scooped up by the cops."

"You're not going back to work this case," my wife told me. "It's done."

Somehow I managed to get her to rethink the whole thing, and she agreed to let me continue on the case. I called Greg later and told him what had happened. As predicted, Greg was angry as to why I had not called him to tell him I was in the hospital. Nat did a great job of keeping this whole ER visit in the background after I showed him a doctor's note that said I was okay as long as I took my medication. Nat made sure that the supervisory personnel only heard his sugarcoated version of what had happened. I went back to Dr. Medavoy, who gave me new meds and another series of exams. What a great doctor! His staff was so professional, I actually felt bad that they had to treat Greg, because he showed up whenever he felt like it. Greg didn't make appointments for doctors—he just went to their office when he wanted to, ignored the people in the waiting room, and went directly to see the doctor. I was always so embarrassed—we'd be walking past ten seniors sitting there waiting patiently and he would be just asking the receptionist, "Is he in?" She would nod, and he would walk right in. He had the biggest sense of entitlement that I had ever seen.

I would say to him, "Greg, don't you ever make appointments?"

"Fuck that!"

Ironically, when I went in by myself for an appointment, the staff would fall all over me, trying to give me the same treatment Greg expected. I would refuse and just wait my turn.

As an FBI agent, I couldn't even get a checkup. But thanks to the Mob, I had access to the best specialist in town.

I really think this whole sequence of events shows my dedication. Not to pat myself on the back, because maybe I'm an idiot. I trusted the doctor I met through the case, so I had to stay with him. That's what this case meant to me. After all, if the Bureau had pulled me from the project, I would have had to find another cardiologist.

There is a postscript to this story, a harrowing incident that happened a couple of days later. We were all having lunch—me, Greg, a few other guys. The whole crew.

Greg was so worried about me—you could see it in his eyes. "Jackie, are you all right?" he asked. "Everybody was concerned about you."

"Yeah, Greg, no big deal," I told him.

And then Greg dropped a bombshell on me. "We got a fucking rat among us."

Suddenly the laughter stopped and everybody was looking around. "We gotta make sure we take care of this guy," Greg insisted.

"What's going on? Who is it?" I asked innocently. "Who is it?"

Greg pointed a long finger at me. "It's you, Jack!" he said.

The whole point of my time in New York Hospital was to get my heart rate down, but now I was sure it was three hundred beats a minute! Suddenly I realized what he was talking about: the little box monitoring and recording my heart rate for twenty-four hours. That's what Greg was referring to. He wasn't referring to the actual recording device I had on me, as always when I was with him and the others.

"Oh yeah, you mean this!" I said, pointing to the medical device, and everybody had a good laugh.

I sat back and I thought to myself, Holy shit! That was a classic!

"You're going to be all right, kid!" the Old Man said, grinning at me, delighted with the extent to which he had terrified me. That was a deciding moment for me. I knew that if I could survive that moment, I could survive anything on the case. Any normal man would have had a heart attack on the spot.

CHAPTER SEVENTEEN

Meeting Robert Vaccaro

As I was providing new puzzle pieces to the Bureau about the Gambinos, the Bureau was also able to share new information with me. On one such occasion, Nat Parisi and Chris Munger informed me that FBI intelligence showed Greg hanging out with a couple of new guys. Our informants identified one of these people as a longtime wiseguy, Robert Vaccaro. On October 7, 2003, Greg came into the La Villetta restaurant, where I was, and introduced me to Robert. What Greg said was striking: "If something happens to me, you are to talk to him. He's the guy you'll be dealing with."

When I first met Robert Vaccaro, I knew very little about him. Even though he was a made guy, the FBI was unaware of his role in the Mob. He was the opposite of Greg DePalma—discreet, the way wiseguys were supposed to be. Greg might talk endlessly on his cell phone, but according to our informants, Vaccaro never used one. We found out later that he had a cell phone, he just never used it. He used a pager with a code system, the same way that dopers do. Everyone in civilized society had moved away from pagers to cell phones, but not Vaccaro. He was very cautious, especially around me in the beginning, until he felt good about me.

He was tall, balding, of average build, in his mid to late forties. He was not a man to be underestimated—there was something in his eyes, a seriousness of purpose, that I found chilling. Robert lived in a halfway house in New York because he was on parole, but he traveled at night, while the parole officers slept, to New Jersey and Connecticut to meet with the Gambino family administration: Squitieri and Megale.

So the question remained, who was this Robert Vaccaro and why was he suddenly in Greg's life? We put together a brief biography of him, based on what Greg said and what we were able to piece together from informants. Vaccaro had just finished serving fifteen years in the New York State prison system for selling heroin. (Once again, so much for the Mob's sanctimonious code against dealing in narcotics.) He then moved to the Gambino family in a trade—once in a while, the Mob traded members from one family to another. Greg told me as much. "He was a Luke"—short for Lucchese—"and now he came over to our side."

As best as we in the Bureau could determine, Vaccaro had two possible roles in Greg's life. One was to learn all of Greg's criminal activities, so that he could take over if Greg retired, died, or moved up the ladder to consigliere, underboss, or even boss. The second possibility was that Robert had been sent by the administration to learn everything about Greg . . . and then to whack him.

I wondered whether Robert intended to recruit me into his crew if Greg was taken out, or if he would whack me for being Greg's friend and confidant.

The funny thing was that Vaccaro took Greg to school on the modern ways of avoiding arrest. "Quit using the phone," Robert told him. "Look around when you're driving to see if you might have picked up a tail." Vaccaro explained that dry cleaning is the term cops use whenever wiseguys make sudden U-turns, changes of route, or even changes of cars to escape from law enforcement vehicles that might be following.

When Greg learned something new from Robert, he would tell me all about it, as if he had received breaking news about how to not get pinched.

"Jackie boy," he growled, "never use the phone when you're talking about business!"

I'd be like, "No shit, Sherlock! You're the guy who's always yapping on the phone."

Initially Greg maintained an ambiguous relationship with Vaccaro. He admired him as a mobster, but at the same time he was annoyed with the new guy's constant presence and potential threat he represented.

Greg was no fool. He didn't survive thirty years as a made member of the Mafia, and into his eighth decade, without being a shrewd judge of character. Okay, he misjudged me. But otherwise, Greg DePalma made very few mistakes.

There was a tension, therefore, between Robert and Greg, and it actually spilled over into my relationship with Greg. When I spent time with Robert, Greg became jealous.

"What are you hanging around with him all hours of the night for?" he would rasp. "Don't forget that I need you to be available for me."

Maybe he felt the two of us were going to gang up on him and squeeze him out. Who knew what was going through his mind? I knew that it was my job to find out more about Robert Vaccaro—who he was and what he was trying to do.

Robert was very close with the Gambino administration, and he was at first strictly business. He talked about Mob business with Greg, but only in the most cautious of ways. He whispered in Greg's ear even when there was practically no one else present, other than me. When other people were around, he took Greg to another table when he had something to say. I admired his coolness.

The small amount of money Robert made in the beginning never filtered through to Greg, which was a constant source of irritation to him. In all honesty, Greg never told me his real take on Robert. After a few months the sense of threat subsided, and he came to take a liking to Robert, but he considered him a brokester, a cross to bear, because he didn't constantly kick money up. Of course, it was unusual for a capo to have a made man in his crew who wasn't bringing in a lot of money, and that's why Robert's relationship with Greg always had its limits. And then, of course, Robert's presence was a constant reminder to Greg that he could be whacked or shelved at any time. No wonder the Old Man never felt completely comfortable around him.

I knew what buttons to push with Greg, but it was more difficult to get to know Vaccaro. That's why I started booking bets with him. He loved to talk about sports, and if you wanted to make him feel at ease, you talked about sports with him. The more time I spent with him, the more it became clear that he was a true blue, old-school mobster. His whole attitude was like he couldn't give a shit, couldn't care less about any of us, Greg, me, whoever. His demeanor practically shouted, "I got put in this crew, I don't know you guys from Adam, and I don't trust anyone, so let's just keep it at that."

Hey, if you're a mobster, that's the way you're *supposed* to act.

So now I was getting to know Vaccaro better, and because of the fact that I was betting sports with him, we had more to talk about. Because I was losing money with him, we had still more to discuss! It turned out that his betting operation was hooked into a multibillion-dollar offshore betting ring centered in Costa Rica. Small-time bookies always have the problem of needing to lay off bets, especially if their clientele is overbetting the favorite or the home team. So the Mob got together and established this computerized betting system in Costa Rica. As a gambler, you would be assigned a code name and code number. You'd call the 800 number, be patched through to Costa Rica, and someone there would ask for your name and number.

I was "the Falcon," and I had a four-digit number that went along with that. Once I identified myself in this manner, I could bet on anything under the sun— not just the outcome of games but all of the "propositions" that can be found in Las Vegas: who will win the coin toss, who's going to score the first touchdown, what the score will be at the end of the first quarter, anything I wanted. Every week the local bookie received a report from Costa Rica indicating how much each person won or owed, and how much the bookie himself owed or was due from the syndicate. It worked like a charm, and this was one of Vaccaro's principal criminal endeavors, as far as any of us could tell.

Vaccaro had a girlfriend who stood by him during his years in prison for his drug conviction. We'll call her Donna. She looked just like Marisa Tomei . . . and she nearly got me killed. Long before the Gambino case began, I frequented a bar-restaurant in New York where I knew a lot of people. I actually met Donna there on numerous occasions because she was a friend of the owner. She was also a niece or cousin of Gigi the Whale, one of the two guys in organized crime who definitely knew who I was.

Donna was always in this particular bar-restaurant in Manhattan. All I knew about her was that she was a girlfriend of a mobster who was doing time. I certainly knew nothing of Robert Vaccaro back then. I'd say hello and we would have brief, friendly conversations. She would always be with other people. I had to assume that she knew what I did for a living, because of Gigi. As it turned out, I was right.

Greg, Vaccaro, and I settled into something between an uneasy truce and an uneasy friendship. It was still a little tense, especially because of Greg's jealousy over anyone taking up any of my time. As my investigation of Robert went along, we discovered that his girlfriend was the same Donna I had known years earlier.

It was vital for me, therefore, to avoid her at all costs. As soon as she saw me, she would undoubtedly recognize me and put two and two together. I'm not suggesting that I'm unforgettable. It's just that there aren't too many guys my size walking around. So I would say to the guys things like "Isn't it great that it's just guys here? Who needs women around, with all those problems? It's simpler this way!" But despite that, I knew eventually the day would come when Donna and I would cross paths.

And indeed that day came. Robert mentioned that his girlfriend was trying to sell some fur coats and she wanted to get together with me to try to move them. Sure enough, the next day, Greg, two other guys, and I sat at our table at La Villetta. I sat where I always did—facing the door. A blue BMW pulled up in the parking lot, and out came Robert Vaccaro and Donna. I swallowed deeply. My mind raced. What was going to happen?

My typical plan—denying that I was Jack Garcia, FBI agent—wouldn't work. I knew she would expose me the moment she saw me. If she did, I would walk out the door of the restaurant, and that would be the end of the case. I can't even begin to describe the frustration and outright fear I felt. Not for my own life. I knew they wouldn't shoot an FBI agent. Greg wasn't that dumb. It's just that we had put so much effort into this case, and the opportunities it presented had expanded exponentially since the first day the owner of the Naked Truth had come to us. In the space of months, I moved from victim to acquaintance of Greg DePalma, one of the leading members of the Gambino crime family, to his associate, and I was on the verge of being made. And now it seemed everything would fall apart as soon as Donna laid eyes on me.

It could have been Gigi the Whale, it could have been Randy Pizzolo, and instead it was Donna. She and Vaccaro walked into the restaurant. He introduced me.

She didn't recognize me. She had absolutely no idea who I was. The meal passed pleasantly, everybody had a good time, a typical lengthy dining experience, wiseguy style. Lots of conversation, lots of laughs, lots of bullshit. But Donna didn't ID me.

Then it dawned on me—she was just playing it

cool, not wanting to make a scene in front of everybody. Of course, she would tell Vaccaro the minute she got out of the restaurant, and then Robert would tell Greg, and it would be all over.

I left the restaurant, grateful that I had not been exposed in front of all of these men. Maybe I was exaggerating my safety—maybe one of them would have pulled a gun on me had Donna fingered me. So that night I made a preemptive phone call to Greg, just to take his temperature, just to see what he had to say.

It was business as usual.

Before long, I realized that Donna actually had no idea who I was; if some memory existed somewhere in the recesses of her mind, it had not surfaced. I prayed it would not, because chances were we would cross paths again. The more I thought about it, the more I realized that every time I had seen Donna when Vaccaro was in prison, she appeared drunk. Certainly we had conversations, but if she was tipsy, it was unlikely that she would have remembered who I was or that we spoke. Thank God for alcohol, I thought. Otherwise, our case would have been cooked, and maybe I would have been, as well.

Or maybe she realized who I was but thought I had some dirt on her. After all, her boyfriend was in the joint and she was hanging around in a bar. To this day, it blows my mind that she didn't recognize me. I was a nervous wreck, and it always concerned me thereafter. Her memory would have to click in sooner or later. And yet it never did.

I survived the shock of seeing Donna, and after that the friendship between Robert and me only deepened. It got to the point where he wanted to do some deals with me. Two things he proposed were extremely intriguing. The first was to open up a Florida branch of the famous East Harlem Italian restaurant Patsy's. This is an old-time Italian pizza joint with a red-brick charcoal oven giving their pizza an extremely distinctive—and most delicious—taste. Vaccaro knew the owner, who told him he could open a branch in Miami. I practically salivated at the thought. Wire that up and we could shut down crime in all of South Florida. We could get to know all of the other guys down there—it would be huge.

The other project in which I believe Robert was trying to involve me was heroin. After he and I got to know each other, he confided that he had been a part of the Pizza Connection case in the 1970s in New York. The Pizza Connection was the name given to a massive criminal case involving the importation of heroin and the laundering of the money earned from it. The case got its name from the fact that pizza parlors were used as distribution points for the drugs that came from Sicily.

"I made a lot of money back then," he told me.

"You used to go to Sicily?" I asked.

He nodded. "Ten, twenty times."

"I'd love to go to the Old Country," I said as wistfully as I could manage. "I want to see it. I've never been there."

"You wanna go, we'll go," he replied.

This got me lit up. "You still know people over there?" I asked.

He nodded again. "Lots of people."

I wanted to go to Sicily to have Vaccaro introduce me to his connections over there. But we both had to dance around the subject very carefully, because of the Mob's taboo against dealing drugs. I was being proposed for membership in the Mafia, so I had to present the facade of an individual who eschewed the drug trade. Bunch of bullshit, but that's how the game was played.

In the space of about six months, Robert went from regarding me as a stranger and potential threat to a potential business partner, all because we talked sports, placed bets, and bounced around together.

One day in October 2004, Greg told me that he had made Robert his acting capo. I asked Greg what that meant. I pretended to be shocked by the news, because I wanted to get information. My role, of course, was to be a guy out of his culture. I knew the Cuban underworld, but I didn't know my Italian roots, so "Fuck, Greg, what's an acting capo?" Greg, as always, took great pleasure in educating me. He was a garrulous guy to begin with, and in me he had the perfect student—I drank up everything he taught me. He wasn't just educating me, of course. He was educating the entire FBI.

Greg explained that the Mafia was designating more and more acting positions because so many guys were getting arrested. If you have an "acting" guy, he's the one who becomes exposed to danger, not the real capo, boss, or underboss. When Greg sensed a problem that he didn't want to handle, or a guy that he did not want to meet, he sent Vaccaro to the sit-down in his place. The acting guy is the one who is exposed to the wiretaps and the informants. And when bad things happen, the acting is the first on the butcher block, the first guy to be cut down. In other words, the acting was the sacrificial lamb or the disposable mobster to the administration.

Vaccaro was present in his new role as acting capo the night we went to Bloomingdale's for the showdown with Petey Chops, which I describe in the prologue. But let me tell you now what happened after that confrontation. Even acting capos like Robert have their limits. Because Robert had struck Petey, a made man in the Gambino family, Arnold Squitieri, the Gambino crime family boss, would have to resolve the matter.

The repercussions of this event were twofold. First, Petey had a right to file a beef with the Gambino crime family boss, because as a made guy, he should not have been hit. And second, I believe that DePalma and Vaccaro questioned my legitimacy. I should have taken some licks on Petey myself. But somehow, they didn't push the issue, or the fact that on several other occasions I failed to beat up or kill other individuals as Greg ordered, and there were no repercussions. They never tried to kill me, and Greg's desire to have me made appeared undiminished. Was it paranoia on my part . . . or just my law enforcement training and experience that led me to think that I had blown my cover? Either way, I survived, and so did the case.

The next day I met Greg at the nursing home. He told me that Vaccaro had gone to the boss to talk it over.

"Jackie boy," he growled, "you don't understand. You're not supposed to put your hands on a made guy. You could get whacked for that. You can't do that."

"Greg, is he going to come out okay with this?" I asked.

"I got no idea," Greg admitted. "If Petey files a beef with the boss, he'd be told first to go to me, since I'm his skipper. And I'd squash the complaint right there and then. So I don't think he can complain to anybody about it."

"What a fucking asshole this Petey Chops is," I said, and Greg nodded sagely in agreement.

Nothing happened that day. Petey Chops didn't come in and report. We later found out he was at the doctor's office, getting bandaged up. He showed up the following day at the nursing home, bright and early, very apologetic. He actually asked Greg whether I was a made guy too. And sure enough, he began to make his payments to Greg. After all, what choice did Petey have? Could he go to the cops and say, "I got assaulted by Robert Vaccaro, Greg DePalma, and this big goon I didn't recognize, because I wasn't kicking up to the higher-ups in the Gambino family for my illegal book-making and loan-sharking operations?" Of course he couldn't.

Before long, Greg and Vaccaro became inseparable. Robert entered numbers in his pager to designate the place where he wanted to meet Greg—one was La Villetta, the restaurant. Two was Agostino's, on the Pelham/Bronx line. Three was Savini's, another restaurant. Four was the nursing home. And five was Bentley's Diner. Mob guys are creatures of habit. They are different from Colombian guys, who, sensing impending arrest, pack in the middle of the night and disappear. Dopers crave anonymity. Mobsters, on the other hand, crave the limelight. We in law enforcement know when they're getting up, we know where they're going, and we know where their girlfriends are. If we lose a mobster in a surveillance, we can find him again in ten minutes. Just like on TV or the movies, the Mob guys know the agents. There's a symbiotic relationship between the bad guys and the agents following them around. The Mob guys hate us, wish us every imaginable death . . . but they miss us when we're not around.

Along those lines, an undercover agent is only as good as his surveillance squad. Fortunately, we had a very good one. A lot of FBI guys think they're acting stealthily because they darken their car windows so no one can see inside. But when a car with darkened windows drives by, it's like having arrows pointing to the vehicle that say, "Here comes the FBI." Okay, people can't see our faces, but they can definitely notice a shiny, late-model, four-door American car with tinted windows!

Vaccaro was a master of countersurveillance. He

always dry-cleaned himself when he drove—sudden U-turns, all kinds of evasive tactics. He toyed with the agents who surveilled him, fucked with us, because that's what he was all about. I give him his due—not respect, but he was a good, quiet mobster and a loyal soldier. Greg, Robert, and I made quite the team.

The single most terrifying moment for me came when Greg called and told me that he wanted to see me right away. I rushed over, and he and Vaccaro piled into my H2 Hummer, Greg in the back and Robert in the passenger seat.

"We've got a rat among us," Greg began, staring angrily at me.

My stomach heaved. I racked my brain, trying to figure out what might have given away my identity as an FBI agent. Maybe it was Donna, or Gigi or Randy Pizzolo, or somebody I never heard of! I couldn't think of anything to say.

"Among us?" I asked, stalling for time, trying to think about my options.

Greg nodded slowly, and he was as angry as I had ever seen him. I could turn around to-ward Vaccaro and pop him in the face, and then I could jab Greg and get out of the car, but they would shoot me before I pulled off something like that. "Well, who is he, one of the guys in our crew?" I asked.

"No, he's a wiseguy," Greg said.

A wiseguy, meaning not an associate like me. A made man.

The sense of relief I felt was palpable. It wasn't me.

"It's the boss of the Bonannos," Greg said with disgust, referring to a rival crime family in New York. "Joe Massino. He's a fucking rat. He's being protected right now by a bunch of marshals. So nobody gets made for now. They're changing the rules. The next one in, it's you."

I had heard from him before that he would make me. He was educating me, but this time he said I was on the list to be made. This is the next step—a list circulated to all the family members and the other crime families to see if anybody had any dirt on the proposed guy. It usually is the last step before getting your button.

"Greg, I'll be honored," I said, as I always did when he said something along these lines.

"Are you sure you want it?" Greg would ask, testing me.

"Of course!"

Vaccaro said nothing—this was the capo's forum, and it wasn't for a soldier to speak.

I nodded, kept my mouth shut, and drove. This conversation left me with a lot to digest. It meant that my apprenticeship with Greg was going so smoothly that he decided to put me up for membership as a fully made member of the Mafia. At the same time, I was still coming down from the rush of emotions that had been triggered by his revelation that there was a rat . . . and then the realization that he hadn't figured out that it was me.

In just a few seconds, I went from believing that

I was in grave danger, to incredible relief, to absolute shock at the idea that he was going to propose me for membership in the Gambino family. To be honest, I didn't know what to think, so I kept my mouth shut. That's always the smartest thing to do.

Naturally, I turned to Nat and Chris and said, "Guys, we gotta record the ceremony!"

They both agreed, but we were all concerned that I would be either patted down at the ceremony or be stripped down naked as Greg had told me some families were now doing during the induction ceremony.

But as the unprecedented event of an FBI agent becoming a made member of the Mob drew closer, there was an even bigger surprise. Maybe they were scared. Or maybe they figured they had already assembled enough cases to advance their own careers. But for whatever reason, the higher-ups in the FBI wanted to shut down the entire case.

INTERLUDE FOUR

The Case of the Curious Cabbie

He was dark-complected, of average height and weight, with a distinctive accent. He walked into a computer store in Queens explaining that he had a problem with his computer—he wanted to make it go faster.

"No problem," the owner of the cramped storefront shop told him. "Anything else I can help you with?"

The man nodded. There was something strange about him to begin with—it was a hot day, and he was wearing an overcoat, practically never taking his hands out of his pockets. He was humorless and had kind of a glazed expression in his eyes. A scary guy.

"There is one other thing," the stranger said. "I'm trying to get to a website called the Anarchist's Cookbook, and I can't find it on the Internet. Maybe you can help me."

This set off alarm bells in the storeowner's mind. "What does that website do?" he asked.

"It teaches you how to make bombs," the guy said, in the eerie flatline tone of voice that told the store owner he was for real.

"Bombs? What do you want to make bombs for? What do you do for a living?"

"I'm a cab driver in the city."

Well, the storeowner took the man's computer and promised to speed it up. He watched the fellow drive off in his taxi, and then he made a phone call to the FBI. As it happens, the store was a sideline for the shop owner, whose main job was with the Department of Corrections in New York.

So there I was, working DePalma and the Mob guys, the bad cops in Florida, Royal Charm and the Asian counterfeiters and currency and weapon importers, and the corrupt officials in Atlantic City. So my friend Tom Donlon, who at the time was the ASAC, Assistant Special Agent in Charge of the Terrorism Branch and the Joint Terrorist Task Force, and SA Todd Renner, the Case Agent, turned to me and said:

"Got a minute?"

I knew what that meant.

"We've got a guy acting squirrelly, going into a computer store, won't take his coat off, he's asking for a bomb book. We think you ought to go talk to the guy."

"I think I should talk to him, too," I said, and the next day I headed out to this mom-and-pop computer store in Queens. I knew that if I became serious about the case, it would be a full-fledged involvement. So I had to fudge the truth with my higher-ups—just tell them it would be a few cameo appearances, so they wouldn't jump to the conclusion that I was stretched too thin. Sometimes I went into the office from eight until noon, just to be seen, and then I'd go home and take a nap, change, and go out and work. That happened a lot, and it wore me down. But I loved undercover work so much that it was worth it to me.

I arrived at the computer store in Queens. The entrance was so small that I had to bend over and I barely fit in. I was there when the cabbie returned to pick up his computer.

As soon as I saw him, I thought to myself, Oh, boy. Here we go.

I'm not trying to engage in any racial or ethnic profiling, but it was immediately evident that the guy came from somewhere in Afghanistan or Pakistan or somewhere like that. What did I know about that stuff? I was just a neighborhood wiseguy. I was playing a guy from the neighborhood who knows everything that goes down. I met the guy and I was pretty free with my *dese* and *dose*—just trying to sound like a local tough guy. Nothing too high up the wiseguy food chain.

"Dis here's my neighborhood," I told him in my best fractured Brooklynese. "You're lookin' for a bomb? You better not be blowin' up bombs around here. I hear you want an Anarchist's Cookbook."

"I'm looking to make explosives," he confided.

"Explosives, for what?" I asked him. "What are you, fucking crazy?"

"I want to knock down something as big as a mountain," he explained, which only set off more alarm bells. This took place in 2003, less than eighteen months after 9/11.

"You're wasting your time with that Anarchist's Cookbook bullshit," I told him. "You need a degree from MIT to navigate that website. Listen, I can get you some C-4 explosives from a construction site."

"Really?" he asked, intrigued.

"Sure," I told him. "Hey, that Anarchist's Cookbook is rudy-mentary,'" I told him. "Gimme your number and I'll get back to youse."

And he did.

A week later I called him and told him to come back to the store. We did a little walk-and-talk over to the McDonald's, where we had a surveillance team in place to photograph him. I told him I could get anything else he needed in addition to the explosives. "What do you want?"

He wanted a lot—night-vision goggles, five bullet-proof vests, a camera that you can put on a car dashboard, and, on top of all that, some sleeping pills. He was having a hard time sleeping, and he needed some pills so he could relax.

Well, this guy looked like a suicide bomber all the way. Now, imagine being on his surveillance team—we had him covered day and night after that meeting. The team would watch him go down into the subway with his coat on, on a scorching hot day. Just plain scary. We followed him around New York, kept an eye on him, as he drove his cab, just watching his other contacts. But despite our best efforts, we lost him.

To our surprise, the guy resurfaced a week later in Miami. He had been arrested after taking a tourist boat tour of Miami Harbor. He asked the guy who ran the tour boat how close they could approach a bridge, or how close they could get to a cruise ship. He took pictures of infrastructures that had nothing to do with the typical tourist sites when you take a boat ride—like Shaquille O'Neal's house, or whatever.

So the guy running the tour boat panicked and called the Coast Guard, which brings in the FBI, who arrested him. They held him and took his film, but they released him. He was here legally, as it turned out, and there was no law against videotaping bridges in major metropolitan areas.

Well, he returned to New York, and now we knew a lot about him. His name was Sayed Abdul Malike, he was forty-three years old, and he had a reputation in his neighborhood in Queens for having a ton of women going through his apartment. He was just a weird guy, according to the neighbors. One neighbor, a sixteen-year-old kid, asked him if he was a terrorist. Sayed looked him dead in the eye and said, "Yes."

"You're Saddam Hussein!" the kid told him, whereupon Sayed went nuts.

"I AM *NOT* SADDAM HUSSEIN!" he exploded. "Never call me that! Your day is coming soon!"

Soon after, I met with Sayed again at the computer store and we traced the same route to McDonald's. I told him that I had ten thousand dollars' worth of C-4 bricks—explosives—that I had from a construction site.

"I can't take it," Sayed said. "I can't keep it in my house."

Now I'm annoyed. "Well, what am I gonna do with it?" I asked.

But he refused to take it. We wanted him to get it so that we could scoop him up for purchasing explosives, which, of course, is illegal unless you have a valid license and purpose. But no dice. We called it a day, and I left.

Then he reached out to me again, asking how he could obtain bulletproof vests, night-vision goggles, a camera for the car, and Valium and Ambien. The kind of camera he wanted was the one that police officers use—they mount it on the dashboard and record everything that happens outside the vehicle. When we put everything together—the vests, the explosives, the camera, the night goggles—it pointed in only one direction. He's planning some sort of operation at night, he's going to blow something up, he's got a team of guys who will be working with him, and he wants to record the whole thing on his camera, so that he can put the video out for propaganda purposes for whatever shadowy organization he represents. Well, this guy was just too freaky for us. We had to take him off the streets.

He was still having sleeping problems, so I told

him that I could get him all the Valium and Ambien he needed. He liked the idea, so we agreed to meet to do the deal.

He showed up for the meeting where I would provide him with the Valium and Ambien, which are controlled substances. You can't just buy them from some guy on the street. So after I gave him the pills, I put my hand through my hair, which was my signal to the guys around me to come and arrest us both, which they did. We had found a very nice, easy way to get this guy off the streets and into jail, and it worked.

They arrested me as well so that he would never make the connection between me and law enforcement. He just assumes I'm some wiseguy who can procure things. That way, when he talks to his friends, he doesn't tell them to be on the lookout for a six-foot-four, 375-pound FBI agent. Incidentally, I never mind getting arrested. I always want the guy to think "Who is this guy who's getting locked up with me?"

Also, this is a great way to test the veracity of a suspect. The bad guy sees me get arrested, so he assumes I'm a bad guy too. Then when the agents interview him, they say, "What do you know about the guy you got arrested with?"

If he says, "I knew him a couple of months and we met six or seven times," then we know he's telling the truth. On the other hand, if he says, "I never saw that guy before in my life," we know he's full of shit. A guy who tells the truth about me is a good candidate to flip and use to get higher-ups in his criminal world.

When Sayed was interviewed after his arrest, he denied ever knowing me. He denied everything—he said he'd never been to Florida, never seen me before, never wanted to find the Anarchist's Cookbook. So he was also charged for lying to FBI agents who also went to his home and found $14,000 worth of traveler's checks and bank accounts containing $41,000. On top of that, we found a list of the license plates of all of our surveillance cars—he made every single one of us.

His neighbors all said the same thing—his hair was always disheveled, and he was always wearing that coat, no matter what the weather was. I often tried to get him to take his coat off—sometimes I'd even blast the heat in the computer store, just to see what he had going on under it. But he never took it off.

It just makes me wonder—if that happy coincidence of him walking into a computer store that happened to be owned by a corrections agent had never taken place, what might this guy and his friends have blown up? Out of all the criminals I've ever put away, this guy concerned me the most. He was up to something very sinister here in New York, and I still wonder what act of terrorism we might have prevented.

PART THREE
Withdrawal

CHAPTER EiGHTEEN

FBI to Falcone: Drop Dead

Get ready for the surprise ending.

One might have thought that the FBI would have been thrilled to learn that one of its own was being proposed for membership in the Mafia.

One would be wrong.

The bureaucracy went crazy when they heard the news, and they immediately sought to shut the case down.

Why? The excuse—the feeble excuse—they gave was that we didn't have enough manpower.

Excuse me? I'm the first FBI agent since Joe Pistone who has been put on record with a Mafia family, and the best the FBI can do is say "We've got to shut it down!" My head spun.

I fought like hell, and before I knew it, we had additional bodies assigned to the squad. So what did the supervisor in charge of the case (the individual to whom Nat, Chris, and I reported) do? He assigned the new people to transcribe recordings I had already made! He could have sent them into the field to help the guys on the case monitor and record new material that I was generating. I wore a wire almost every single day for nearly two and a half years among the Gambinos. But instead of keeping the case moving forward, the supervisor wanted to use the new manpower to tie up loose ends and prepare for ending the case.

Every new agent coming out of Quantico would have killed for the opportunity to monitor the wiretaps and develop new information derived from the Bureau's biggest organized crime investigation. But the supervisor didn't care.

He wouldn't assign anybody to listen to the bugs. We kept fighting, because we were just trying to work the case. And yet the people who were supposed to be helping and supporting us weren't helping. If anything, they hindered us.

Once it became clear that management wanted to shut down the Gambino case, we had a meeting with the FBI higher-ups to find out exactly why. They said that since we had identified the bosses and the players in the Gambino family, we had "fulfilled the objectives" of the investigation.

I went ballistic.

"Are you kidding me?" I demanded. "Look at what we've accomplished in such a short period of time! I'm about to be made! Greg says that soon they're going to make me a member of La Cosa Nostra!!"

They blew that off. "Well," one of the bosses in the case said, "it's not a crime to get somebody made."

What? Was I hearing right? We were not talking about whether it's a crime to be made. Everybody knows that! We were talking about the incredible benefits that could have flowed from my being inducted as a full-fledged member of the Mafia. I could have vouched for undercover agents from one side of the country to the other. But they were far too shortsighted to see the value in what we were building. Even getting into the inner sanctum of the Gambino family meant nothing to these people. Greg told me that I would meet all the big bosses, be part of the sit-downs, and I was being groomed for full membership. Again, this meant nothing to the bureaucrats, who insinuated that I tried to keep the case alive only because I enjoyed the job of pretending to be in the Mafia! How ridiculous! This was my role, the main purpose of the whole case. I was doing my job and producing results greater than anyone's expectations, with the possibility of gathering even more invaluable intelligence after I was made.

I had to respond to the supervisors.

"Let me make this clear," I told them. "I don't want to just keep this case going because I'm having so much fun! This is dangerous work! I'm not trying to prolong this to benefit myself. We're making a major case here, and we can have a powerful effect on all of organized crime if we can continue to do our job.

"I'm doing this because this is what needs to be done. This is an opportunity that arrives only as often as Halley's Comet! If we dismantle the Gambinos and the other crime families in New York, we can cause them to lose their credibility with the Mob in Sicily and with the public. We've got our foot on the neck of organized crime, and all you want me to do is walk away. I can't believe it."

I couldn't stop myself—all my feelings poured out.

"There are bad guys in this case who don't exist in your minds," I told them, "because they aren't on your beautiful chart. How many guys out there aren't on your chart who are in fact made guys? You subscribe to the idea that your charts are accurate? Greg De-Palma himself told me there are twenty-six capos in the Gambino family. You've only got twenty-one on your chart. Where are the other five? You are missing a lot of soldiers! Where's Robert Vacarro? Where's Louis Filippelli, Vinny Pacelli, Peter Vicini, Andrew Campos, Nicky LaSorsa, to name a few? We also identified the post-Gotti administration in this investigation. You didn't have Squitieri, Megale, or JoJo Corozzo as the boss, underboss, and consigliere?"

Maybe I should have tried to calm down a little bit, but I was incensed. Others tried to interrupt me.

"What happened?" I continued, enraged. "You said you didn't have the manpower, and when we finally get some manpower assigned to the case . . . what do you do? You just try every which way to shut it down. Hey, this is the first penetration into the Gambino crime family! This most likely would never happen again that an FBI agent is proposed for membership into La Cosa Nostra! Don't let this opportunity pass you by!"

And so on and so forth.

When I was new in the Bureau, my attitude was, "If you're my superior, I salute you." But as time went on, I came to realize that some of the people who were in charge of cases I ran had little to no actual experience of what it meant to be an agent on the street. It got to the point where I asked a new supervisor, "How many years have you done on the street? What did you do there? Did you put in the long hours on surveillance? Did you have an informant who wore a wire? Were you ever an affiant on a wiretap? Did you testify in court?" If a supervisor can answer all those questions correctly, I'll listen to him. I'll go the extra mile for the guy who's proven himself on the street. But if he thinks he can become an experienced agent by reading about other cases, he's insane. Don't tell me what you've read. Tell me what you've done.

Sometimes a newly hatched supervisor will say, "Yeah, I worked cases. I went on arrests." Big deal. You might have one agent kicking the door open and risking his life and another agent hanging around the perimeter. Sure, that agent was technically out on the arrest. But was there anything that would actually make his or her eyes widen? Did he or she see or do anything that required courage, split-second timing, or coordination with their fellow agents? All too often, the answer is absolutely not. If you want a safe career, go work in a library. Leave law enforcement to the professionals. But that's not how it works out. A small group of guys just want their junior G-man ID badges so they can impress the neighbors or draw a federal pension one day while getting another salary working in the private sector. They aren't genuinely productive during their Bureau careers.

I'm not the only one—a lot of agents with whom I've spoken, especially the undercovers, feel that same sense of frustration about a few FBI managers. The FBI is like anything else, any other organization of human beings. We've got guys who are actually doing the work, and then we have a few guys who hang around, run their mouths, and pretend to be more than what they really are.

Mistakes can happen, especially if more than one law enforcement agency is involved in a given case. Take Operation Reciprocity, a huge dope case that involved not just the FBI but DEA and Customs, since the case involved international narcotics smuggling. Charlie Cunningham, a case agent at that time and now recently retired as an SAC in Richmond, Virginia, is also a buddy of mine. He worked in Washington on Operation Reciprocity, and he was reviewing what the FBI analysts have put together about all of the dopers, money launderers, smugglers, and so on in the Mexican cartel. All of a sudden, one of the phone numbers looked really familiar to him.

It *should* have looked familiar; it was *mine*.

The alphabet agencies (DEA, ICE, FBI, etc.) that

worked the case had somehow gotten into their collective minds the notion that I was a bad guy, not an FBI agent. Charlie straightened them out. "Jack's one of us! He's only playing the role of money launderer as an undercover agent in another investigation!"

"Oh, sorry."

If Charlie hadn't been there, the FBI might have taken out a wiretap on my beeper and my cell phone! They thought I was a major member of the Mexican cartel!

The real problem with dope cases is that you've got this whole alphabet soup of agencies that could be working any one case. This means that I could show up on a set—a location where I have a meeting with a bad guy—only to find it overrun by agents and cops from other agencies.

"What are you doing here?"

"What are *you* doing here?"

"I'm lookin' to launder some money."

"Oh yeah, us too. We're going to be laundering some money for some dope dealer."

It can be a real mess. Law enforcement is in theory a small world, but there are so many different agencies working dope that it becomes hectic. There are the FBI, the DEA, the New York Police Department, the Joint Task Force, the District Attorney's Office, the State Police, Customs, the IRS, and the ATF—the Bureau of Alcohol, Tobacco, and Firearms of the Treasury Department. There are more people working dope than there are dopers!

There's also a lot of what I call the nonsharing of information. People jealously guard whatever power or knowledge they have, lest somebody else get the credit. When one agency confides in another, the second agency often steals the informant. It happens all the time. Ideally, there should be just one agency working dope and that's it. But people and organizations have their own separate fiefdoms and agendas, so I don't count on that happening anytime soon.

My performance in front of the supervisors somehow didn't win me friends with management, which really didn't bother me. Instead, I was able to buy some more time. But it is so ridiculous to have to buy time from your FBI bosses when you have a unique opportunity to deal a serious blow to organized crime.

CHAPTER NiNETEEN

"I Love to Get Kissed When I'm Getting Fucked"

The interference from the supervisors was eating me alive. Despite the cases we were building against several dozen top mobsters, the proximity of my initiation into the Mafia as Jack Falcone, and the constant flow of information we generated regarding organized crime, the New York field office and Washington remained dead set on shutting down the operation. Yet according to Greg, I was just weeks away from getting made. What to do?

At undercover school, they taught us that if you have a situation you can't resolve, "We're here to help you." Okay, I thought. I've got a situation I can't resolve. We have a great case, and somehow I can't get the Bureau to pay attention.

I learned of the FBI decision to shut the case down in two months during a phone call with my supervisor, who was against this case moving forward. He said, "We've been blindsided by the higher-ups in the Bureau."

By this he meant that the boss in Washington had stepped in to tell him what to do.

I acted like I had no idea what he meant.

"Really?" I said, my tone dripping with sarcasm. "What happened?"

"They've decided that the case is going to end in two months instead of six."

"Wait a minute!" I exclaimed. "Cases run in six-month increments. What is this two months thing that you're talking about?"

"That's what they've decided," he said. "Instead of the case going on for six months, we've got to shut it down in two months. I'm sorry, Jack. There's nothing I nor the FBI headquarters supervisor could do."

This sounded like utter bullshit to me, because I knew how much they hated this case in the first place. I'm not some crazy hothead who just made things up.

I called the undercover unit in headquarters, and I said, "You're here to help me? Then help me. They're trying to shut me down."

Fortune was smiling on me, and I got a great guy, Mike Costanzi, the same individual who later took over Operation Steal Pier, the Atlantic City public corruption case. I told him what was going on.

"They're telling you *what*?" he asked, outraged. "But wait a minute! They can't do that!"

He called for a meeting in New York. When headquarters gets involved, especially with an undercover issue, nobody in the office in New York is too happy. We then had another meeting to address the issue of why the case was being shut down prematurely.

For this meeting, I sought the assistance of the organized crime coordinating supervisor in the New York office, Mike Campi, who is an expert on La Cosa Nostra. In addition to individual squad supervisors, large FBI offices around the country have a coordinating supervisor who makes sure that everything is running on track. I told Mike about what was going on.

I then asked both Nat Parisi and Chris Munger to do me a solid. I wanted them to pick me up near the White Plains FBI office and drive me down to the Manhattan office. I wanted them to park in the basement—so I would not be seen and would be able to take a different elevator, as opposed to having to badge myself in the building.

My concern was that if I went in the normal entrance, other agents would greet me as one of their own. And if one of the subjects of the many investigations that I was involved in saw me, my cover would be blown, and along with it my entire career as an undercover. This would not only endanger the investigation but would put my life at serious risk. I wanted to avoid blowing my cover or risking my life.

Chris and Nat agreed to come get me, but then they called back a few minutes later.

"We've been ordered not to pick you up by the supervisor," they told me, shocked and dismayed. "He told us not even to talk to you."

"What are you talking about, you can't pick me up?" I asked, amazed.

"On top of that, you're gonna get fired for insubordination for calling in headquarters!" they told me.

"Are you shitting me?" I asked, incredulous. "I'm within my rights calling in headquarters! They've got an office to support the undercovers, and I'm an undercover! That's not insubordination!"

"We are so sorry, Jack," they said, disappointed and angry. "There is no way we can pick you up."

"They expect me," I asked, outraged, "to walk into the fucking FBI building and badge myself, and put my life at risk and possibly compromise all my other undercover investigations, just because I called for a headquarters meeting?"

This was so bizarre! Who ever heard of that—not being allowed to give another agent a ride! I couldn't believe it. The supervisors at the New York office were actually willing to put me in harm's way because they were angry that I had gone to headquarters with a complaint. And yet going to headquarters when I had a problem is exactly what they taught me to do back in Quantico. I reached out again to Mike Campi.

Mike went ballistic. He reamed out the supervisor and ordered him to have Nat and Chris pick me up and bring me to the meeting. I was driven to the office and taken upstairs through the back, protecting my identity.

We walked into the meeting, which was held at a long table in a conference room. On one side were the guys who wanted to shut the case down—the ASAC of the New York office; the supervisor of the FBI White Plains office who was running the case; the FBI headquarters organized crime supervisor (who was best friends with the New York squad supervisor); and another co-case agent. I don't want to mention their names.

On the other side of the table were those of us who wanted to keep the case open: Mike Campi; my handlers and case agents, Chris Munger and Nat Parisi; Joe Della Penna, an agent on our task force who worked for the Department of Labor*; Mike Costanzi, the undercover unit supervisor from headquarters; Mike Pollice, another agent assigned to the case; and myself.

"We got blindsided," the White Plains supervisor began. "Headquarters told us to shut the case down. We don't support this. We're just doing what we've been ordered to do." The HQ supervisor said that he also knew nothing about it and that the decision must have been made way above him.

The guys across the table denied that they had anything to do with shutting the case down! This was a total lie!

"You guys are freaking lying to me!" I exclaimed. "*You* originated the demand to shut the case down, not headquarters!"

---

* Joe Della Penna is a great guy who worked his tail off on this case and deserves special commendation. Joe is brilliant in making union and labor cases against wiseguys.

"Headquarters wants to shut it down, not us," they insisted. I knew that was an outright lie. So did the guy from HQ.

"Wait a minute!" the undercover supervisor exclaimed. "You're saying *we* told *you* to shut the case down? I've got a communication from *you guys* making the request to shut this undercover operation down!"

Now, that was a hard hit! It was hilarious! The White Plains supervisor and the FBI HQ supervisor both were rendered speechless. They had been caught with their pants down in front of all of us.

Both the FBI HQ guy and the White Plains supervisor then switched to denial mode.

"Okay, then explain it," the undercover unit supervisor said.

They couldn't explain, of course, and it was embarrassing to them and to all of us. The ASAC, by the way—the guy who's in charge of the entire organized crime branch of the FBI for New York—wasn't saying anything. That's just his management style. If *I* were the ASAC, I would have had a serious problem with the two guys who had made this claim. It was actually sad to see the ASAC sit there and not take command.

They went back and forth, and then the White Plains guy changed his story. "We wanted to shut the case down," he now said, "because it met and exceeded all of its objectives. It was the right time to close it out."

I had heard enough. I told them how I felt about all this bullshit.

"First, I don't appreciate you guys making me get my own ride," I began. "Second, I object to the fact that you guys are upset that I called Headquarters. You've been trying to shut this case down for a year!"

Well, there were denials all around, and then we discussed the case and its potential value in the fight against organized crime. And nothing was done. People should have been reprimanded at a minimum for not being truthful. Blindsided by Washington? Give me a break.

I could see the writing on the wall. The case was becoming too hot to handle for the supervisory staff at New York and FBI HQ. That's the only reason it was shut down: These guys couldn't take the heat. And there wasn't even all that much heat to take! All they had to do was let the thing run its course. Joe Pistone had six and a half years in the Mafia as Donnie Brasco. I was begging for just a fraction of that amount of time. I realized I would have to do what Roberto Durán had done against Sugar Ray—raise my hands and say "*no más.*" I knew that I was beaten.

The bottom line for them was how they could just bask in the glow of the case. Trying to talk some sense into them about what the case meant and where it could go was like talking to a two-year-old. Had they given me just a couple of more months, there would be a chapter in this book about the ceremony in which I became a made member of the Mafia and another whole section about how we placed undercovers on my vouch into all five New York crime families.

A lot of guys put a lot of sweat equity into this case. It was a team effort. We fed off each other. Together, we were invincible. Well, maybe we could stand up to the Mob. But when it came to the FBI's bureaucracy, I guess we weren't that invincible after all.

The counterargument is that if I had stayed in the Mob and gotten made, I could have gotten killed or been ordered to kill someone. The case could have gotten too big and unwieldy, and the cases against the original targets could have gone stale. To that I say bullshit. I could have gotten killed any day in my career in undercover, and that's the risk I ran. As for the case getting too big, I say, the bigger, the better! Why take down just thirty-two guys when we can take down the whole five crime families, or at least put a serious dent into the way they terrorize the people of New York? Why should the FBI even bother investigating organized crime if they're just going to do it in a half-assed manner?

The day they shut the case down, I lost the opportunity to travel with Robert Vaccaro to Miami and then Sicily, to meet with the Mob over there. This was just two years in. What would have happened if I had had the opportunity to go to Sicily? I never had a single moment of mistrust with the Gambinos. There wasn't a moment when Greg or anyone else thought I was anything other than what I claimed to be, Jack Falcone.

Conveniently, after the case ended, the ASAC moved up to become a section chief in Washington.

The guy from headquarters also moved up—he got a coveted desk as supervisor in New York. The supervisor on the case also got a promotion to a big job at headquarters in Washington, D.C. So everybody in the FBI who managed this case advanced. The entire institution of organized crime dodged a bullet as never before. The big winners were the supervisors and bureaucrats on the FBI side and the mobsters. I hate to say this, but the two big losers in this whole deal were me, because I was playing the role I felt I had been born to play, and the people who live in New York: the people who pay a "Mob tax" on every piece of construction, whose schools are built by Mob-controlled construction companies, who spend endless hours in needless traffic delays on the city's highways because make-work projects have been doled out to Mob-related companies, and so on. The FBI and the Mob won. The citizens of New York and I lost. To quote the mobsters, "Kiss me, kiss me! I love to get kissed when I'm getting fucked."

CHAPTER TWENTY

The People v. *Greg DePalma*

Now that the undercover operation was over, it was time to begin work with the U.S. Attorney's Office to build cases against the thirty-two Gambinos and other Mafiosi we were preparing to prosecute. The respect I have for the U.S. attorneys we worked with is immeasurable. During the investigation, we had consulted with them constantly about the various violations we were witnessing. I occasionally met with them personally, but it's the case agent who normally does that. We had to obtain the U.S. attorney's okay regarding the creation of wiretaps or the placing of bugs in restaurants. Also, whenever the FBI renews an undercover's role, an endorsement letter must come forth from the U.S. attorney's office.

On this case, the U.S. attorneys had to read through thousands of pages of rough transcripts of all of the evidence, looking for language that indicated the many violations that created the case. They were going to prosecute the defendants based on the RICO statute, which makes it a criminal offense to be part of an ongoing criminal enterprise. The first part of a RICO violation is to admit that you belong to a crime family. They read through all the transcripts to find the places where Greg DePalma says the words "the Gambino crime family" in a way that suggests that he admitted he was a part of it.

They worked nonstop. It's amazing how hard they worked and how detail-oriented they were—and had to be. I went from hanging around with Greg DePalma one day to sitting with the AUSAs—the assistant U.S. attorneys—the next. They worked twelve- to thirteen-hour days. They'd say, "This is what I need. Tell me where it is." Then it would be my job to help them find it. It was an honor to work with these AUSAs: Ed O'Callaghan, Chris Conniff, and Scott Marrah. They supported the case throughout and wanted it to continue, but they knew the Bureau was not supporting it with the necessary manpower that it needed.

Once the cases were created, the AUSAs presented evidence against the thirty-two Gambinos before a federal grand jury, which indicted all of the suspects. We then created an arrest plan under which teams of FBI agents and Department of Labor special agents were assigned to each of the thirty-two subjects. Early on the morning of March 9, 2005, teams of agents fanned out across the greater New York/New Jersey area and arrested all but one of them. They also held search warrants for the recovery of stolen items—the watches and televisions we had given away or sold to the bad guys during the investigation—which were seized.

Ironically, the only person to evade arrest at that time was the first guy I met in the course of the investigation, Chris Sucarato. Once we began the arrests, the "Mafia telegraph" started clicking like crazy. Let's say one suspect was shacking up with some girl. He gets arrested—and she starts making phone calls. They also heard about the story because it was all over the news. Chris ran—and didn't turn himself in for nine months. But, ultimately, we got him, too.

Each of the suspects was told that I was an FBI agent, an action we took for my protection. When they were brought as a group before the magistrate to hear their charges, I was told they all ostracized Greg— because I was Greg's boy! Some of these guys chose not to believe that I was an FBI agent, which would lead to a contract taken out against me. They thought I was exactly what I claimed to be: a knockaround guy from Florida who flipped and was now on the side of law enforcement.

In the days before the trial, everyone but Greg pleaded out—all thirty-one of the other mobsters and associates we indicted. I was amazed but somehow not surprised that Greg had not taken a plea. He had taken a plea in the Scores case, but I think that was for his son and because John Gotti, Jr., urged him to do so.

Greg was old school. Of his own volition, he would never admit guilt.

I expected that Greg would try to pull a fast one on the judge and jury regarding his medical conditions. Now, I knew Greg. He really had all of the conditions he claimed. He was a diabetic, he had half a lung, he was a cancer survivor, and he had survived a heart attack. But with all of those ailments, nothing slowed him down. He always had an extra step in his walk. He always hustled. He was a strong man who turned on that charm and then suddenly switched to the "I'm sickly, deathly ill" for the sympathy vote. He made that switch with a snap, like turning on a light. He went from tough guy to what we in Spanish call a *pobrecito*, a pitiful one.

When we went to trial, my first concern was that my identity would be compromised, since the case had been covered extensively in the media, and the trial would be too. We knew it would be a media circus. We figured that someone would take my picture and blow my identity with regard to the other cases that I was working. We also argued strenuously that my name should be redacted from the proceedings, in order to protect my identity. The judge disagreed. He said that my name was already out there. As much as I hated having my name given out, I couldn't argue with him. We should have edited the tapes to conceal my identity. That was my mistake, but who was thinking about that kind of thing when we were still working the case?

The day of the trial, I hoped Greg would take a

plea. I've been to court many times where a guy takes a plea in court at the last minute for leniency in sentencing. I looked at Greg and thought, This poor guy, he's seventy-three. He's going to risk dying in prison— for what? For what principles? For the unity of the Mob? Not a single individual out of the other thirty-one we had indicted did the old-school thing of facing trial and jail time. They all cut deals, from the boss on down. DePalma's family never showed at any of the court proceedings. His wife and his other son washed their hands of him. They did the Pontius Pilate thing— they were done with him. He was truly the last mobster standing, the last person to put the honor, such as it was, of La Cosa Nostra above his own freedom.

I was especially shocked that his wife turned against him. She wore a gold Rolex President—I knew she wore that watch, because I was the one who gave it to her. Again, from the envelopes I saw and from the businesses in which he had sunk his claws, she dressed nicely, could afford nice jewelry, the whole nine yards. And yet she let him hang. Greg should have had his family there. That was the only time I ever felt kind of bad for him. He loved being a made guy, but nobody was there for him. They all left him. He paid his dues, but when it came time to collect, there was nothing for him. That was the sad thing.

His Mob family was done with him because he took me around. He was responsible for the dismantling of the post–John Gotti Gambino family hierarchy and also for taking down members of the Lucchese and Genovese families, which this case did as well. None of that mattered in Greg's mind. He would roll the dice—he was going to trial.

The trial took place in the Federal Courthouse in Foley Square in Lower Manhattan. The twelve jurors were a younger crowd, and racially mixed. They were told to expect a two- to three-week trial. For us, it was easy. We had everything ready to go, our case all lined up. At first we didn't understand what DePalma's defense was, because his attorneys admitted at the beginning that he was in the Gambino crime family. The first predicate for a RICO or racketeering conviction is to belong to a criminal enterprise or organization, and they stated that that was exactly what he did. DePalma had never acknowledged that he was a Gambino in any of his previous trials. I assume he did so here because I made so many recordings with him where he states that he is a Gambino.

As it happened, their defense was that Greg De-Palma was an old man, one who was prone to exaggeration, an individual who lived in the past. All of the threats and boasts he made to me in the course of the investigation, his attorneys told the jury, were strictly the exaggerations of an old man whose memories were more vivid than his current existence. It's true, Greg didn't look like much of a threat. His physical appearance was pitiable. Every day in court, he appeared with two EMT guys standing behind him. It was all a big show to influence the jury. He would doze and drool throughout the trial, slumping in his wheelchair, sucking on oxygen. His attorneys fought for the right to allow Greg to attend the trial on a gurney, but the experienced judge, Alvin Hellerstein, refused this transparent sympathy plea.

One of our witnesses was a contractor in his thirties whom Greg had shaken down for $50,000 over two years or more.

"Are you afraid of Greg DePalma?" the prosecutor asked him in front of the jury.

"Yes," he said. "He wasn't an old man. He was a tough man."

"Do you think you can handle yourself if Greg came at you?" Greg's defense attorney asked him.

"Honestly, no," he replied, which triggered a burst of laughter from the jury.

They glanced over at Greg, a man in his seventies, sitting in the courtroom with oxygen tubes up his nose, begging for sympathy. The newspapers called the witness a coward, but by his mere presence Greg invoked the spirit of the Mob. The witness was no coward. He wasn't referring to a personal fear of Greg. He had legitimate fear of what Greg *represented*. With the wave of a hand, you could be gone. They would just take you out. I knew this witness personally from working the case. He was definitely a tough kid. But his personal toughness meant nothing when it came to fear of the Mob. When the witness said that he was afraid of Greg, he meant that he was afraid of what Greg represented: La Cosa Nostra.

Ironically, whenever the jury left the courtroom,

Greg suddenly snapped to, becoming animated. I'm sure that didn't play very well with the judge.

I entered the court before Greg did. When he was rolled in in his wheelchair, I just had to laugh to myself. Greg, man, I thought, you're unbelievable. As soon as I saw him, I felt as if we were back out there together. You're good, Greg. You're trying. You're doing what you have to do—to get away with it. He had a knitted blue blanket on his lap, his hair was all messed up, and he had some Oreo cookies on the table. Not to mention those oxygen tubes in his nose. He acted as if he were ready to die, leaning to one side, looking deathly ill, doing what he did best—manipulating, trying to get his way.

Greg never quit. The U.S. marshals even found a stash of cigarettes in his hospital room. While he was in prison, they also found, on top of his hairpiece, two fifty-dollar bills. You can't have cash in prison! But that's just Greg. In a way, I thought, as I studied him in the courtroom, you have to respect the guy for being such a gangster. As a human being, he was a train wreck, a failure, a leech on society. But as a criminal, he was a great gangster, because that's what his life was all about.

Again, he's the only one who went to trial. He would never admit to anything, never copped a plea. He denied everything, like the good mobster he was. As far as his going away, I'm glad about it. The world is a better place with him behind bars. Businesses aren't being shaken down, people aren't being slapped around—everything's better. At least until the next guy steps up to the plate in his place.

When it came time for me to testify, they cleared the courtroom. A SWAT team picked me up and transported me from a hotel in Midtown in the black SUV normally used only for the director of the FBI. They brought me into the courthouse through the back way, through the basement, up the back elevators, and into the rear entrance of the court, the SWAT team alongside me throughout. Since I was still doing other undercover cases, the judge had to have my testimony piped into another room, where reporters could listen, so none of them ever saw me.

Our legal system grants defendants a right of confrontation—the person who is accusing someone of a crime almost always must be present in the courtroom. At the same time, the judge had to balance the right of the community at large to know what was going on in the trial against the government's need to keep my identity a secret. That's why he chose to clear the courtroom of anyone except himself, the courtroom officials, the attorneys, the jurors, the defendant, and me, with the reporters in the next room.

The U.S. attorneys played tape after tape that I made, absolutely burying Greg. There was no way the jury could have concluded that Greg's comments were those of a has-been. Greg was just simply too current in his knowledge of what was happening in the streets and too garrulous to keep his mouth shut. He talked about absolutely everything he did, he talked about it in detail, and he talked about it over the phone, in person, with whoever was beside him. The U.S. government didn't convict Greg; Greg convicted himself.

The judge had a sense of humor about the whole thing. On the tapes, Greg could be heard talking with his mouth full, and the judge would admonish him not to do so, that it was bad manners. Greg's language left much to be desired. It was a constant flow of expletives—cocksucker this, motherfucker that. But the tape that really did Greg in was the one where he told me that he should have gotten the Oscar at his last trial, that he had completely snowed the judge into believing that he was an invalid when in fact he was getting along just fine. Greg told me, loud enough for the recording device strapped to my body to pick up, that he hadn't shaved for four days, that he wore a blanket, that he lay on a gurney, and then, most destructive to his own case, he even started making fun of the judge.

"He gave me a downward departure," Greg said, referring to the sentencing guidelines that permitted a judge to reduce a sentence in light of a defendant's failing health. "I should have won the Academy Award! He gave me five years instead of twelve!"

That was the moment, I believe, when the jury convicted Greg, right there in the courtroom. Greg turned red as the tape played, and that was when the prosecutor said, "We have no more questions for Mr. Garcia."

When Judge Hellerstein said, "Okay, Mr. Garcia, you can leave," I had to walk right past Greg. It was the first time he had spoken to me since the beginning of the trial. I could hear him mumbling "You cock-sucker!"

I had to laugh.

Keep in mind that the reporters couldn't see any of this happening, and they never got to see me. Of the fifteen tapes that we played for the judge, all of them took place while we ate. The judge asked me at one point how much weight I had gained during the case, and I told him eighty pounds. Well, the reporters had a field day with that one. They assumed that I was a regular-size guy who had gained eighty pounds, not a big guy who had gotten bigger. The headlines the next day read: "Fat Fellas—Undercover Agent Gains 80 Pounds as He and Blobsters Eat Their Way Through New York." The story in the *Daily News* was hysterical. Thomas Zambito wrote on May 17, 2006:

The man who infiltrated the Mob gained more than 80 pounds in his first two years—learning that the GoodFellas were more like FatFellas, eating their way through New York. On their menu every day were steaks, pasta and fresh seafood. They dined at places like La Villetta in Larchmont, Westchester, where they contemplated the pork tenderloin with Portobello balsamic reduction or risotto with porcini and white truffle oil.

When they felt like red-blooded meat eaters, they would go to the Ye Olde Tollgate Steakhouse in Mamaroneck, also in Westchester, a place that the New York Times *once wrote had "steak that a sumo wrestler would love."*

When they wanted less-fussy Italian, they would hit Spaghetti Western in Bronxville, where they would eat under an Italian poster of The Good, the Bad and the Ugly.

And in just twenty-four months, the once-svelte FBI undercover agent Joaquin Manuel Garcia suddenly found himself needing pants with a wider waist—much wider.

I have to say, I loved that comment that I was once svelte! Not in a long, long time, Mr. Zambito!

David Hinckley, also writing in the *Daily News,* wrote that it was no surprise that I gained eighty pounds in the course of the case. "There may be no worse culinary regimen anywhere than the Mob Diet," Hinckley told his readers. "When 'Sopranos' characters . . . walk onto the set, New Jersey tilts."

And Greg DePalma went back to prison.

CHAPTER TWENTY-ONE

Hit Parade

After the Royal Charm case involving the Asian counterfeiters and potential weapons smugglers concluded, I got a call from my fellow undercover agent Lou Calvarese with some surprising news. He and I were the subject of a hit!

It happened this way: A Canadian member of the smuggling group was put in prison here in the United States for his role in the ring. He told his cellmate that he had organized crime contacts and that he had ordered a hit on Lou and me. Bureau policy requires that a "threat assessment" be conducted in such situations. They typically send in another prisoner wearing a wire to try to get the threat recorded on tape; that way we can tell how serious the threat is and bring charges against someone who threatens the life of a law enforcement agent. Another crucial step is notifying the agent whose life has been threatened so he can take the precautions necessary in protecting himself. I was kept completely in the dark, and to this date, I have no idea whether such an assessment was ever carried out. If it wasn't for Lou telling me, I wonder if anyone would have ever called me.

And then, on August 8, 2005, it became known that a $250,000 contract had been taken out on me. The *New York Post* headline that day read: "Mob's FBI Hit Plot—$250K Price on Head of Infiltrator." The article suggested that wiseguys ought to "pray for the good health of Jack Falcone." If the hit had been carried out, the lives of New York's organized crime family members would become a "living nightmare." The government paid "lightning fast visits" to the bosses, underbosses, and consiglieres of all of the five families, to let them know that any attempt on Jack Falcone would result in unprecedented heat . . . plus the death penalty for anyone involved.

People ask me what it's like to know that there is a Mafia contract taken out in my name. Having a hit is actually a very frightening thing, not so much for me but for my family. Had my mother been alive, she would have had a very difficult time dealing with the idea that there was a hit on her son. I would never have told her, of course. My wife was petrified, as was everyone else concerned. As for me, my reaction was the same as pretty much anyone in that position. I assumed a more protective role for my family, and I became more aware of situations that were potentially risky.

But I didn't really think that somebody would come and whack me. Nevertheless, today I always carry a gun. My house is fully wired. My car starts with a remote. I have motion sensor cameras that go off all the time when deer and other animals invade "the compound."

Having a hit on me changed my life dramatically. I don't take the same route home every day. I'll deviate, I'll alternate, I'll look in the rearview mirror a lot. I do drive-bys through neighborhoods where I don't belong. Where it used to take an hour and a quarter to get home from the city, now it takes an hour and three-quarters because I'm doing all this dry cleaning.

I am more careful about whom I tell about my work in law enforcement, and I am cautious about where I go. I can't go to a country club, for instance, for a wedding or some other celebration or even just to sit by the pool, because I never know who I'll run into. For a while, I walked around my house with my gun in a shoulder holster. The Supervisory Special Agent of the Gambino squad, Phil Scala, a dear friend and great FBI manager, told me he would send his whole squad to camp out in my house if need be. I sometimes wonder how differently the case would have gone had Phil been running it out of the Gambino squad in Queens, instead of out of the White Plains office. I'm sure it would have been managed much more sensibly, and with much more impressive results. My handlers, Chris and Nat, got the local town cops to do regular patrols. My house is like Fort Knox—there are so many cameras everywhere I feel like I am on my own reality show!

The one thing I can count on is the support of my fellow agents. "You can call us," they told me. "We'll hook you up with the state police, whatever you need." The guys helped me feel protected. I don't let it dominate my life. It's just part of the cost of doing business on Team America.

I do have to take management to task for the way they handled the contract on me. Their approach was piss-poor. The FBI got a letter from an informant in jail, an individual we'll call Pete. Pete wrote in the letter that he heard from another guy we'll call Al, who was connected to the Colombo family and was in prison for murder, that a hit had been taken out against me. It seems Al was boasting that he and his associates had accepted a contract from embarrassed Mob bosses to get Jack Falcone. So what happened to the letter?

The FBI lost it in the routing system! It finally reached the hands of Nat and Chris weeks later.

I know it sounds incredible, and I'm sure that the bureaucrats who lost the letter will come up with a nifty story that has nothing to do with reality, but the fact is that they plain and simple lost it. They didn't tell me about it. It never crossed their minds to say "Hey, Jackie boy, there's a guy in the pen who says the Gambinos took a contract out against you."

Somehow, weeks later, they found the letter, and then somebody brought it to my attention. I suggested they wire up Pete, the guy who wrote the letter, get him back into contact with the Colombo guy, Al, and see if there was any truth to it. But management didn't opt for this. They told me that they were pursuing the situation in their own way.

I said no—the easiest thing is to simply wire the guy up, put him in contact with Al, and you're done! They could find out quickly, once and for all, whether there was any truth to it. Instead, management came up with this crazy story about how they tried to find some guy who had been released, that he had gone down to Florida, that he knew something, some cocka-mamie thing. Nat, the case agent and a man totally in my corner, was on vacation at the time. The overall case was now in the capable hands of Chris Munger. He's a great guy, an aggressive and very experienced and competent agent, so naturally the brass didn't want to give the business about the hit to him. Instead, they took it away from him and assigned it to another agent, also a very fine agent, but one who mostly did foreign counterintelligence work throughout his career. That's the spook world! It's different from criminal matters! I'm not trying to demean that agent or what he sought to accomplish, but I had a bond with Chris, who had considerable experience in this area. I wanted to say, "Hold on—the fucking contract's out on me! Don't I get a say in how it's handled?"

Of course not. They told me they didn't know where to find Pete, that he had been transferred by Corrections to somewhere else, that the whole thing was a big mess. In any event, even if they knew where he was, they didn't have grounds to move him.

"But wait a minute!" I exclaimed. "They're prisoners! You don't have to give them a reason! You just call Corrections and you say 'Transfer the guy!'"

Greg DePalma told me over and over that there'd be a knock on his cell door in the middle of the night and he would be taken to a different prison. This is just what he lived with—what every inmate faces.

Yet my arguments fell on deaf ears. We're going to approach him, I was told.

Approach him? What do you think he is going to tell you? He's a hard-core criminal, a murderer! My arguments were unavailing, so they outright asked him. Of course he denied it, and after some back-and-forth decided to take a polygraph test. The first question was the obvious.

"Is there a contract on Jack Falcone?" he was asked.

"No," he responded. The needle flew off the charts! There was absolutely no way on earth that he told the truth when he denied the existence of the contract.

Now I was livid. I was waiting, pacing, sweating, to hear the results of the polygraph, and they came and said, "Hey, guess what! The guy took the polygraph and he failed!" So immediately I called the ASAC and said, "You see? We should have wired the guy up instead of this bullshit. Now we'll never know."

Then the ASAC told me, "Oh, we knew that he would fail! You know how these guys are."

"No, I don't," I replied, disgusted. "But if you knew he would fail, why were you so adamant in giving him the polygraph test!"

"We had to," they told me. The bottom line—management never believed this was a credible hit.

"So what are you gonna do?" I asked. "What are you gonna do to protect my safety? Or my family's safety?"

They just gave me the typical hand-job bullshit routine. And why not? It wasn't their lives, or their families' lives, at risk! The whole thing was ridiculous. The Gambino crime family of the Mafia had put out a quarter-of-a-million-dollar hit on me, and these guys were treating it like a departmental requisition for extra Coca-Cola. The whole thing was a joke to them, but my life was on the line. Maybe the hit hadn't been sanctioned by the Commission, the gathering of the five bosses of the five Mafia families. But what if some freelance asshole trying to make a name for himself wanted to come after me? He wouldn't have been doing it for the money. Where's he gonna collect? At the nearest Mobs-R-Us? "Hey, I killed Falcone! Where's my 250 large?" He would have done it to show what a tough guy he is, which is why I'm very careful about my whereabouts to this day.

I told them, "I know why you had the guy do a polygraph. So you could just wash your hands. That's why you did it. You wanted him to show that there was no contract, so you can say, 'See? There is no contract! It was all bravado!' But now what?"

They had no answer to that one. They knew it was true, and that was the story.

The reality is that I had embarrassed the Mob. I walked among them. I infiltrated them. Worse, I'm not even Italian—I'm a Cuban American! People had to ask each other, "How stupid are these guys!" That's the ultimate insult—to have a non-Italian pass himself off as an Italian so convincingly! The Mob tries to be all-wise, all-knowing, all-powerful. In Sicily, they must have torn their hair out. They probably laughed at their American counterparts, viewing it through the lens of their stereotypical idea of a Hispanic. Of course, Andy García did a great job playing an Italian in *The Untouchables* and in *The Godfather: Part III*. He's Cuban too. But that was the movies, and this was real life.

I'm not just blowing off steam when I say that the investigation into the alleged hit was poorly handled. The outcome in fact remains open, due to the ineptness, idiocy, incompetence, and above all the inexperience of some of the managers in the investigation. Not all of them; just the ones who managed my case. So if you and I ever meet, don't walk too close!

CHAPTER TWENTY-TWO

The Unmaking of Jack Falcone

I always say, "The day you can say, Been there, done that and got the T-shirt, is the day you have to retire."

I retired from the FBI on March 3, 2006. The real insult to an agent comes the day we retire. We go in on our last day and they take our badges and credentials. The New York Police Department does it the right way: On the last day, people get a photo ID card indicating that they're retired NYPD. At the FBI, though, they just take our picture—and it takes nine to ten months to process the retired credentials.

I've been undercover for the last quarter of a century. There are bad guys everywhere that I've put in jail who have since gotten out. By now, either they've been returned to jail a couple more times, or they've had a kid who's gone to jail already. I still look in the car next to me at a red light, look to see who's behind me on the highway. I have to carry a gun, and, of course, I don't look like an agent. Let's say I get stopped by a cop and I try to explain that I'm former FBI. They're not going to believe that. If the cop finds my gun, I'm on freaking Rikers Island before you can say J. Edgar Hoover. I actually went ten full months before I got my retired FBI credentials. Did I carry a gun every day of those ten months? I'll never tell!

On my last day, in addition to turning over my badge and my FBI credentials, I had a few other things to turn in as well. As Jack Falcone, I wore all kinds of nice jewelry and watches. Those all went back to the Bureau, of course. I was fine with that—the one good thing about wrapping up the case was that I no longer had to get dressed up every day to be with DePalma. That was so wearing. I turned in the pinkie rings, the jewelry, the Rolexes, and I was a civilian for the first time in almost thirty years.

At least in terms of the FBI official records, I was a civilian. In my head, it took me a little longer to adjust to the fact that I was no longer Joaquin Garcia of the FBI or Jack Falcone of the Gambino family. The danger with undercover work was that the role I played was such a seductive mistress. My wife tells me that from time to time, I still act like a mobster! It happens in restaurants mostly. Now when I tell the maître d' that I have a reservation, he checks his book and tells me to wait in the bar. If I went in there as Jack Falcone, believe me, he would never have sent me to the bar, regardless of whether I had a reservation or not. He would have found a table for however many I demanded that instant. But I'm not in the FBI anymore and I'm not Jack Falcone anymore, so I trot off to the bar and wait my turn, like the rest of the citizens.

Sometimes the waiting gets a little too much to endure, especially if I see other people getting seated ahead of us. That's when I stomp over to the maître d' and growl, in my best Jack Falcone voice, "Hey, pal, what did you do, put me on the 'pay me no mind' list? There's other people who have been seated ahead of us! Do we understand each other?"

With that, we always get an apology and a table right away, but I also get a look from my wife as if to say, You're not Jack Falcone anymore.

It really burns me up, though. Bad guys walk into a restaurant and get a table right away. Honest citizens really should be seated first. The guy who's out there busting his butt to take care of his family. The police-man, schoolteacher, or fireman. *Those* are the ones who should be taken right to the head of the line! But in our topsy-turvy society, we honor the mobster and dishonor the honest individual who is protecting soci-ety or just taking care of his family.

Why did I retire? First, I could see the writing on the wall. After the Gambino case ended, I wasn't get-ting handed any new undercover cases. I had a sense that my superiors wanted to shift me out of under-cover work, after all those years, and the idea of being a regular agent held very little appeal for me. At the same time, I realized that after playing the role of Jack

Falcone, there was really nowhere to go but down. How do you go back to any other case? The Bureau continues to call me in as a "consultant," and even as I write these words I am still doing undercover work for several divisions. By the time this book comes out, all of those cases should be wrapped up, and that will most likely be the end of my career, whether officially on the Bureau payroll or as a consultant. But I really wanted to leave at the top of my game, like a Jim Brown or a Tiki Barber in football, instead of those athletes or individuals in other fields of endeavor who don't know when to quit. I wanted to go out on top.

At the same time, I wanted to spend more time—a lot more time—with my wife and daughter. My daughter was six when I stepped down from the Bureau, and she honestly had no idea whether I was a good guy or a bad guy. I had never explained to her exactly what I did for a living, because she was simply too young to understand. I wanted to give her a childhood that was free of the Greg DePalmas of the world. I also wanted to spend more time with my wife, who is the real heroine of this story. Just think about the amount of sacrifice that she made over the years, allowing me to work seven days, long hours, in dangerous situations, and with extremely violent people, the most violent individuals and organizations in society.

She's the one who endured worrying about me, wondering where I was, if I was all right, whether I was in the Badlands of Philadelphia posing as a dope dealer or in the company of mobsters with DePalma and his crew. I'd like to take a moment and salute all the spouses—and the children—of law enforcement officers. They never receive medals or commendations for the sacrifices they make, but they are truly equal to those of the agents, police officers, firefighters, and others whose careers they so selflessly support.

The day I left the Bureau, therefore, was a day of mixed feelings for me. This was an organization to which I had given my entire adult life, and as part of it, I had truly lived the American dream. Remember that I'm a Cuban émigré, a person who came to this great country as a boy not even speaking the language. Now here I was, described in a column by the noted organized crime reporter Jerry Capeci, titled "Meet the FBI's best undercover agent." That's quite a leap for a kid whose family had fled from Cuba. This country gave me an amazing opportunity, and I had the good fortune to run with it and to succeed.

Of course, I had countless friends among the agents and managers in the Bureau. While I certainly had my run-ins with the bureaucrats and paper pushers, there were so many outstanding managers and great agents that their names alone would fill a book. It was painful knowing that I would not be in daily contact with them as in the past. On my last day, I got a ride home from Sean McMullen, Jimmy Lopez, and Rich Shaw, three good friends and great case agents on my drug squad. It was an odd feeling to be dropped off at my home without a job to go to the next morning. Indeed, for the next couple of weeks, I found myself getting up at the usual hour, getting dressed, mentally preparing for another day at the FBI. I guess all retirees go through something like that. I was calling in to the office so frequently about this, that, and the other thing that the guys started to tease me. Didn't I realize I was retired? they would ask.

Back when I started, new agents were assigned to a bullpen. You'd bullshit with the other guys—his wife would call and you'd tease him, "Hey, I love you too, sweetie!" We had a steno pool, young kids who did the paperwork. We became like a family—we'd all go out after work, have drinks, pizza, whatever.

The bullpen is gone and so is the steno pool. Now it's much more sterile. You're assigned to work in a "pod"—a little workstation with high walls so you never get to meet and interact with your fellow agents. As for the stenographers, agents became typists! Now they spend hours on the computer, typing reports. They shouldn't be typing—they should be out there on the street, working! And it's all voice mail today—it's no longer a guy picking up the phone and saying "Hey, he's not here, can I take a message?" We're no longer on top of each other the way we used to be.

Guys come out of Quantico all piss and vinegar, ready to take down the bad guys. And they instead get assigned laptops and cameras . . . and seats in those fucking pods . . . and suddenly they've been trans-formed into little IBM guys. Active agents don't even know who some of the new guys are!

"Hey, who's the new guy?"

"I don't know!"

"What's he doing?"

"Beats the shit out of me!"

When I was coming up, if something was happening, I could say to the rest of the squad, "Hey, come on, I gotta go lock up this guy—let's all go!" And everybody would ride off together. Today guys don't go out on arrests like that, because you can't find anybody—all the agents are stuck in their little walled-off pods! Hey, where is everybody?

I hear this complaint a lot from the guys today. I used to love going into that bullpen—if anyone came in depressed, everybody would get on him, make him feel better. They really ought to go back to the way we were then. Wishful thinking? Wistful thinking? Okay, a little bit. But from a strictly professional point of view, we're losing the camaraderie that made the FBI such a great law enforcement agency. Mr. Director, tear down those pods! And bring back the steno pool, while you're at it!

There were certain benefits to leaving law enforcement. Instead of chauffeuring Greg DePalma all over the New York metropolitan area, I now take my daughter to and from school. If that's not a radical transition—from DePalma and the wiseguys to the first grade—I don't know what is. But I love her so much, and I'm so happy to be able to spend this time with her.

A month ago I was awakened by coyotes. I grew up in the Bronx! What the hell am I doing with coyotes!

Out in the distant suburbs where we now live, we've got turkeys, we've got deer, we've got bobcats, we've got coyotes. I'm in hell! This is my cross to bear!

One night some neighborhood kid rang the doorbell at 11 P.M. My wife went crazy, and I went out and got my gun, until we figured out that it was just some kid fooling around ringing doorbells.

"Oh my God," my wife cried. "They know where we live. They were checking us out."

Another time she went into a panic when our mailbox was knocked down. I told her, "Would you take it easy? Nothing happened."

Am I afraid every day? No! The main thing is this: If I live in fear, they win! Yes, I have to take a few extra precautions, but that's the price I pay. Let them be embarrassed. They are all bad guys, the criminals. They all took guilty pleas. We had them all by the balls. And now they're doing time.

I visit Manhattan occasionally but not often. There are still plenty of bad guys out there who remember me and who might not mind taking a shot at me. I have to be very careful where I go and how I get there. That's a small price to pay for the privilege of having been on the right side of the law all these years.

At the same time, job offers came in. Perhaps the most attractive came from Major League Baseball. They wanted me to travel to the baseball academies in Latin America and speak to the young pro prospects and draftees about the dangers that awaited them when they reached the United States. There would be gamblers who wanted to befriend them, wiseguys who might be seeking information or even trying to bribe them or to get them in trouble somehow.

The job was alluring, but the fact that it required me to spend 60 percent of my time traveling made me turn down the offer. People said, "How can you turn down Major League Baseball?" The fact is, I'm a football guy and not that much of a baseball fan, so it didn't mean all that much to me. The main thing at this point in my life is that I wanted to be with my family. Most FBI agents who have a second career after their time in the Bureau tend to go into private security. In my mind, I'm done with all that. I want a completely new challenge. That's one of the reasons I wrote this book! I'd also love to go into acting. After all, undercover work is acting. Undercovers inhabit a role more dangerous than actors. We can't step out of character. It's not just a career on the line if people don't find you credible, it's your life. I sit home with my wife and watch *The Sopranos,* and I say to her, "How hard can that be? Those people have all the takes they need to get the scene right! An undercover only has one take!" So if Hollywood is looking for a six-foot-four, 375-pound leading man, look no further!

It's sobering to realize that all of the people I "befriended" in the course of my time working the Gambino case are now in prison. That's where they belong—they're bad guys who deal drugs, contrary to the "image" of the Mafia. They extorted unions and legitimate businesses and turned otherwise law-abiding businessmen into not just victims but willing participants in organized crime. They loan-sharked, they did billions of dollars' worth of illegal gambling, they broke into stores, and they hurt and killed people. I have no compunction about the fact that all of these individuals are in prison. If anything, I wish they could stay in even longer. I'm definitely not sentimental about these "friendships," because they never were friendships at all. From my first undercover case, when I knocked on the door of the massage parlor in Manhattan, through my last day with DePalma and even into the cases I am still working, I've never been out there to make friends. I've been out there to put bad people in jail and make the world a little bit safer for everybody else.

They say that everything happens for a reason, and who knows? Maybe my luck posing as Jack Falcone wouldn't have lasted forever. It's easy to focus only on the positive side of what might have been—the ability to insert undercover agents into every organized crime family not just in New York but across the country. It's hard not to dwell on the fact that we could have dealt that hydra-headed being a crippling or even a fatal blow. But the reality is that Robert Vaccaro's girlfriend Donna could have put the puzzle pieces together at any time, and that would have been the end not just of the case but of Joaquin Garcia.

Or Gigi the Whale could have turned up at an inopportune moment, or Randy Pizzolo, or any one of the thousands of bad guys and associates I've encountered in my decades in the FBI. Brother agents, of course, have given their lives, and while I will carry regret to my grave about the early termination of the Gambino case, I know that I am fortunate to have survived among the mobsters for as long as I did.

There's no way to know whether either of the contracts taken out on my life was ever rescinded, and who's to keep any of the thirty-two Gambinos we sent away from continuing to plot against me? It was a wild ride, in those Escalades, Hummers, and other vehicles at my disposal in the role of Jack Falcone. This was just one case in my career, albeit a big one. There are a ton of other cases I didn't have time or space in this book to write about—Russian organized crime, corrupt cops in Boston and San Juan, Puerto Rico . . . I could go on and on. But perhaps the most satisfying coda to my career is this: We took down the top thirty-two members of one of the most powerful organized crime families in the country. For a moment, in the ongoing war between the good guys and the bad guys, the good guys finally won.

Not bad for a refugee kid whose family came to this country with little more than the shirts on our backs. Okay, getting yanked from my role as Jack Falcone was the ultimate nightmare. But everything else in my career, up to and including wearing the badge of the FBI and putting all these bad guys behind bars . . . I gotta tell you, it's been the American dream.

EPILOGUE

Where Are They Now?

The following are some of the dispositions of the individuals involved in the various cases described in the book.

Randolph "Randy" Pizzolo, one of the two Mafiosi who could have identified me in the Bronx, was killed on December 1, 2004, in an industrial section of Brooklyn. There were four bullet wounds in his body, which lay next to his brand-new BMW. Indicted for Pizzolo's killing was acting Bonanno family head Vincent "Vinnie Gorgeous" Basciano, who took his nickname from the beauty salon his family owned, "Hello Gorgeous."

    Willy Falcon and Sal Magluta, "Los Muchachos," Miami's most powerful cocaine cowboys, avoided prison during their trial for importing 75 tons of the drug into the United States. They were subsequently found guilty of bribing jurors on that celebrated trial. Sal Magluta was sentenced to 205 years in prison for his role in the jury tampering. Willy Falcon pleaded guilty before his trial began and received twenty years for money laundering and a $1 million fine. Neither was ever convicted in the murder of any of those scheduled to testify during their first trial. Forty others in their importing operation also went to prison.

Operation Royal Charm and **Operation Smoking Dragon** resulted in the arrests of eighty-seven defendants on racketeering and other charges, with four indictments out of Los Angeles and six out of Newark. The FBI seized more than $5.3 million of Supernotes, the largest seizure of its kind; 36,000 Ecstasy pills; and almost half a kilo of crystal meth. Defendants were charged with arms trafficking and conspiring to import more than $1 million worth of silenced pistols, submachine guns, assault rifles, and other weapons, including rocket launchers, according to the FBI.* Charges included RICO violations, dealing in counterfeit U.S. currency, narcotics trafficking, money laundering, conspiracy to defraud the United States, and illegal weapons trafficking. The FBI called it a "one-stop shopping criminal organization that had the will and the

---

* From the prepared remarks of the Acting Assistant Attorney General John C. Richter, Criminal Division, at the press conference for Operation Smoking Dragon and Operation Royal Charm, Washington, D.C., Monday, August 22, 2005.

means to smuggle virtually every form of contraband imaginable."*

Gambino underboss **Anthony "the Genius" Megale** pleaded guilty on September 6, 2006, to racketeering and extortion charges and received a sentence of 135 months in jail.

Gambino boss **Arnold Squitieri** pleaded guilty on April 20, 2007, to racketeering and extortion charges. He was to have been tried with DePalma just a few weeks after he pleaded out. He was sentenced to ninety-two months in federal prison.

Sayed Abdul Malike, the cabbie/terrorist who wanted explosives, was found guilty in January 2004 and sentenced to thirty-seven months and three years supervised release and was recently deported back to his homeland of Afghanistan. The story made the front page of the newspapers, as it was a joint takedown involving the New York Police Department, the FBI, and the Joint Terrorism Task Force. The guy who created the case—the corrections officer who owned the store—should have gotten an award for his concern and for the fact that he reached out to the FBI.

The **Hollywood Police Officers** were sentenced as follows: Kevin Companion, fourteen years; Jeffry Courtney, nine years; Stephen Harrison, nine years; Thomas Simcox eleven years plus a $100,000 fine.

---

* Department of Justice press release, Federal Racketeering Indictments Target International Smuggling, Counterfeit Currency Operation, August 22, 2005, and Department of Justice press release 06-044, dated April 19, 2006.

Simcox received a reduction in his sentence because he cooperated with the FBI in the investigation.

According to the *Miami Herald* of July 20, 2007, a weeping Kevin Companion told the court at his sentencing, "I was a good police officer for a long time and a good man. I'm no longer a police officer, but I'm still a good man."

Craig Callaway, disgraced president of the Atlantic City City Council, was sentenced to forty months in prison for accepting bribes. Calloway defended his actions this way: "What I did was wrong, but I just wanted to try to help people who had been left out." In other words, members of the minority community in Atlantic City that had previously been shut out of the bidding process for construction jobs. Callaway apparently believed that accepting bribes from them was a legitimate means of helping their businesses succeed.*

Al Alvarez, a Lucchese crime family associate, a Cuban, and earlier in his crime career a member of the Tanglewood Boys, received eighteen months for gambling violations. Bail had been denied. The judge in the case, Alvin Hellerstein, twice allowed Alvarez to go trick-or-treating with his daughter. According to the New York *Daily News* on January 5, 2007, the judge forbade Alvarez from attending his five-year-old daughter's birthday party at a "swank" Eastchester country club. "Denied," Hellerstein wrote, according

---

* "N.J. Politician Behind Sex Tape Is Jailed," *Philadelphia Inquirer,* George Anastasia, March 14, 2007.

to the *Daily News.* "A birthday party at home, school or church is one thing. A celebration outing on the eve of going to jail is another. Bail conditions were set for a reason, and the celebration is not consistent with those reasons."

Ramón Rosario, Atlantic City City Council member, admitted accepting bribes in exchange for offering influence in October 2006 and was sentenced to ten months of confinement.

Chris Sucarato, Gambino associate and soon-to-be-made Gambino soldier, to whom I made the initial shakedown payment at the Naked Truth, received twenty-five months for RICO violations and extortion.

Joe "Machines" Fornino received ten months for gambling violations.

Johnny "Hooks" Capra, a Lucchese capo, received eighteen months for extortion and gambling.

Tommy "Sneakers" Cacciopoli, a Gambino capo, received twenty-four months for conspiracy to commit extortion.

Pasquale "Scop" DeLuca, a Genovese capo and acting street boss, received twenty-one months for conspiracy and gambling violations.

Louis Filippelli and Nicky LaSorsa each received sentences of forty-six months for racketeering. Both were made members of the Gambino family who were identified as acting capos as a result of this investigation.

Alphonse "Funzi" Sisca, a captain in the Gambino crime family, received seventy-five months.

Peter Vicini aka **"Petey Chops"** was not charged in any of the cases in which I was involved, although he probably no longer dines at Bloomingdale's. Because of this investigation, Vicini has now been identified as a made member of the Gambino family.

Robert Vaccaro, Gambino soldier and DePalma's acting capo, was sentenced to ninety-six months in prison for RICO violations and extortion.

Joe Moray, Greg DePalma's one-time driver and a Gambino associate, received twenty months' probation. Had he stuck around Greg instead of parting after their disagreement, he might have been looking at more serious time.

Greg DePalma was convicted on June 6, 2006, and sentenced on September 25, 2006, to a term of twelve years in prison. He is currently an inmate at the Federal Prison at Butner, North Carolina.

DePalma and Judge Hellerstein were roughly the same age. At sentencing, DePalma said that the judge, then seventy-two, appeared to enjoy better health than DePalma.

The judge agreed and added, "Then again, I haven't lived your life."

At the sentencing, Hellerstein said, "Clearly, being sentenced to this type of time at seventy-four years of age is not enticing. But in a sense, one earns what happens." According to the *Daily News*, Hellerstein also ordered DePalma to pay $70,000 in restitution to two companies from which he had extorted money.

"Can I give them my Social Security check?" he joked.

On October 2, 2007, a group of agents received the Department of Justice's Attorney General's Award for Excellence in Law Enforcement for penetrating the Gambino La Cosa Nostra crime family. Honorees included FBI Special Agents Natale Parisi, Michael Pollice, William P. Ready, and Joseph A. Della Penna. Five distinguished individuals who were also responsible for making the case so successful did not receive recognition: FBI Special Agents Chris Munger and Bim Liscomb, and AUSAs Ed O'Callaghan, Chris Coniff, and Scott Marah. One other person who played an integral role was left out as well—Special Agent Joaquin "Jack" Garcia. Must have been a bureaucratic oversight.

ACKNOWLEDGMENTS

I would like to acknowledge and thank the following individuals for making this book possible: My attorney, Stephen Sheppard, of Cowan, DeBaets, Abrahams and Sheppard LLP, for all his guidance and support throughout this amazing journey. My editor, Zachary Schisgal; copyeditor, Deborah Manette; attorney Eric Rayman, Esq.; editorial assistant Shawna Lietzke; and all the people at Touchstone Fireside, a division of Simon and Schuster, for their fantastic ideas and influence in the publishing of this book. My writer, Michael Levin, for his tireless efforts and dedication to this project, and Michael's outstanding assistant Nicole Rhoton and typist Terrie Barna, for their help in making this a great book. To Paul Fedorko, of The Trident Media Group, for getting this project off the ground. To John Henson, Special Agent Christopher J. Munger, and Retired FBI Section Chief Thomas G. Donlon, retired NYPD captain and actor Joe Lisi, and bestselling author Stan Pottinger, for their enthusiasm and encouragement that prompted me to write this book.

Many thanks to the following individuals for their role in my graduation from the FBI Academy in Quantico, Virginia:

My first New Agents Training Class 80-4, especially to my class counselor, James R. Pledger, and Reynold Selvaggio, for all their support and positive encouragement that inspired me to return to Quantico and successfully complete my training. From my graduating class, New Agents Training Class 80-12, special thanks to Thomas "TJ" Murray, may he rest in peace. Thank you, TJ—without your help at Quantico, this book would not have been possible.

I would like to thank the following individuals I had the pleasure of working with during my first FBI assignment in Newark, New Jersey, for their training, friendship, and most of all, the impact they had in shaping my career:

Thanks to all the special agents and support employees of the FBI Newark Division, specifically the elite Bank Robbery, Fugitive, Terrorist Squad known as C-1: Special Agent in Charge (SAC) Robert McCarthy, Supervisory Special Agent (SSA) James E. Hoffman, SA Edwin Petersen, SA Daniel P. McLaughlin, Supervisory Special Agent (SSA) George "Pat" Johnson, SA Rene Amaya, SSA Bernard Thompson, SAC Andre Stephens, SA Thomas Menapace, SSA Ron Romano, SA Edward White, SSA Jim Swayze, SA Dick Sikoral, SA Ronald Butkiewicz, SA Barry Martino, SSA James Dougherty, SA Maureen McAvoy, SA Jose Reyes, Intelligence Analyst (IA) Theresa Delloiacovo-Minovich, NJSP Detective Robert Vasquez, and SA Thomas Freidman.

Thanks to all my friends in the Philadelphia Division, and the following individuals with whom I had the pleasure of working in the BT Express/Metroliner Narcotic Investigation: SSA Wilbert Van Marsh, SSA Jerome Peters, SA Ed Sims, SA Robert Nettles, SA Annette Vogts, SSA Randez Hadden, SA Reynold Selvaggio, Assistant United States Attorney (AUSA) David Fritchey, AUSA Al Wicks, AUSA Paul Mansfield, Community Outreach Specialist (COS) Tanya Jeter, Intelligence Analyst (IA) Michele Goebig, SA Thomas Tierney, and SA Gerry Williams.

Thanks to all my many friends in the New York Division, in particular, all the current and former members of C-13, the FBI's Premier FBI/NYPD Narcotics Task Force, whom I enjoyed so much working with and being a part of: I would like to recognize the following Agents and Detectives: Assistant Director (ADIC) Lewis Schiliro, Assistant Special Agent in Charge (ASAC) Charles Domroe, Section Chief Charles J. Rooney, ASAC Thomas Nicpon, ASAC Diego Rodriguez, ASAC Don Ackerman, ASAC Dennis Buckley, SAC Pedro Ruiz, SAC Charles Cunningham, SSA

Robert Joyce, SAC Michael Tabman, SA Craig M. Arnold, SA Reynaldo Tariche, SA Steve Hubeck, SA Salvatore Lomonto, SSA James A. Gagliano, SA Danielle Messineo, SA Sean McMullen, SSA Robin Gazawi, SA Richard Shaw, SSA Niall Brennan, SSA Richard Walsh, SA James Lopez, SA Stephen B. Morley, SA Matt Womble, SA David L. Coletti, SSA Paul E. Cassidy, SSA Fernando Llanos, SA Edgar "Rusty" Wright, SA Don Bean, SSA Juan "Sunny" Grajales, SA Holly Meador-Barille, SSA John Scata, SSA Kim Clinton, SST Sharon Steinhauer, SA Andrew DeCicco, SST Julia Stutzbachs, ECT Arlene McKenna, SA James Gregorio (ICE), ASAC D. Shepard Rabbiner, and our first squad secretary who took care of us all, Barbara Ferchland. NYPD Detectives: Paul Caroleo, Det. First Grade Steve Casazza, Michael Costello, Det. First Grade Francis Berberich, George C. Daley, William Mitzeliotis, Wayne Behnken, Kevin Dunleavy, Sergeant Peter J. English, Marie Ward, Sergeant Robert Sotero, Lieutenant Michael Geraghty, Pete Crespo, John Lawlor, Patrick O'Shea, Wayne Callahan, Sergeant Daniel C. Evans, Rafael DiLone, John Segovia, Mariano "Dee" D'Christina, Michael Parker, Jim Murphy, Kathy Mugan-Coletti, Lt. Chris Hannon, Assistant United States Attorney (AUSA) Elaine Banner, AUSA Jody Avergun, and AUSA Jed Davis. Thanks also to Lt. Jim Fisher and his officers at the Special Investigation Division, Danbury Police Department and former justice of the N.Y. State Supreme Court, The Honorable John Diblasi.

Thanks also to the following individuals whom I

have had the privilege of knowing and working with during my tenure in the FBI: FBIHQ Section Chief and friend Thomas G. Donlon, ADIC Richard T. Garcia, ADIC Mark J Mershon, ADIC Pat D'Amuro, SAC David Cardona, ASAC David Shafer, SSA Richard Frankel, SAC Kenneth T. McCabe, SA Ronald J. Moretti, SA John T. Dugan, SA Chris Anglin, SA Carmine A. Esposito, SA Jose M. Flores Jr., SA Johanna Loonie-Esposito, SA Beamon L. Kendall, SA David R. Orozco, my good friends, SSA David Sebastiani and SA Joseph A. Cincotta, NYPD Det. Frank "Big Frankie" Manzione, SA Joseph "Donnie Brasco" D. Pistone, Section Chief Stephen A. Salmieri, SA Edmundo Mireles, SSA Robert M. Hart, SA Charles "Bud" Warner, SA James Macintosh, SA John L. Kapp, NYPD Det. Mario Cardona, SSA Michael McKinney. To my good friend SA Giraldo "Jerry" Bermudez, SA Michael McGowan, SA Antonio Dillon, Detective Eddie Dominguez, Boston Police Department SSA Kevin J. White, SA Carlos Fernandez, and SA Jenny Espinosa (DEA). Thanks to SA Richard Meade and SSA James Gagliano and the elite N.Y. SWAT Team, for their professionalism shown during my protection detail in the Greg DePalma trial. To SA Martin Suarez, SA Carlos Castello, SA Vincent Pankoke, SA Jerry Hester, SA Gary Moore, SA Dave Roberts, SA Daisy Clemens, SA Richard Stout, SA Kevin Conroy, SSA Gary Loeffert, SSA Chris Piersza, SA James Margolin, SA Robert Booth, SSA Dawn Bruno, SSA Mark Horton, SA Richard Defilippo, SSA Neil Moran.

To SSA George M. Hanna, SA Eileen O'Rourke,

and all the members of the Bonanno squad—your hard work and perseverance in making quality cases against the Bonannos should be commended. To SA Stephen Byrne, SA William McCarthy, SA Todd Renner (the Case Agent on the Terrorist Cabbie case), SSA Kevin M. Hallinan, and to SA Rico Falsone, for his great work in the dismantling of the Albanian Rudaj Organized Crime Family. Thanks to SA John Sereno, for his outstanding work in the Anthony Megale investigation in New Haven, Connecticut. Thanks to SSA John Foley, SSA Kevin Constantine, SA Giraldo "Jerry" Bermudez, SA Michael Carazza, and Lieutenant Detective Frank Mancini of the Boston Police Department Anti-Corruption Division; I would like to thank you for the opportunity of working with you guys in your investigation into three corrupt members of the Boston Police Department.

Thanks to my good friend SSA Phil Scala and his C-16 Gambino OC squad. Thank you for all your support throughout the years, especially during my undercover days in the Mob investigation. Also, special thanks and acknowledgment to SA Theodore Otto, SA Rita Steiner, SA Cindy Peil, SA Gerry Conrad, SA Beth Ambinder, and SA Chris Lamanna, for their exceptional work in the FBI's biggest consumer fraud investigation ever perpetrated by members of the Gambino Crime Family on the Internet, Banking and Telecommunication Industries. Outstanding work!

For the "Tarnished Badge," Hollywood, Florida, Police Corruption Investigation, special recognition goes to the hard work and support of many individuals: they include in part SAC Jon Solomon, SAC Michael Clemens, ASAC Tim Delaney, SSA Mario Tariche, SA Kevin Luebke, SA Michael Grimm, SA David Sebastiani, SA Joseph A. Cincotta, SA Tony Velasquez, SA Geoffrey Swinerton, SA Antonio E. Castaneda, Jr., SA John Jones, and AUSA Edward N. Stramm.

Thanks to those who worked the Willy Falcon and Sal Magluta Jury Tampering Investigation. I would like to commend SSA Mario Tariche for his hard work and dedication. I would also like to acknowledge ASAC Michael Anderson and SA Dennis Donnell (IRS), who along with Mario Tariche's tenacity and tireless work ethic sent out a message to the criminal world—that "you cannot buy Justice in the American legal system." Also for the hard work of the United States Attorney's office in Miami, specifically the following prosecutors: AUSA Pat Sullivan, AUSA Edward Nucci, AUSA Julie Paylor, and AUSA Michael Davis, who successfully prosecuted the subjects of this investigation.

Thanks to those who worked so tirelessly in the Newark Division, Atlantic City Investigation titled "Steal Pier." I would like to commend the following individuals: SSA James Mallon, SSA Michael Costanzi, SA James Eckel, SA Edward Corrigan, SA Robert Gilmore, SST Donna Craven, and SA Michael Grim.

To my friends, Big Lou, Kent, Peter, Jimmy, Howie, Chris, Little Louie, Dr. Frank, Walt, Jack, George, Ramon, Pat, Ski, thank you for everything, especially your friendship. To all my high school and college friends and teammates, thanks for teaching me the importance of being a team player. To Chairman Anthony Bergamo and all the distinguished members of the Federal Law Enforcement Foundation, who for over twenty years have supported our law enforcement community, thank you for bestowing such a distinguished honor upon me on Novmber 1, 2007.

To all those listed above and to those whom I may have forgotten to include, I thank you for your support and friendship. My professional success is due, in large part, to you and the hard work that took me from being an FNG to a UCA in the FBI! Thank you!